MUSIC IN LONDON
1890–94
CRITICISMS CONTRIBUTED WEEK BY WEEK
TO THE WORLD

IN THREE VOLUMES
VOLUME III

©

BERNARD SHAW

BERNARD SHAW

MUSIC IN LONDON
1890–94
CRITICISMS CONTRIBUTED WEEK BY WEEK
TO THE WORLD

IN THREE VOLUMES
VOLUME III

NEW YORK
VIENNA HOUSE
1973

MUSIC IN LONDON 1890–94

I HAVE to congratulate the Philharmonic Society on having at last made a resolute and fairly successful effort to give a concert of nearly reasonable length. Instead of the usual two or three concertos, five or six symphonies, selection of overtures, suite from the latest "incidental music" composed for the theatres by one of our professors, and a march or so, besides the vocal pieces, we had only about two hours' music; and though that is a good half-hour too much, still, it is better than two hours and forty or fifty minutes. We also had the orchestra under the command of conductors who, as their own works were in hand, were strongly interested in making the most of the occasion; and the result was instructive.

Saint-Saëns' Rouet d'Omphale is trivial enough to satisfy even the weariest of the unhappy persons who go to the Philharmonic for the sake of culture, under compulsion of fashion or their parents, and who invariably betray themselves by the rapture with which they greet any of those bogus concertos or symphonies which are really only very slightly developed *suites de ballet*, with episodical barcarolles disguised as "second subjects." But it afforded the relief of contemplating a broad expanse of finely graded sound between the *fortissimo* of the band as Saint-Saëns handled it and its *pianissimo*. There were ten degrees of color and force in the gradation where there is usually only one; and even these did not exhaust the possible range of effect, for the orchestra is capable of a much more powerful *fortissimo* than Saint-Saëns required from it.

Again, in the scherzo of Tchaikowsky's symphony, a movement of purely orchestral display, the quality of tone in the *pizzicato* for the strings and in the section for the brass was wonderful. Probably Tchaikowsky could not have achieved such a result anywhere else in the world at equally short notice. But why is it that but for the occasional visits

1

of strangers like Grieg, Tchaikowsky, and Saint-Saëns, we should never know what our best London band can do? Solely, I take it, because the visitors are virtually independent of that impossible body of hardened malversators of our English funds of musical skill, the Philharmonic directors. For their displeasure the distinguished foreign composer does not care a brass farthing: he comes and instals himself at the rehearsals, making their insufficiency suffice for his own work by prolonging and monopolizing them.

On the other hand, the official conductor is the slave of the directors: if he complains to them they take no notice of his complaints: if he complains to the public, as Mr Cowen did in desperation, they dismiss him, knowing, unfortunately, that there will be no difficulty in finding someone else to take his place, which, except artistically, is a highly desirable one.

This season, thanks to the scandal of Mr Cowen's complaint and dismissal, and to such tweaking of the Philharmonic nose, and tripping up of its heels, and unexpected hurling of sharp cornered bricks at its third waistcoat button as those critics who have the Society's interests really at heart can find time for, there has been an improvement, of which I, for one, have given rather exaggerated accounts for the better encouragement of the directors in the right path; but, after all, here I am face to face with a concert in which the band did admirable work under the batons of Russian and French strangers, whilst, under the official conductor, it played the accompaniment to Isolde's Liebestod in a way that would have fully justified poor Miss Macintyre in sending for the police.

To make that song produce no effect whatever may seem hardly feasible; but the Philharmonic band—this very same band that distinguished itself so remarkably in Tchaikowsky's symphony a few minutes later—did it quite easily. I need not describe the familiar process—the parts read off with businesslike insensibility at a steady *mezzo-forte*, and

2

with just enough artistic habit to make the result presentable to those who were unacquainted with the work. That is the sort of thing that turns me from a reasonable and indulgent critic into a mere musical dynamitard.

Of Tchaikowsky's symphony apart from its performance I need only say that it is highly characteristic of him. In the first movement, the only one with a distinctly poetic basis, he is, as ever, "le Byron de nos jours"; and in the later ones, where he is confessedly the orchestral voluptuary, he is Byronic in that too. The notablest merit of the symphony is its freedom from the frightful effeminacy of most modern works of the romantic school. It is worth remarking, too, considering the general prevalence in recent music of restless modulation for modulation's sake, that Tchaikowsky often sticks to the same key rather longer than the freshness of his melodic resources warrants. He also insists upon some of his conceits—for example, that Kentish Fire interlude in the slow movement—more than they sound worth to me; but perhaps fresh young listeners with healthy appetites would not agree with me. The symphony, brilliantly performed, was handsomely received; and neither Saint-Saëns nor Tchaikowsky can complain that they were not made as much of as they deserved, especially Saint-Saëns, who was recalled again and again after playing his G minor concerto in the hope that he would throw in a solo. This, however, he evidently did not understand; and the audience had at last to give over the attempt.

On Saturday afternoon the Albert Hall was filled by the attraction of our still adored Patti, now the most accomplished of mezzo-sopranos. It always amuses me to see that vast audience from the squares and villas listening with moist eyes whilst the opulent lady from the celebrated Welsh castle fervently sings, Oh, give me my lowly thatched cottage again. The concert was a huge success: there were bouquets, raptures, effusions, kissings of children, graceful sharings of the applause with obbligato players—in short, the usual exhibition of the British bourgeoisie in the part of

3

Bottom and the prima donna in the part of Titania.

Patti hazarded none of her old exploits as a florid soprano with an exceptional range: her most arduous achievement was Ah fors e lui, so liberally transposed that the highest notes in the rapid traits were almost all sharp, the artist having been accustomed for so many years to sing them at a higher pitch. Time has transposed Patti a minor third down; but the middle of her voice is still even and beautiful; and this, with her unsurpassed phrasing and that delicate touch and expressive *nuance* which make her cantabile singing so captivating, enables her to maintain what was, to my mind, always the best part of her old supremacy. She was assisted by Mr Santley; by Mr Ben Davies, who distinguished himself in an excellent delivery of Deeper and deeper still; by Madame de Pachmann, whose talent was thrown away in the Albert Hall, where a pianoforte is worse than useless; by Miss Clara and Miss Marianne Eissler with harp and violin; and by Mr Lemare, who revelled among the stops of the organ, which are mighty ones and millions, but who does not understand—what organist does?—how very disagreeable are those sudden pianos which are produced by stifling the organ with the swell shutters. Lastly, there was Miss Alice Gomez, now become a ravishing singer, with high notes of delicious quality and an exquisite delicacy of artistic treatment, not to mention all her old feeling and her rich contralto tones.

An orchestral concert was given by Herr Benno Schönberger last week. Instead of the Mozartean band for concerto accompaniments usual on such occasions, we had Mr Henschel with an orchestra on the scale of the London Symphony Concerts; and very pleasant it was, I must say, to hear the power and breadth produced by the firmly sustained wind playing upon which Mr Henschel insists, after months of the Philharmonic band, with its inveterate habit of pecking at the chords instead of holding them. He turned the opportunity to account by introducing a new symphony by Emmanuel Moor, which was, on the whole, well worth

4

the trouble.

I do not know the composer's nationality; but he seems to me to have that warm-blooded racial disqualification for orthodox symphony-writing which consists in having no musical impulses except passionate ones. A perfectly tranquil andante, a purely humorous scherzo, a continent or reflective first movement, seem out of the question with Mr Moor. He is clever and self-possessed enough; but he is always more or less vehement and ardent, and would, I should imagine, succeed better at a Lisztian "symphonic poem" than in sonata form. Herr Schönberger played Beethoven's fourth concerto and Saint-Saëns' Concerto in G minor with the dexterity which he has so resolutely cultivated. His passion for the mechanical part of his art seems to have filled him with an ambition to play like clockwork; and all I can say is that if he is not very careful he will succeed. I did not hear the Beethoven concerto, as I was detained at the *matinée* of Captain Thérèse given by Miss Emmott-Herbert at the Criterion as a specimen of the work she has been doing in the provinces. The company consisted of performers not less capable and comely by nature than those who, under fair artistic influence, achieve success in metropolitan centres. They had, however, habituated themselves to the influence of the provincial gallery; and the London critic, fresh from the Savoy, woke up grinning from his jaded apathy and enjoyed what was to him something of a novelty.

The concert given by Miss Edith Blyth and Miss Mabel Wood at Steinway Hall introduced an able and brilliant Italian violoncellist, Ronchini, who played the inevitable Chopin nocturne and the equally inevitable Popper morçeau, but played them *à l'Italienne*, impetuously and originally, with Southern accuracy of intonation and richness of tone, besides delicate and swift execution. Miss Edith Blyth was very nervous; but she may take courage: her performance of so difficult a piece as the cavatina from La Gazza Ladra was highly creditable; and she need no

5

longer fear that great booby, the public, which, in its helplessness, will always respond warmly to honest service in
such pleasant and easily intelligible forms as Miss Blyth's
singing. Miss Mabel Wood, keeping on the smoother
ground of sympathetic ballad singing, acquitted herself
with good sense and feeling, and, helped by a pleasant voice
and good musical endowment, made an excellent beginning. Miss Ada Wright, the pianist, played Schumann's
Faschingsschwank with adequate manual skill and truly
English coolness—that coolness which, in people who feel
deeply, is really shyness. Miss Wright must give herself
away to her audience more freely if she wishes to change
their respect into enthusiasm.

Mr Ernest Kiver gave his annual concert last week at
Prince's Hall, and, with his usual enterprise, introduced
two new trios for pianoforte and strings, by G. J. Bennett
and Eduard Schütt. More I cannot say, as I was, unfortunately, unable to be present.

14 June 1893

IF many concerts make a good season, the present must
be of the best. There are not only concerts, but audiences; and these audiences include a certain proportion
of persons who conceivably pay for their tickets. One of the
novelties of the year is a new concert-room in the depths of
the Grafton Gallery, very pleasant in this weather, whatever
it may prove in winter, and offering to the critic an opportunity of sneaking away from the music to look at the pictures. A caged bird, with no change of air except as between
two perches and a ring, must feel much the same as I do
when caged in London in June hopping restlessly from St
James's to Prince's Hall, and from that again to Steinway
Hall. The Grafton Gallery is an extra perch for me; and I
offer my blessing to Mr Farley Sinkins, the enterprising
concert agent who has discovered it. I visited it for the first
time last week to hear Madame Swiatlowsky's concert,
where I found Madame Haas and Max Reichel playing a

sonata presentably, but with no extraordinary solicitude, Herr Reichel giving himself no more trouble than a good first violin in the orchestra would take over a rather difficult score. Madame Swiatlowsky sang a florid air of Handel's in an original and very un-English fashion. Instead of making it as like a foot rule as possible, with the minims, crotchets, quavers, and semiquavers all mechanically marked off, she managed to strike out a purely musical treatment in which the hard outlines vanished and the aria, though somewhat jellified (if I may so express myself), came to life as a song instead of remaining a mere *"étude de la vélocité."* She also sang a serenade from Saint-Saëns' Ascanio, greatly to my surprise; for, though I well remember conscientiously sitting out that solemnly manufactured grand opera in Paris, I can recall no such alleviation of my prodigious boredom on that occasion as this serenade would certainly have been had Madame Swiatlowsky sung it. She has the merit of inventing her own way of singing a song, and realizing it how she can, without preoccupying herself with academic considerations: for example, the quaint contrast between her lowest and highest register is a quality which she exploits instead of a defect which she tries to conceal. After the serenade I went to look at the pictures, as I seldom lose an opportunity of deserting my post at a miscellaneous concert.

If one may judge by their success in filling St. James's Hall, the combination of Eugène Oudin and Tivadar Nachez has been a fortunate one. I must frankly say that I should not care to listen to Oudin for more than, say, twenty-nine or thirty songs in succession; for he now specializes himself remorselessly for melancholy ditties, sung very slowly so as to admit of the most minute examination by the ear of the quality of one particular stop on his voice. No doubt it is a luscious stop; but its charms are not inexhaustible: after a while it becomes rather monotonous, later on decidedly monotonous, then very monotonous, and at last exasperatingly monotonous. It sets up an itching to hear him sing The Vicar of Bray, or Non più andrai, or Hans Sachs' cobbling song. If he has no turn for the humorous, and prefers his refined vein of lovesickness, *siècle de Louis Quatorze*, I make bold to remind him that there is plenty of English music in that vein and of that period, and that no concert singer ever reaches the very front rank in England—the Sims Reeves, Santley, Patti rank—by persistently singing in a foreign language. Tivadar Nachez paid homage to the great by playing a good deal of Bach—the chaconne in D minor, etc.—but he was not in a classical humor, and, I thought, trotted his *chevaux de bataille* round with a certain forcing of his inclination. The Beethoven romance was the first piece which he played as if for its own sake. The Beethoven concerto I was unable to wait for, and indeed unwilling, in view of the fact that there was no orchestra. What with the way in which concerts are jostling one another at present, and the circumstance that the influenza fiend has left me in a condition quite incompatible with prolonged doses of concert-room air, my appearances just now are unusually fragmentary. From the point of view of ventilation my most terrific recent experience has been the concert of the Handel Society, a hospitable body which takes St James's Hall once a year, and invites an overwhelming audience, without reservation of seats. When I entered, the temperature was about two hundred and fifty in the draught; and I deemed myself fortunate in securing an angle of the wall to lean against whilst August Manns, in the centre of a sort of Mahometan paradise of lady violinists, with a trusty professional lurking here and there, mostly in the wind department, was bringing off a very creditable performance of the overture to Lodoiska. After this we had an admirable little cantata for band and chorus called The Storm, by Father Haydn, who, if he gave it to his children the public indulgently as a piece of claptrap, certainly took good care that it should do them no harm. The instrumentation and the vocal harmony sounded much fresher than they would have done half a century ago; and I waited for the last note before I fled, gasping for air, into Regent Street. Had I come

8

earlier I should have heard the only Beethoven symphony I never yet heard an orchestral performance of: to wit, number one. I was prevented by Miss Dora Barrington's concert at Prince's Hall, where I heard, besides various songs from Miss Barrington, Mr Reginald Groome, Mr Ben Grove, and Mr Brockbank, a fine performance of Franz Abt's Schlaf wohl from Madame Belle Cole, who was in one of her finer artistic moods, and a rather impatient handling of Svendsen's Romance and Wieniawski's Scherzo Tarantelle, by Henri Seiffert, a violinist of remarkable talent, who nevertheless generally plays either as if he were heavily preoccupied with something else, or at best as if he had not quite made up his mind whether he cared for the violin or not.

Miss Marie Roberts, who gave a concert at Steinway Hall last Thursday, is one of those artists who sit down at the piano and play their own accompaniments at their ease. In this way they offer me, not an orthodox feat of concert singing to be measured by the regulation standards, but an entertainment to be judged on its own merits as a method of pleasing an audience. All I can say of Miss Roberts is that she does this successfully. She can sing a bit, and play a bit, and compose a bit, and eke out these little gifts by acting a bit in the character of a fully accomplished musician; so that everyone finds her very clever and agreeable. It is not "legitimate"; but then, why should it be? Only I would say this to all singers who accompany themselves in public, from Mr Henschel and Mr Shakespear downwards. It is undoubtedly better to be accompanied well by oneself than accompanied badly by somebody else. But nobody can do two difficult things at a time as well as they can do one. If an accompaniment is so simple that the singer can play it and yet have more than enough attention to spare for the song, well and good; but this means that both song and accompaniment must be very easy relatively to the singer's capacity; and this consideration must limit the repertory of the self-accompanying singer, who is likely to sing The Lass of

9

Richmond Hill rather more successfully than Adelaide.

Mr Edgar Hulland's recital at Prince's Hall began at about ten minutes past three with a violin sonata by Rubinstein. Sauret played it very well; but after about twenty minutes or so it struck me that the first movement was rather diffuse. However, I sat there patiently, noting that Mr Hulland, though not an exquisitely delicate or sentimental pianist, was an intelligent and ready one, and wondering whether Sauret was completely reformed, or whether he would relapse into Vieuxtemps or Ernst before the end of the concert. Then I thought over my past life exhaustively, and elaborated several plans for the future. Finally I had a long and delicious sleep, from which I woke to find by the change in the light that the afternoon was now far advanced. But the Rubinstein sonata was still in a comparatively early stage of performance. I respectfully suggest that it be treated henceforth as a tetralogy, like Der Ring des Nibelungen, and spread over four concerts, one movement to each. When it at last came to an end, Miss Evangeline Florence, whose style has been considerably smartened by her stay in London, sang an air from Handel's Alessandro, which takes a good deal of singing, to which Miss Florence proved equal. She was followed by Mr Hulland with the fifteen variations and fugue on the Prometheus-Eroica theme, played with the impetuosity and inconsiderateness of youth, the general effect being to make them appear insufferably long. When he retired Sauret appeared, and cast, I thought, a dark look in my direction. I glanced at the program; saw the name Ernst there; realized Sauret's fell design; and fled from the hall.

I do not know whom I have to thank for the invitation to hear Mr T. A. Wallworth's lecture at Trinity College on Wagner's compositions and their influence on vocal art as compared with those of the earlier composers; nor do I exactly know what I am expected to say about it. The lecture had already been delivered to the Guildhall students; so that the Trinity College authorities must have known precisely what it was going to be like. Besides, Dr Turpin took the chair in his academic gown, and wound up with a benediction on Mr Wallworth which was meant, I presume, as an official sanction of the lecture on behalf of the College.

Mr Wallworth informed us that the peculiarity which differentiates Wagnerian music-drama from opera as composed by the great masters consists in the fact that Wagner attempted to express all the incidents and emotions of the drama by means of the orchestra alone, reducing the singers to mere lay figures. This method led him to so overwhelm the voice with unsuitable instrumentation that his singers speedily lost their voices in their attempts to shout down the band; and the real reason why the Bayreuth performances have been suspended this year is that all the singers are disabled permanently, and an interval is necessary in order that a new supply of artists may be grown, to pass in turn to their doom. (Continental papers, please copy.)

These deplorable results were brought about by Wagner's conceited contempt for all the great composers who preceded him. He was totally indifferent to the setting of words to music (like Beckmesser), and whenever in his works the musical accent follows the verbal accent, the agreement is to be regarded as a fortuitous coincidence, unintended by the composer. Mr Wallworth then sang, as an example of perfect setting of words to music, the recitative to The trumpet shall sound from The Messiah, and gave the phrase "in the twinkling of an eye" exactly as Handel wrote it: that is, with the accent on the "of." Altogether it was a very remarkable lecture, well worthy the consideration of those who may have an interest in estimating the value of Trinity College as an educational institution.

21 June 1893

A CONCERT of chamber music selected exclusively from the works of Johannes Brahms is not supposed to be the sort of entertainment to put me into the highest good-humor. Herein, however, I am wronged.

11

Such a reputation as that of Brahms is not to be won without great talent. Unfortunately, music is still so much of a mystery in this country that people get bewildered if they are told that the same man has produced an execrable requiem and an excellent sonata. There seems to them to be no sense in going on in this inconsistent way; for clearly a requiem is a musical composition, and if a man composes it badly he is a bad composer; and a bad composer cannot compose a good sonata, since that also is a musical composition. Yet these very people can often see plainly enough that in pictorial art the same man may be an admirable decorative designer, colorist, or landscape painter, and an atrocious figure draughtsman; or, in literature, that good stories and bad plays, charming poems and fatuous criticisms, may come from the same hand.

The departments of music are not less various than those of the other arts; and Brahms is no more to be disposed of by the condemnation as tedious, commonplace, and incoherent, of those works of his which profess an intellectual or poetic basis than—well, the comparisons which offer themselves are numerous and tempting; but perhaps I had better leave them alone. Suffice it to say that whilst Brahms is successful neither as an intellectual nor a poetic composer, but only as a purely sensuous musician, his musical sense is so much more developed than that of the average audience that many of the harmonies and rhythms which are to him simply voluptuous and impetuous, sound puzzling and imposing to the public, and are therefore surmised to be profoundly intellectual.

To me it seems quite obvious that the real Brahms is nothing more than a sentimental voluptuary with a wonderful ear. For respectability's sake he adopts the forms academically supposed to be proper to great composers, since it gives him no trouble to pile up *points d'orgue*, as in the Requiem, or to call a childishly sensuous reverie on a few simple chords, arranged into the simplest of strains for chaconne purposes by Handel, a set of variations on a theme by that master, or to adapt a ramble in search of fresh delights more or less to sonata form; but you have only to compare his symphonies and quintets with those of Beethoven or Mozart to become conscious that he is the most wanton of composers, that he is only ingenious in his wantonness, and that when his ambition leads him to turn his industry in any other direction his charm does not turn with it, and he becomes the most superficial and irrelevant of formalists.

Only, his wantonness is not vicious: it is that of a great baby, gifted enough to play with harmonies that would baffle most grown-up men, but still a baby, never more happy than when he has a crooning song to play with, always ready for the rocking-horse and the sugar-stick, and rather tiresomely addicted to dressing himself up as Handel or Beethoven and making a prolonged and intolerable noise. That this masquerade of his has taken in a considerable number of persons in Berlin and London is easily explicable on the hypothesis that they see no more in Handel or Beethoven than Brahms can imitate; but again you have only to compare the agonies of lassitude undergone by a Requiem audience with the general purring over his violin concerto, or the encores Miss Lehmann gets for his cradle songs, to see that Monsieur Tout-le-Monde is not in the least taken in, though he does not venture to say so in the teeth of eminent counsel's opinion to the effect that he ought to be.

These being my views, I accepted Mr Ernest Fowles's invitation to his Brahms recital without misgiving, especially as the program did not include any of Brahms' enormities. It is true that I did not arrive in time for the first piece, nor wait for the whole of the last, as I should certainly have done had they been by Mozart; but that was because, being a more farsighted voluptuary than Brahms, I know that the pleasures of sense should be tasted with a fresh palate, and not wallowed in. So I left the audience wallowing the moment the sweetness began to pall; and they may be there still for all I know.

What I heard was the twenty-five variations and fugue

(save the mark!) on that theme which Handel has already furnished with quite enough variations to supply the world for some centuries to come. Brahms' variations might, however, just as well be called variations on the key of B flat as on Handel's air. Mr Ernest Fowles played with much devotion and enjoyment; and though his technique and style are not of the calibre by which huge assemblies can be seized and carried away, being distinctly a chamber technique rather than a concert-room technique, yet, on that very account, the concert being one of chamber music, he gave the right feeling to several passages which would certainly have been knocked on the head by a fully equipped Rubinsteiner or Leschetitzkeian, especially in the violin sonata in G, which he played with Joseph Ludwig, who handled the violin part with discretion and sympathy, if not with a very ardent appetite for its luxuries.

There was a tremendous crush at the Philharmonic to hear, or possibly to see, Paderewski. Gangways were abolished and narrow benches substituted for wide ones to make the most of the available space. Paderewski took advantage of the occasion to bring forward for the second time his own concerto, which is a very bad one. No doubt it was "frightfully thrilling" to Paderewski himself to fly up and down the keyboard, playing the piccolo and the cymbals and the big drum and every instrument except the pianoforte on it, and driving the band along, in spite of Dr Mackenzie, as if it were a coach-and-seventy thundering down a steep mountain road; but to me it was simply a waste of the talent I wanted to hear applied to some true masterpiece of pianoforte music.

I could see that he felt like a Titan when he was threshing out those *fortissimos* with the full band; but he had the advantage of me, for he could hear what he was doing, whereas he might just as well have been addressing postcards for all that reached me through the din of the orchestra. I do not want ever to hear that concerto again. It is riotous, strenuous, bold, vigorous, abounding in ready-made themes and figures, scored without one touch of sympathetic feeling for any instrument—least of all for the pianoforte, pardonable on the plea of youth and stimulating wilfulness in the first movement, clever and pleasing in the andante, and vulgar and cheap in the finale, which repeatedly made me rub my eyes and ask myself whether I was not really in the Empire Music Hall listening to a rattling ballet scene.

Perhaps the most exasperating feature of the work is that, with all its obstreperousness, the form is timidly conventional. Besides, Paderewski did not play it at all as well as Sapellnikoff, for instance, would have done. His almost insolent masterfulness of execution and his anxiety to get the last inch of effect out of the work destroyed his artistic integrity as pianist. At the end there came a contest of obstinacy between him and the audience. He, very naturally, only valued the torrent of applause as an acknowledgment of the merits of his concerto, whereas many of the applauders plainly meant, "We have sat out your confounded concerto like angels: now give us a nice little solo."

Over and over again he came up the steps only to retire again after that curious bow of his which is so like the action of a critic who, falling asleep at a concert, nods forward until he overbalances himself and recovers himself just in time to avoid falling with a crash on his nose. At last he relented and gave us a commonplace of his own which at least shewed that his power of treating a melody is unimpaired—though this had already appeared in the slow movement of the concerto. His recital this week, however, must settle what America has done or undone for him in other respects. It will also enable us to turn from his immature and second-hand achievements as an orchestral composer to his really creative achievements as the greatest of living pianists.

As for the rest of the concert, it was, of course, most horribly long, a second concerto (Max Bruch in G minor, conducted by the composer and played by Gorski) having been wantonly thrust into it in order that the audience might enjoy their Turkish bath as long over two hours as possible.

15

I therefore take a malign pleasure in recording the fact that the extra concerto had very poor luck, Gorski being bothered from the first by the high pitch. When he found that he was agonizingly out of tune in the first solo, he took advantage of every *tutti* to screw up; but as the wind got sharper and sharper in the heat, whilst he, standing amid the strings, could not quite realize how flat he was, he never completely remedied matters; and the warm applause he received was a recognition that he was not to blame, and had heroically made the best of a bad job, rather than an expression of any very exquisite pleasure experienced during the performance. Bruch's Achilleus spectacle music was brilliantly fired off by the band; but it contained nothing fresh. The Haydn symphony (E flat, with the drum roll) was so mechanically and unaffectionately played that it was hardly possible to pay any attention to it. The strings lumbered over the andante like a traction engine; and the one moment of relief was when the flattened-out major subject breathed for just a moment in the hands of the oboe. Madame Melba did not appear: her place was taken by Miss Palliser, who sang Divinités du Styx, a great air, too little known here, like all Gluck's music; also Grétry's Plus de dépits, which ought to have been sung more neatly or else not at all.

The concert ended with Sir Arthur Sullivan's new Imperial March, which will undoubtedly have a considerable vogue in the suburbs as a pianoforte duet. This finished the Philharmonic season, which has been, on the whole, one of improvement in the value and prospects of the Society. All that is wanted to accelerate the improvement is a rigid restriction of the duration of the concerts to a hundred and ten minutes at the outside, and the compulsory retirement of all directors at the age of ninety-five, into a lethal chamber if possible.

I remember wandering into a theatre one oppressively warm evening in Munich, and seeing a comic opera, which presented the novel feature of a chorus in ordinary evening dress. It was a rollicking, Bohemian, naïve affair enough, good fun for a willing audience admitted on a modest scale of charges, but hardly suited for a London house with half-guinea stalls and a half-crown pit. There was a comic man whose sallies were immensely laughed at; and as I could not understand one of them I fell into a deep melancholy, and at last went out and sentimentally gazed on Iser rolling rapidly by moonlight for the rest of the evening. This coat-and-waistcoat comic opera has turned up again, much glorified, at the Prince of Wales Theatre as Millöcker's Poor Jonathan, himself none other than the comic man, now become intelligible to me and very funny into the bargain, in the person of Mr Harry Monkhouse. The additions made by Señor Albéniz and Mr Brookfield have made the work more pretentious; but they have also, I am afraid, weakened it by making it far too long. It contains much talk about music-halls and opera companies which might pass if it were satire, but which, being in fact nothing else than theatrical "shop," ought not to have survived the first rehearsal. Mr Monkhouse is a coster who obtains a place as *chef* to a millionaire by writing himself a flattering testimonial, having learnt the necessary accomplishment in a reformatory. The millionaire first discharges him for making an ice pudding with mottled soap, and then, finding him about to commit suicide rather than face destitution, hands him over all his property. What is wanted to give the piece a chance of success is a vigorous blue pencil, to be wielded with a frank recognition of two facts: first, that Millöcker wrote quite as much vocal music as the piece will bear; and, second, that the parts on which Messrs Denny and Kaye waste their ability are worthless, and should, with the contingent parts for their pupils and prima donnas, be cut down to the barest cues for Miss Schuberth's songs and for such of the dances as the public shew any interest in. It will be a pity if Señor Albéniz' enterprise should suffer for want of a little energetic revision; for his management is an example to London in point of artistic aim and liberal spirit.

28 *June* 1893

MR ALBERT BACH'S Loewe recital at Steinway Hall was rather a propagandist demonstration than a concert. Just as the late Walter Bache preached Liszt, so does Mr Bach preach Loewe. I have every sympathy with him in his work; but this is just why I submit that such a recital as that of Thursday last may do Loewe harm as well as good. Mr Bach is a powerful German basso cantante, with much more dramatic force than lyric charm, and with a robust German conscience in the matter of intonation. Loewe was a tenor singer, probably of exceptional compass, as he often wrote with a wicked disregard for the normal limits of the human voice.

In nearly all the ballads of his which are known to me there are smooth lyric passages of intense expression (as in Archibald Douglas), and stirring excursions into the high, clear, ringing vocal regions where the least mixture of the earthy roughness of the heavy bass is not to be tolerated. Some songs lie in this region altogether, notably that charming ballad, Des Glockenthürmers Töchterlein, the notes of which should soar like those of a carillon in a Flemish tower two hundred and fifty feet above the plain. I agree with Mr Bach that this happiest of songs should be made known to the benighted British public; but I ask him whether he really achieved that end the other evening by transposing it into a subterranean key and almost growling it at us. The audience may have been previously unconscious of the existence of the ballad; but surely that state was more blessed than their present one of believing it to be a dull, clumsy, unmanageable tune in the wrong place.

The fact is, Mr Bach, by undertaking the whole program himself, was placed in this dilemma, that he had either to make his presentation to Loewe one-sided, or else to vary it by introducing songs not suited to his voice and style. It seems clear to me that he would have done better to have secured the co-operation of other singers, if only to relieve the monotony of his own voice. A concert on the fourth string makes one long for the *chanterelle;* and I confess that after hearing Mr Bach sing twelve times in succession, I would willingly have exchanged the thirteenth item, though it was no less a ballad than the famous setting of Uhland's Die drei Lieder, for Miss Palliser's song from The Gondoliers or any other frivolity that would have brought me a breath of clear soprano air.

I do not believe the most versatile bass singer in the world, however perfect his intonation and great his lyric gift, could carry off a Loewe concert single-handed; and Mr Bach's overwhelming dramatic bent deprives him of versatility, whilst, as I have already said, he is comparatively careless as to his intonation, and sometimes shews so little lyric feeling that his tone, instead of being sustained, breaks out and lapses from syllable to syllable almost as much as it would if he were making a vehement political speech. It is with some reluctance that I press Mr Bach thus hardly on the shortcomings of an enterprise which engages my entire respect; for he carries the banner of Loewe with ability and enthusiasm, and in interpreting some of the most striking and difficult of the ballads—the Hochzeitlied, the Three Songs, and Henry the Fowler, for instance—attains a remarkable degree of success, which would, I think, be heightened if he accustomed himself to study the peculiar fastidiousness of London audiences whilst taking care to preserve his force and freshness.

But the fact remains that his recital, interesting as it was, did not altogether do justice either to Loewe or to himself. I should shew myself even more ignorant of Loewe than I actually am if I passed over the important share taken in the recital by Mrs Bach at the piano. Playing, as she does, with a most un-Lisztianly stiff wrist, she rather failed to maintain the swing of such galloping accompaniments as that to The Erl King; but in the sparkling, tinkling, busy merriment of the Hochzeitlied, and indeed in almost all the daintier traits, she distinguished herself highly.

Before leaving the subject, it may be as well to mention, for the benefit of the uninitiated, that Loewe was a Westphalian, born 1796, deceased 1869. The ballad poetry beloved of Sir Walter Scott, with its witches, warlocks, and freebooters, was in vogue in his young days; and Loewe, by saturating himself with it and seeking musical expression for it, produced a store of perfectly original and very clever and imaginative settings of the ballads of Goethe, Uhland, Herder, etc.

Schubert, saturated with the music of Haydn, Mozart, and Beethoven, and using all the songs and ballads he came across as excuses for his music (thus reversing Loewe's process), never, even in The Erl King, succeeded in growing his music from the ballad stem as Loewe did, although Loewe was, as far as I can judge, less gifted as a musician. Intellectually and dramatically, however, he had powers of the Gluck-Wagner order, and might possibly have done something for the stage if his vocation for it had been stronger and his opportunities wider than those of a provincial organist. I speak, however, without first-hand knowledge of his operas; and my opinion is, therefore, worth exactly nothing.

Mrs Henschel, giving a recital the night after Mr Bach, was assuredly not, like him, hampered by an unpopular and neglected cause. She took St James's Hall, brought her husband (an incomparable accompanist), brought his choir, brought her audience, and took her success without effort or anxiety. She certainly sang admirably, some of the Irish and Scotch folk-songs being quite irresistibly given, not in point of national color or dialect, for neither of which has Mrs Henschel any genius, but solely in pure feeling for the melody—the only feeling, by the bye, she ever condescends to display, and one which she possesses in a degree that would make the fortune of a violinist, especially if his touch were as delicate and sure as hers.

With her complete and self-contained individuality, her cool superiority to sentimental or devotional moods, and

20

her susceptibility to absolute music, she presents a fascinating subject to the critic, and one which I will not pretend to have mastered. If the gentlemen who talk about "analytic criticism" will make me a complete psychology of Mrs Henschel, explaining why she will sing a folk-song or a Schubert or Liszt melody with exquisite feeling, and then go through a prayer by Mendelssohn or an elegiac tone-poem by Beethoven quite hardheartedly, then I will give them credit for knowing something more of a critic's business than can be gathered from their ready grasp of Professor So-and-so's view as to the root of the seventh on the supertonic.

Paderewski's recital was so crowded that the fall of the thermometer the night before must be regarded as a special providence. In spite of the crowd, the final degrees of excellence in his playing remain a secret between himself and those of us who would very willingly have let him off those brilliant but shallow numbers in his program which plenty of other players can play as well as they need or can be played, but which are applauded at his recitals more noisily than those greater compositions in which he applies all his insight, judgment, and skill most intensely to every phrase and progression.

I did not hear the whole recital; but what I did hear was, humanly speaking, faultless; by which I do not mean that I liked all his mannerisms, and would have played the pieces exactly as he did if I had the skill, still less that his way is the only right way, and every other way consequently wrong. I simply mean that all the work he did was exhaustively studied, and that the reading founded on the study was successfully executed, and was in no case trivial, cheap, or unworthy of a great artist. And I would recommend all singers and players, no matter what their instruments may be, to hear Paderewski, and carefully consider the secret of his pre-eminence.

Infant phenomena have been rife lately; but I managed to avoid them until last week, when, at Mr Strelitski's concert at Portman Rooms, a bright, nimble, sure-fingered boy pupil of his, in the usual black velvet tunic and antimacassar, rattled off Mendelssohn's violin concerto. He evidently did not think much of it, and, no doubt, deemed us fools for wanting to listen to it—in which he had my hearty agreement.

I strongly object to the practice of using works of this class as stalking-horses for children. It is possible to teach a small boy the sword-exercise; but that would not justify his immediately taking part in a cavalry charge; and, cleverly as this youngster had picked up all the difficult passages in the concerto, he should not have been allowed to play it at a concert. Mr Strelitski himself, though announced as flautist and violinist, only played the flute, on which he executed the usual feats, labial and digital, without, however, displaying that exceptional lip-power of correcting the machine into something like perfect tune which, combined with excellence of style, alone justifies a flautist in taking so imperfect an instrument out of the orchestra.

Still, Mr Strelitski shewed a good deal of the right artistic spirit in the pains he took to make his concert a success. He had engaged a band which did not give itself too much trouble on his accoun t, but which enlivened a very hot afternoon with some new and pretty pieces by Mr Silas, and by the overture to William Tell, which I did not wait for, as it is not such a novelty to me as it is to the generation born when I was twenty. Miss Duma, by the way, sang Mascheroni's Ave Maria with a vigor and grandiosity which would not have overcharged Rossini's Inflammatus.

Sir Arthur Sullivan's Golden Legend was done at the Crystal Palace on Saturday afternoon on the Handel festival scale, with Albani, Miss Marian Mackenzie, Messrs Ben Davies, Henschel, and Grice. I look with indulgence on The Golden Legend, because I know that the composer really loves "those evening bells" and all that sincerely sentimental prettiness, with a dash of piety here and a dash of fun there (as in Lucifer's comic song with the Kneller Hall accompaniment), not to mention the liberal allowance of blissful but indeterminate meandering for mere love of musical sound.

I am not that sort of person myself; but I must not therefore churlishly withhold my blessing. The chorus was good, especially the men; but the dainty orchestration was for the most part wasted on the huge scattered band, always the weak point in these monster performances.

Miss Elsie Hall, still in comparatively short frocks, but tamer than of yore, gave a concert at Lady Stanley of Alderley's, with the assistance of Mr Stanley Blagrove. It was, to tell the truth, a somewhat jejune affair; and the sooner Miss Elsie takes her undeniable talent and intelligence off to Leschetitzky to be seriously trained, the better.

5 July 1893

THE utilization for concerts of the very convenient room of the extinct Meistersingers' Club, at 63 St James's Street, reminds me to ask what has become of the mushroom-crop of clubs which sprang up a year or two ago, and were nothing more than co-operative concert-giving societies. The Meistersingers alone, though described as "the late," have escaped dismantling; for their concert-room is still available; and very glad I was to take refuge in it from the rain at Mr Hirwen Jones's concert, where I found Mr Shortis playing the banjo with a delicacy and conscientiousness that ought to have been devoted to some musical instrument. Also there played a Mr Squire, who gave us a couple of tunes of the more obvious sort, with some trick effects, prettily executed, on the violoncello. The concert-giver sang a couple of songs by Mr Cowen, who accompanied in person; Mrs Mary Davies sang one good song and one trumpery one, both by Sullivan, with her fine natural artistic faculty; Miss Rosa Leo chaminaded as well as a lady can who has the wrong temperament for that *genre;* and, the rain having intermitted, I made off.

The Begum Ahmadee's concert at the Grosvenor Club must have puzzled some of the audience a good deal. It was undeniably a novel experience; and I am afraid that some of us thought that the Begum sang a good deal out of tune. She certainly gave a very Oriental version of the intervals of our scale, the keynote itself being so modified when it was approached in certain ways as to suggest doubts whether it had the character of a keynote for her at all. But there is a great difference between a young Englishwoman trying to sing our major or minor scale and doing it inaccurately through defect of ear, and a young Oriental with a good ear tempering our scale with the intervals to which she is accustomed. I found the effect interesting and by no means disagreeable.

Still, my toleration for foreign intervals must not be abused. I bar duets between the Begum tempering the scale in her Indian manner, and Mr Joseph O'Mara tempering it in our native manner. Una notte in Venezia, sung under these conditions, inflicted such exquisite anguish on the more sensitive persons present that they had to set their teeth and hold firmly on to their chairs to endure it with outward calm. I think this was partly due to a gallant attempt on Mr O'Mara's part not to sing obtrusively in tune from the European point of view, and to attenuate his tone as much as possible so as not to drown the Begum, who was suffering from the effects of an attack of influenza; but the result, however well meant, was disastrous.

It was in a solo that the Oriental peculiarity first asserted itself as a charm. The influenza had produced an inharmonious pallor which deprived the Begum of the great personal advantage of "the shadow'd livery of the burnished sun"; but when this passes away she will be powerfully aided by her appearance. Her voice is a mezzo-soprano of agreeable quality.

Among the artists I heard during the few minutes I was able to spend at the Grosvenor Club was Mr Charles Copland, who treated Stradella's Pieta, Signore, so as to exhibit a good voice and some skill in using it, without the slightest regard for appropriate expression. If I were an Olympian deity, and a mere mortal were to demand "pieta" from me with the peremptory incisiveness of Mr Copland, I should certainly reply with the heaviest thunderbolt I could lay my hand on.

I also heard a couple of violin solos from Johannes Wolff, who has carried his spontaneity, his initiative, his freedom of expression, and some (though by no means all) of his neatness of execution unimpaired through a thousand drawing rooms. But the enervating atmosphere of these artistically noxious places, the confined space, the stifling carpets and curtains, the cross-currents of wandering attention and contrary squalls of whispering, have left their mark on his tone. His bow is nothing like so patient and sensitive as it used to be; and he plays his *pièces de salon* as if he had worn out every sensation they could give him except that of astonishing private audiences with his execution of them. He was quite another man in the evening at Steinway Hall, where he led a Beethoven pianoforte trio with some real artistic enjoyment, and instinctively got back some of his old fineness of tone. This was at a concert given by Alfred Gallrein, a competent executant on the violoncello, but not an extraordinary musician, as I judged by his rather commonplace treatment of a suite by Corelli. Miss Liza Lehmann sang Vieni, Dorina bella, known to this generation, as far as it is known at all, by Weber's pianoforte variations. The disappointment caused by the absence of Mr Bispham was relieved by the appearance of Hugo Heinz, a cultivated, intelligent, and sympathetic German singer, whom I occasionally hear at concerts, never without pleasure.

An excellent concert was that given by Mr Maud Crament at the Town Hall, Kensington. This I may say with a clear conscience; though I am, I confess, strongly biassed in Mr Crament's favor by an act of extraordinary and benevolent intrepidity performed by him years ago. This was nothing less than an entirely disinterested attempt to teach me counterpoint, an art to which I am constitutionally impervious. Lest this statement, now published for the first time, should ruin him professionally, I hasten to add that he is in no way responsible for my present attitude towards the academic training in music. When I think of the appalling facility with which he could write canons at all sorts of intervals, and choruses in an unlimited number of real parts, so that even the piously contrapuntal Friedrich Kiel could teach him no more, and an Oxford musical degree cost him nothing but the fees and a hasty look at the date of Monte Verde's birth or the like, I cannot help admiring him from my soul for all the oratorios and festival cantatas he has *not* written. For if he had chosen to abuse his powers, "analytic criticism" would certainly have pronounced him another Handel. Unfortunately for the analysts, he was not only a contrapuntist; but a musician and a man of sense, and so lost his chance of a nine days' immortality. At this concert he did not put a single composition of his own in the program; and there was, unluckily, no organ in the building: else I should certainly have got up and moved that the concert-giver play a Bach fugue. It is odd, by the bye, that even in St. James's Hall nobody ever seems to think of varying a concert with an organ piece.

Saint-Saëns, for instance, is an excellent organist: I heard him play Bach's Fugue in A minor at a concert in St James's Hall more than a dozen years ago; and he might most opportunely have repeated the experiment at the Philharmonic the other night; but nobody dreamt of suggesting it. The stock objection, "They [the audience] get enough of it on Sunday," does not appear to me to be conclusive as against the value of a great mass of organ music which is quite unknown to the public, and, I may add, to myself. I am thinking, not only of the fugues and passecailles of Bach and Handel, but of works by Sweelinck and other brilliant composers of the old Netherlands school, of which I have heard just enough to make me believe that a specimen or two would be more refreshing, even to a miscellaneous concert audience, than the forty-thousandth repetition of Popper's Papillons.

Two singers who had the advantage of Popper in respect of novelty appeared at Mr Crament's concert. One, Miss

26

Minnie Tracy, a soprano from the Opera at Nice, did due credit to that establishment, being a very capable young lady. The other, Mr Fawcett, is a tenor with two strong points in his favor—a distinguished presence, and an unmistakeable devotion to his art. In aiming at a style much above that of the ordinary rough-and-ready robust tenor or the pretty drawing room tenorino, he is still a little preoccupied by his method, which has not yet become automatic with him; and for the moment he is put at some disadvantage as compared with less scrupulous singers by his altogether dignified and artistic determination to fall short in trying to sing finely rather than succeed by shouting his way out of every difficulty.

His voice, though its quality is uncommon and expressive, is at present a little careworn, so to speak, by study: he lacks freshness of tone, complete certainty of execution, vigor of attack—in short, mastery, which, however, is slow and difficult of attainment on the plane on which he is striving for it. In a year or two more Mr Fawcett will be able to challenge a final criticism; meanwhile, he can make himself acceptable to an audience, and so can afford to wait.

I heard also a few pieces from Tivadar Nachez, who was in the vein and played very well; a renewed success of Norman Salmond's with that charming old song, My love is like the red, red rose; and an admirable delivery of Grieg's remarkable little tone landscape called Autumnal Gale by Miss Agnes Janson, one of the best examples of this particular kind of concert singing I have heard this season.

To Jan Mulder, the Dutch 'cellist, who introduced a string quartet by A. Borodine at his concert at the Meistersingers' on Saturday, I can offer only my old excuse for absence—that I cannot be in more than four places at most at the same time. The Patti concert also escaped me, though I got as near it as Palace Gate, where Mrs Charles Yates, who might very well have ventured upon a pianoforte recital, was led into a concert by the assistance of such a stupendous array of artists—Carlotta Elliot, Clara Samuell, Agnes Janson,

27

Madame Valda, Nachez, Oudin, Norman Salmond, Lawrence Kellie, Claus, Thorndike, Brandon Thomas, and a score or so more—that I can only express a hope that they all sang and played and recited excellently; for the program so far exceeded my ideas of a reasonable day's work for a critic that I fled after hearing Mrs Charles Yates play Grieg's rococo suite, Op. 40, which she handled to the greater advantage as her school of pianism, which is that of Theodor Kullak and Madame Schumann rather than that of Liszt, Leschetitzky, or Rubinstein, is also that of Grieg himself, his countrywoman Agatha Backer Gröndahl being, as far as I know, the greatest living exponent of it.

Miss Estrella Belinfante, who gave a concert at St James's Hall on Friday, and who is built on the lines of Signora Duse, is not, as well as I could judge from hearing her sing one song, which she appeared to be reading at sight, a concert singer, but rather a stage singer who has had to resort to the concert platform as a means of introducing herself to the London public. I should not be surprised to find her, on the stage, a dramatic artist of exceptional force and charm. Hollmann, with the air of a man introducing a striking novelty to an awestruck nation, played Popper's Papillons. Hollmann is, on the whole, and without any exception, the greatest violoncellist I have ever heard; but I wish he would learn a new piece. He clings to those Papillons as Sims Reeves does to Come into the garden, Maud, or Patti to Home, sweet Home.

On Saturday evening the Lord Mayor of London invited me to the Mansion House to meet about three hundred and forty representatives of Art and Literature. Music, the art for which England was once famous throughout Europe, was represented by the police band, Mr Ganz, Mr Kuhe, Sir Joseph Barnby, and myself. I fully expected that one of our names would have been coupled with the toast of Art; but no: the City, which should before this have built that Wagner theatre on Richmond Hill for me, has not yet discovered that music is an art. I could not eat: my feelings as a musician and vegetarian were too much for me; and save for some two or three pounds of ice pudding I came away empty, unless I take account of the great feast of chin music afterwards, which I cannot criticize without unpardonable breaches of politeness to the most distinguished of my fellow guests. Our host apologized for the absence of Sir Frederick Leighton. It never occurred to him to allude to the absence of Dr Mackenzie or Sir George Grove. Poor Music!

12 July 1893

LAST week was one of almost complete immunity from concerts, every musical person being engaged in playing the Wedding March in one form or another. Madame Inverni, however, ventured on a concert on Monday afternoon, with a rather strong program, which attracted a comparatively large audience. Slivinski played Mendelssohn's Variations Sérieuses, and some other pieces which I did not hear. He has resolved to join the ranks of the bearded so recently that he presents, for the moment, an alarmingly neglected appearance. Somehow, Slivinski has not, so far, been very handsomely treated here. When he first appeared he shewed technical powers of an altogether extraordinary kind: his mere displays of execution— in some of Liszt's operatic fantasias, for example—were intensely interesting and brilliant. His style and force were essentially of the order needed for large audiences and large halls; and one felt that the strain of these was essential to his continued development as an artist. He came, too, at a moment when what was wanted above all things, from a business point of view, was a rival to Paderewski. Slivinski, on the whole, might have played that part better than anyone else had he been vigorously seconded. But we have no great captains in the concert industry nowadays: our agents wait, dreaming Alnaschar dreams, until some single mighty artist makes a success, and then content themselves with running that artist for all he has made himself worth. This is very well as far as it goes; but it leaves to the artists and the public the work that should be done by the *entrepreneur—*

the work, that is, of making them acquainted with one another. And when the public is very full of an established favorite, and is convinced that when it has heard him play it has heard everything it ought to hear, and may now go home and have done with the classics, any later arrival, however remarkable, cannot get adequately recognized without some determined, skilful, and longsighted business handling—unless, indeed, he is a supreme genius, and can oust the favorite. Now, a player good enough to oust Sarasate or Joachim, for instance, is not reasonably possible. When a player like Isaÿe comes to London, he finds that Sarasate and Joachim are supposed to represent all the first-rate violin-playing there is in the world; and when he suggests that he too can fiddle a little, he finds only two sorts of agents: the one who says, "But I have got Sarasate, and I shall be ruined if the British public discovers that there is any other violinist extant"; and the one who sighs, and says, "Ah, if only I could get hold of Sarasate, what could I not make him!" The net result being, of course, that Isaÿe, unaccustomed to be treated as a second-rater, and tired of agents who throw away the king of trumps because they cannot have the ace, gives up London as a bad job, to our infinite artistic loss. Slivinski has hitherto, it seems to me, been in much the same predicament. The business of making a reputation for him, as far as that is a business matter, has not attracted British enterprise, either because he is not Paderewski, or because he would be a dangerous rival to Paderewski. Of course this may be a sound business policy for anything I know to the contrary; but from the point of view of the interest of the public, which is the one I am bound to take, whether the public understands its interest or not, it is altogether unsatisfactory, since it ends in a little pianoforte-playing by Paderewski at doubled prices, and a great deal by third-rate players at practically no prices at all; whilst artists like Sapellnikoff, Stavenhagen, De Greef, Sophie Menter, and Agatha Backer Gröndahl (to mention only those whose names occur to me hastily) seem, after a

30

trial or two, to prefer every other musical centre in Europe
to London. Instead of getting our reasonable annual share
of the best European art in all departments, we find the
business of organizing the supply monstrously overdone
one year, not done at all for the two years following, timidly
underdone the fourth year, profusely but cheaply done the
next year if the underdoing has proved encouraging, and
finally overdone again the following year out of mere
business jealousy—with, of course, a recurring cycle of
depression following as before. All this, by the bye, is
somewhat wide of Madame Inverni's concert. Besides
Slivinski, there was a composer who announced herself
as Guy d'Hardelot, a name in which I confess I do not
altogether believe. She accompanied Madame Inverni and
Mr Isidor de Lara in a cycle of her love-songs—fluent
and pretty outpourings of a harmless Muse with an unsus-
piciously retentive memory. The two singers were quite
equal to them, Mr de Lara, in fact, being considerably under-
weighted. Madame Inverni, who has a voice of nice quality
and a good ear and method, has been a little too severely
trained. Although English is evidently her native language,
she has acquired a diction so artificial that I have no doubt
that many of her hearers took her for a foreigner who had
made a very close and conscientious study of English for
artistic purposes. Whatever her natural delivery may be,
she has thrown away its qualities as well as its faults. It is
greatly to her credit that she has studied singing and diction
so resolutely; but she must now study music and her own
self with equal determination, in order to get rid of some of
those over-refined vowels, and to recover her own artistic
individuality, which she seems to have been taught, in the
usual professorial fashion, to regard as a department of
original sin.

A N autumnal delight will be the Norwich Musical Festival, which will rage with unabated fury from the 3rd to the 6th of October. The most splendid feature in the announcements is the engagement of both Paderewski and Sarasate, Paderewski to play a new Polish fantasia of his own composition for pianoforte and orchestra, and Sarasate the well-worn rondo by Saint-Saëns, and Mackenzie's pibroch. Everybody except Santley will sing —Albani, Helen Trust, and Anna Williams; Lloyd and Ben Davies; Marian Mackenzie and Belle Cole; Norman Salmond, Bantock Pierpoint, and Henschel.

The choral diversions will be of the most festive kind. Judith will have a whole evening to herself, the East Anglians being curious to hear whether so famous a work can possibly be as bad as I think it; and three cantatas will be performed for the first time under the batons of the composers themselves, though only one of them hall-marks his opus as "composed expressly for the festival." Mr Cowen and Mr Barnett have not claimed that speciality for The Water Lily and The Wishing Bell. There will be a new symphony, "composed expressly" by Mr Edward German; and the dizziest heights will be scaled in The Golden Legend and St Paul. Handel's Messiah is also in the bill, with a clear day between it and Judith, so that the older work may not be hopelessly put out of countenance by a too close comparison with the new.

Mr Randegger will conduct; and it will unquestionably be "all werry capital," and well worth six guineas for a patron's stall or three for a seat among the patronized in the gallery. I note that the committee includes twenty-five peers or sons of peers, nineteen baronets, sixteen members of Parliament, four knights, three mayors, a high sheriff and an ordinary sheriff, two judges (of law), a dean, an esquire, a colonel, and not a solitary musician or artist of any degree— not even a critic to see fair. There will therefore be no danger

of having the festival spoiled by the interference of special-
ists.

The proceeds will be handed over to the principal
charities in Norfolk and Norwich instead of being used, as
they ought to be, for the endowment of art in the county.
If the inhabitants wish, for instance, to celebrate the first
performance of Judith in their midst by giving some
rising local sculptor a commission for a public statue
in honor of Holofernes, they will have to do so by subscription. Art, being a beggar in England, is to be robbed
of her casual earnings to save rich East Anglians from
supporting their local charities. I never heard a meaner
proposal.

I must offer my apologies to Mrs Lynedoch Moncrieff,
of whose songs, as far as I know them, I am an admirer, and
to Bentayoux for having missed their concerts last Thursday, the invitations not having reached me until the performances were over. I may as well take this opportunity of
repeating my periodic plea for at least a few days' notice of
concerts. The notion that I live on the premises, and that
my attendance can be instantly secured at any hour by ringing the night bell, is one which a reflective mind ought to
reject without any prompting from me; and yet it must prevail very largely in the musical profession, if I may judge
from the fact that when invitations do not reach me through
a regular agent, in which case I get them a fortnight or so
beforehand, they are as likely as not to reach me the day
after the fair. Another precaution which I recommend to
concert-givers is the sending of a program. All experienced critics assume, in the absence of evidence to the contrary, that a miscellaneous concert is not worth going to—
or, to put it more gracefully, that it will contain nothing
new. Besides, when it happens, as it often does at the height
of the season, that the utmost time that can be spared to any
one concert in an afternoon is fifteen minutes, a critic duly
supplied with programs can arrange his engagements so as
to avoid happening upon Popper's Papillons and On the

Ling ho four times over by the same artists, and not hearing a single note from any one of the concert-givers. And, be it noted, what is convenient for the critic is convenient for everybody else too. If it is good for me to know a fortnight beforehand that I have to be at such and such a place at such and such a quarter of an hour on such and such a day, it is no less good for the artists and for the hostess—I say the hostess, because it is in the case of concerts at private houses that the tendency to leave everything to the last moment is strongest, the public halls being only obtainable on condition of being booked for a long time beforehand. I have no doubt that often, when I have been invited to a rather good concert and not accepted the invitation, whilst in the same week I have paid some attention to a rather bad one, the neglected giver of the better concert has wondered whether the opposition management enclosed me a ten-pound note along with the ticket. But the ten-pound note, though I should like it extremely, would make no difference, whereas a week's notice accompanied by a program would make all the difference in the world; and I ask those concert-givers who have misinterpreted my partialities to consider whether they have not deprived themselves of the solace of my criticisms by indulgence in business habits of the same pattern as my own. I have enough to do to struggle with the effects of my incorrigible procrastinativeness without being hampered by that of others as well.

The most considerate artist I have yet met is Mrs Aylmer Jones, who gave a concert last week in Stanhope Gardens. She not only gave me timely warning, but when I arrived she immediately sang all the items set down for her in the first part of the concert, one after the other. I do not suggest that this was done on my account; but it made me acquainted in the shortest possible space of time with Mrs Aylmer Jones's merits as a singer, which are, a soprano voice of nice quality, a sensitive ear, a refined style, and an intelligent delivery. I do not recommend Mrs Aylmer Jones to go on the stage and play Carmen: she is too ladylike for that sort of success; but at this concert she was quite equal to the occasion.

26 July 1893

THE musical season took advantage of the nuptial festivities at Court to fall down in a swoon; and it may now, I suppose, be regarded as stone-dead. It ended piously with a cantata at the Crystal Palace, on the Handel Festival scale, at popular prices, relieved by a mild fling at the Criterion in the evening, where Mr Wyndham has revived La Fille de Madame Angot for the benefit of the autumnal visitor. Whether it has been a good season or not I cannot say: the usual number of assurances that it has been "the worst ever known" are to hand; but it has been quite busy enough for me, even though my labors have been lightened by the retirement of some of our *entrepreneurs* from an unequal combat with my criticism. On looking back over it I recall, with a certain hopeful satisfaction, the failure of innumerable comic operas. They were not worse than the comic operas which used to succeed—quite the contrary. On the musical side, both as to composition and execution, there has been a steady improvement. The comic-opera stage now exchanges artists with the grand-opera stage and the oratorio platform; and the orchestras, compared to their predecessors, are exquisite and imperial.

The difficulty lies on the dramatic side. I have often expressed my opinion of the average comic-opera librettist with pointed frankness; and I have not changed my mind in the least. Mr D'Oyly Carte's attempt to keep the Savoy stage up to the Gilbertian level by calling in Messrs Grundy, Barrie, and Conan Doyle is part of a sound policy, however this or that particular application of it may fail. But for the moment the effect on our younger comic-opera artists of having been trained so extensively at bad dramatic work is that the rank and file of them cannot act; and when good work is put into their hands, they are unable to execute it effectively. On the ordinary stage the incapacity of the actors is got over by the ingenuity of the authors, who, by adroitly contriving a constant supply of effective lines, situations, and passages of pure stage management, reduce the function of the actor to the display of fairly good stage manners; but the ordinary opera librettist has not the skill thus to substitute good parts for good acting, nor the imagination to write drama of the order which stimulates actors to genuine feats of impersonation, and eventually teaches them their business.

And so a comic opera, on its dramatic side, has come to mean mostly an inane and occasionally indecorous play, performed by self-satisfied bunglers who have all the amateur's ineptitude without his disinterestedness, one or two experienced and popular comedians being thrown in to help the rest out by such fun as they can improvise.

The effect on the public of the long degeneration from La Grande Duchesse, with its witty book and effervescent score, down to the last dregs of that school (tainted as it was from its birth, one must admit, with a certain dissoluteness which we soon turned into graceless rowdiness) seems now to be nearly complete. In the days when La Grande Duchesse was shuddered at as something frightfully wicked, when improper stories about Schneider formed the staple of polite conversation, and young persons were withheld from the interpolated *can-can* in the second act as from a spectacle that must deprave them for ever, the many-headed received a rapturous impression of opera bouffe as a delightful and complete initiation into life—the very next thing, in fact, to a visit to the Paris of Napoleon III, represented in the British imagination chiefly by the Mabille Gardens.

Now the theatre-going public may be divided roughly into three classes. First, a very small class of experts who know the exact value of the entertainment, and who do not give it a second trial if it does not please them. Second, a much larger class, which can be persuaded by puffs or by the general curiosity about a novelty which "catches on," to accept it at twice or thrice its real value. Third, a mob of persons who, when their imaginations are excited, will accept everything at from ten times to a million times its real value, and who will, in this condition, make a hero of everybody who comes within their ken—manager, composer, author, comedian, and even critic. When a form of art, originally good enough to "catch on," begins to go down hill as opera bouffe did, the first class drops off at once; and the second, after some years, begins to follow suit gradually.

But the third class still worships its own illusion, and enjoys itself rather more than less as the stuff becomes more and more familiar, obvious, and vulgar; and in this folly the managers keep speculating until that generation passes away, and its idols are too degraded to attract fresh worshippers. Managers are still trying to pick profits out of the dregs of the Offenbach movement; and the question of the day for Mr D'Oyly Carte is, how to keep the Gilbert-Sullivan movement from following the Offenbach movement into the abyss.

This being the situation, up comes an interesting question. Why not go back and begin over again? Generations of playgoers are happily shorter than generations of men; for most men only begin to go to the theatre when they arrive at the stage of having a latchkey and pocket money, but no family; and they leave off when they arrive at the stage of a family and (consequently) no pocket money. As for myself, I can be proved by figures to have completely outgrown that boyish shyness which still compels me to regard myself as a young man; but I am not so very old—nothing like what you would suppose from the wisdom and serenity of my writing. Yet I have the flight of time brought home to me at every theatrical "revival" by the number of men, to all appearance my contemporaries, for whom the operas and plays and artists which seem to me those of yesterday are as Edmund Kean's Richard or Pasta's Medea. I have hardly yet lost the habit of considering myself a child because I never saw Charles Kean, Macready, or even Grisi; yet I am confronted already with a generation which is in the same predicament with regard to Titiens and Costa, Julia Mathews and Stoyle.

37

Twenty years of playgoing makes you a veteran, an oldest
inhabitant, an authority to your face and an old fogey behind
your back—all before you are forty—long before you begin
to be spoken of outside as a callow young man. Under these
circumstances La Grande Duchesse and La Fille de Madame
Angot may surely be produced today as absolute novelties.
La Grande Duchesse and La Belle Hélène belong to the
sixties, Madame Angot to the early seventies. Compared to
them Madame Favart, Le Voyage dans la Lune, and La Fille
du Tambour Major are quite recent works, although these
last three are also ripe for revival—that is, if revival proves
a practicable expedient. Somehow the Zeitgeist, as it stalks
along, brushes the sparkling bloom off operas just as it does
off pastel drawings; and even an "opera buffa" like Mozart's
Don Juan, which turns out to be not for an age but for all
time (meaning a few hundred years or so), survives as a repertory opera, to be heard once a year or so, instead of being
boomed into a furorious run of five hundred nights.

And Don Juan is a very different affair from Madame
Angot. I wish I had some music type at my disposal to shew
exactly what Lecocq would have made out of La ci darem la
mano. To begin with, he would have simply composed the
first line and the fourth, and then repeated them without
altering a note. In the sixties and seventies nobody minded
this: Offenbach is full of it; and Sir Arthur Sullivan was not
ashamed to give us a most flagrant example of it in the sailors'
chorus which opens H.M.S. Pinafore. It not only saved the
composer the trouble of composing: it was positively popular; for it made the tunes easier to learn. Besides, I need
hardly say that there are all sorts of precedents, from The
Vicar of Bray to the finale of Beethoven's choral symphony,
to countenance it. Still, there is a difference between the repetition of a phrase which is worth repeating and one which
is not; and the song in which the market-woman describes
the career of Madame Angot in the first act of Lecocq's opera
may be taken as a convincing sample of a series of repetitions of phrases which are not worth hearing once, much

38

less twice. They delighted 1873; but I am happy to say that on last Saturday 1893 saw through their flimsiness at once, and would have damned the whole opera as *vieux jeu* if the rest of it had been no better.

Probably Wagner has a good deal to do with this advance; for even our comic-opera composers have become so accustomed by him to associate unprecedented persistence in repetition with apparently inexhaustible variation and development, that they are now too sensible of the absurd woodenness of the repetitions of Offenbach and Lecocq to resort to them so impudently. Anyhow, it was clear on Saturday night that the old quadrille padding, in spite of its mechanical vivacity, will no longer pass muster, even in an opera bouffe, as lyric or dramatic music. As to the conspirators' chorus, its original success seems to have vaccinated the English nation against a recurrence of the epidemic; for it was not even encored.

And we nourish our orchestral accompaniments so much better nowadays that the score sounded a little thin; although that was partly due to the fact that Mr Wyndham, who, as frequenters of his theatre know, is not a judge of a band, has made no such orchestral provision as would be a matter of course at the Lyric or Savoy. Still, the band did well enough to shew that we now expect more substance and color in accompaniments, and will not be put off with mere movement and froth.

In other respects the opera stood the test of revival very well. The mounting was, for a West End theatre, decidedly modest, the whimsicalities of the *incroyable* period being cheaply and uninventively represented. The choristers sang but little: they for the most part bawled, screamed, and shouted in a manner that would have been trying in a large theatre, and was intolerable in the Criterion. The men were especially objectionable; and I implore Mr Wyndham to send them all for a week to a respectable cathedral, to learn how to make some passably civilized sort of noise. The success of the performance was due altogether to the principals.

Everything depends in Madame Angot on Clairette and Lange; and Miss Decima Moore took unsparing trouble with Clairette, and brought off the first act triumphantly, though in the third her attempt at the gay vulgarity and braggart combativeness of the daughter of the market was rather forced, and, as far as it was successful, hopelessly British.

Miss Amy Augarde, as Lange, was the only one who seemed to breathe the national and historical atmosphere burlesqued in the piece. She took her part in thorough artistic earnest, and brought down the curtain at the end of the second act amid the most solid applause of the evening; although the famous waltz finale was robbed of much of its illusion, not only by want of imaginative inscenation, but by the execrably rough singing of Augereau's hussars behind the scenes, and the ridiculous effect of their trumpet being sounded in the orchestra instead of in its proper place. Miss Augarde was perhaps more tragic and dignified than Lange is meant to be; but she was quite successful in imposing her reading on the part.

Mr Courtice Pounds was a neutral sort of Ange Pitou, bringing out neither the humor nor the naïveté of the part; but he was at least inoffensive; and his singing, thanks to a liberal mixture of head voice, was rather pretty. Mr Blakely amused himself and us by a sufficiently outrageous Louchard; and Mr Sydney Valentine made a courageous operatic essay as Larivaudière. Pomponnet was impersonated by an eminent composer, who is too much of a musician to be surprised at my confessing that I thought him the very worst Pomponnet I ever heard. The last act was liberally cut, and diversified by a grotesque quadrille and a skirt dance which, like most skirt dances, was not a dance at all.

2 August 1893

SHALL SIR AUGUSTUS HAVE A TESTIMONIAL?

I HAVE received a circular letter, which I give here in full, although some of my readers will have already seen it elsewhere. Its reappearance in this column may be the means of adding a few more donations to the one which it announces.

Proposed Testimonial to Sir Augustus Harris

To the Editor

Sir,—As a very old musician, and one that admires talent, energy, and perseverance, I have watched with keen interest the extraordinary success which has attended the efforts of Sir Augustus Harris to establish in this country an opera worthy of the name, and in accordance with the best traditions of its history. This, in my own opinion, deserves some sort of public recognition, and I have therefore ventured to suggest that all lovers of high-class music, and all admirers of managerial enterprise, should be invited to subscribe towards an appropriate souvenir which shall serve as a testimonial to the Impresario of our Royal Opera House, who, for the reasons just stated, I cannot but regard as a benefactor to his country.

Except for the unceasing exertions of Sir Augustus Harris, and his persistent determination to revive our Covent Garden Opera at any personal cost or sacrifice, that time-honored institution would have long since died a natural death. Indeed, at one period it gave sufficient promise of becoming for ever extinct, in spite of the repeated attempts of La Porte, Lumley, E. T. Smith, Gye, and Mapleson to save it from this doom. At last people began to believe that the failures were due not so much to want of managerial enterprise as to want of operatic attractions, and it was said that the "palmy days" of opera—which I myself so well remember—were completely over, never to be

41

revived again. This was, however, by no means the view
taken by the present Manager of Covent Garden. In his
own estimation, there were as many good fish in the operatic
sea as were ever produced out of it. So Sir Augustus Harris
betook himself to the Continent, and ransacked every leading opera-house there, with the result that he returned
triumphant with a company which, regarded as a whole, I
have no hesitation in pronouncing the completest and most
brilliant that has ever yet appeared upon the boards of
Covent Garden during her Majesty's reign.

It is in view of these circumstances that I have proposed
to open the fund for the souvenir already referred to, under
the title of "The Operatic Testimonial Fund," and I shall be
pleased to head the list of subscribers to it by a donation of
ten guineas. Should the readers of this letter be disposed to
follow my example in any way, their contributions, whether
in the form of cheques or otherwise, will be received by the
National Bank, Oxford Street Branch, if sent on behalf of
"The Operatic Testimonial Fund."—I am, Sir, yours, etc.

(Signed) HENRY RUSSELL.
18 Howley Place, Maida Vale, July 26th, 1893.

Now I have no objection on general grounds to a testimonial to Sir Augustus, though I would not, if I were Mr
Russell, call it an "operatic" testimonial. Let it by all means
be a genuine, enthusiastic, munificently subscribed and
influentially patronized tribute; and since Sir Augustus
knows what is due to himself, let us not insult him with anything meaner than a life-size statue of solid gold, with suitable quotations from the opera criticisms in the Sunday
Times on the four sides of the pedestal. And let Mr Henry
Russell, as the leader of the enterprise, inaugurate the
monument by once more singing I am not mad; by heavens!
I am not mad.

But it would be a mistake, as well as a very left-handed
compliment, to attribute to our illustrious impresario any
design to revive the palmy days. Mr Russell was born more

42

than forty years before I was, and so belongs to a younger period of the world's history. I am therefore to all intents and purposes his senior; and I can assure him, as one who remembers the end of the palmy days, and whose youth was blighted by their accursed traditions, that they deserved their fate, and are not only dead, but—I use the word in the profoundest serious sense—damned. If you discuss them with one of their veteran admirers, you will find that all the triumphs which his memory fondles are not feats of management, but strokes of genius by individual artists. Indeed, so far is he from being able to conceive an operatic performance as an artistic whole, that he will describe the most absurd *contretemps* and the most disastrous shortcomings in the stage management, the band, chorus, dresses and scenery, as excellent jokes.

My readers will remember the examples of this which I was able to give from Santley's Student and Singer, culminating in his playing Don Giovanni for the first time after one rehearsal, at which the tenor (Mario) did not turn up until it was half over. As to the mutilations, the spurious scorings, the "additional accompaniments," and the dozen other violations of artistic good faith which were played off on palmy nights as a matter of course, you will find the average veteran either unconscious of them or utterly unconcerned about them. He is content to remember Ambrogetti as "the Don" (an almost centenarian reminiscence), Piccolomini as Zerlina, Taglioni as La Sylphide, Malibran as Amina, Grisi and Rubini, Tamburini and Lablache in the Puritani quartet; and so on up to Titiens and Giuglini, and those post-Giuglinian days when "the mantle of Mario" was tried on every trooper, porter, or ice-barrow man who could bawl a high C, until at last the jeremiads of Berlioz and Wagner were fulfilled, and palmy Italian opera, which had been corrupt even in its prime, openly putrified and had to be embalmed, in which condition its mummy still draws audiences in the United States and other back-eddies of civilization.

43

Mr Russell, under the impression that he is paying Sir Augustus a compliment, accuses him of having tried to play the resurrection-man. I believe this to be unjust. I admit that there are certain scattered materials for Mr Russell's case—tentative Favoritas, Lucias, and Trovatores (palmy style, with Signor Rawner as Manrico), which had a somewhat retrograde air; but they cannot outweigh the broad fact that the Italian operas which were the staple of the old repertory are the mere stopgaps and makeshifts of the new. If the testimonial is to be given for palminess, then let it be transferred to Colonel Mapleson, whose gallant attempt to revive the old repertory in competition with Sir Augustus a few years ago utterly failed. And the failure was so certain from the first, that for the sake of old times I refrained from attending a single performance, although I have no doubt that I could have had three or four rows of stalls any night for the asking. No, Covent Garden has its defects, as I have had occasionally to remark; but such as it is, it has been created by Sir Augustus, and is no mere revival of the palmy imposture which still takes in Mr Russell.

Is Sir Augustus then, as Mr Russell says, "a benefactor to his country"? The standard definition of a national benefactor is "the man who causes two blades of grass to grow where one grew before." Now Sir Augustus, on the contrary, has caused one opera-house to keep open where two kept open before. But I do not think he ought to be disqualified on so highly technical a point. He established an opera where, for the moment, there was no opera at all; and if this was not a benefaction I do not know what is.

Therefore, instead of churlishly asking why he should have a testimonial, let us rather ask why he should not have one, and why Mr D'Oyly Carte should not have one, and why Signor Lago should not have one, and why, above all, I should not have one? Signor Lago discovered Giulia Ravogli and Ancona, Orfeo and Cavalleria; and although Sir Augustus is no doubt right in preferring to take his own discoveries ready-made, still, the original discoverer is useful in his little way too, and should not be overlooked. Mr D'Oyly Carte founded a new school of English comic opera; raised operatic inscenation to the rank of a fine art; and finally built a new English Opera House, and made a magnificent effort to do for English grand opera what he had done for comic opera, with the result that Sir Augustus is now conducting a music-hall on the ruins of the enterprise.

As to my own claims, modesty forbids me to ask whose pen has done more to revive public interest in dramatic music during the past five or six years than mine. It is true that I have done it because I have been paid to do it; but even Sir Augustus does not play the public benefactor for nothing. A man must live. Take the case of August Manns, whose enormous services to music in England do not need the penetrating eye of an octogenarian to discover them: even he does not scorn to accept his bread-and-butter. If there is any spare cash left in the country when the Harris testimonial is fully subscribed, some little token—say a cheap conducting stick—might be offered to the untitled Augustus of Sydenham.

But now that I think of it, such a proceeding might be construed as a slight to the conducting staff at Covent Garden. And we must not thoughtlessly appear to undervalue what Sir Augustus has done for us in placing his orchestra in the hands of three such *chefs* as Mancinelli, Bevignani, and Randegger. Although they are so devoted to the traditions of the house that Sir Augustus has to send to Germany for help whenever the Nibelungen dramas are performed, yet Mancinelli can conduct Die Meistersinger and Bevignani Tannhäuser in a way that I am sure I for one can never forget. Why not give them testimonials? The stage manager, too—he who staged Gluck's Orfeo and Das Rheingold—that "damned pantomime," as somebody is said to have called it—why should not something be done for him! But I am opening up too vast a field. There are so many public benefactors about.

45

I should be less than candid on the subject, however, if I were to take the proposal quite uncritically. I do not see how it is possible for an impresario to maintain Covent Garden in such a fashion as to deserve a testimonial as a public benefactor. As I have often pointed out, fashionable grand opera does not pay its own expenses in London any more than it does in Paris or Berlin. A subvention is necessary; and if the State does not provide it, a body of private guarantors must. In England there are so many irrational people who think the National Gallery and the British Museum virtuous and Opera vicious (because it takes place in a theater), that the State leaves Covent Garden to a knot of rich people for whom Opera is not a form of art but simply an item of fashion. These people pay the piper; and they naturally expect to call the tune.

Now suppose an artist or a clique of artists get at the guarantors behind the impresario's back, they can make it very difficult for him to do anything that they disapprove of, whether it be in the public interest or not. To such means of resistance to the manager must be added the already enormous powers possessed by leading artists in virtue of their personal monopoly of voice and talent. The impresario's one defence is his own monopoly of the power of making London reputations. To preserve this monopoly and at the same time to provide for the danger always latent in the fact that London will support one guaranteed Opera handsomely, but not two, he must strain all his commercial genius to suppress competition; and this means not only taking every theatre large enough to be used as a rival house, but engaging several superfluous artists for the sole purpose of forestalling their possible engagement by someone else, the result being, of course, to waste their talents most frightfully.

Finally, he must by hook or crook, by conciliation or intimidation, gag independent criticism, because his greatest need is prestige, and this the press can mar if it chooses. His prestige is his life-blood: it convinces meddling guarantors

and mutinous artists that he is the only possible man to run
the Italian Opera; and it paralyses his competitors, making
their attempts to raise a rival guarantee unavailing, and
stamping them from the outset as second rate. And this
prestige, which is at once his sword and shield, propagates
itself by all the operations which he undertakes for its sake.
The theatres leased and kept closed, or sublet on conditions
which bar opera; the magnificent list of artists engaged
apparently out of an insatiable artistic enthusiasm which
takes no account of salaries; even the running of two sets of
performances to prevent the superfluous artists from eating
their heads off: all these master-moves, with the huge turn-
over of money they involve, heap prestige on prestige, until
at last the public gets dazzled, and ancient men call for
testimonials to the national benefactor.

Then there is only one enemy left; and that is the un-
hypnotizable critic who, having his own prestige to look
after, persists in explaining the situation to the public and
criticizing the performances for just what they are worth,
and no more. And such critics are scarce, not because of
their Roman virtue, but because they must have an eye for
the economics of the situation; and a musical critic who is a
bit of an economist as well is a very rare bird.

Under these circumstances I do not see how the public
services of Sir Augustus as impresario can run to a testimonial. However high-mindedly and ably he may have
struggled to do his best within the limits of his very narrow
freedom of action, or however Napoleonically he may have
faced and fought the opposing economic forces, the fact
remains that Covent Garden, with all its boasted resources,
could not put the four Nibelung dramas on the stage last
year except by the pure showman's expedient of sending for
a German company, orchestra, conductor and all.

I do not blame Sir Augustus for this: I pointed out again
and again (before the event as well as after) that the real
difficulty was the incorrigible *fainéantise* of the De Reszkes,
with their perpetual schoolboy Faust and Mephistopheles,

47

Roméo and Frère Laurent, and their determination to make Covent Garden a mere special edition of the Paris Grand Opera. Sir Augustus did contrive to get one triumph out of Jean de Reszke and Lassalle—Die Meistersinger. But from the moment when Jean allowed Alvary to take Siegfried from him, and Edouard left Wotan to Grengg (I hope I have the name correctly), there was an end of all possibility of a testimonial for Covent Garden.

Give me one performance of Die Walküre or Siegfried by the De Reszkes, Calvé, and Giulia Ravogli, with the orchestral work done by the regular band of the house, and a competent conductor of the calibre of Richter or Faccio in permanent command, and then Mr Russell may apply again. At present I am not at home.

Let me point out, however, that there may be an opening on the dramatic side, as to which I, of course, cannot speak. Sir Augustus is famous for his pantomimes and popular dramas, in producing which he is unhampered by guarantors or tenors, and can face competition without misgiving. My duties as musical critic make me a stranger to his work in this department. There, where his qualities have fuller scope, no doubt they take effect in the high artistic temper and wholesome moral atmosphere of his productions. If so, perhaps my friend W. A. will give Mr Russell's project his blessing and his subscription.

9 *August* 1893

A LETTER which is quite a masterpiece of inconsiderateness has come to me on the subject of the Norwich Festival and my late remarks thereon. Those remarks were precisely accurate; were based on the prospectus issued to the public by the committee along with the usual forms of application for seats; and were, in my opinion, of first-rate importance. I therefore jump at the opportunity of rubbing them in. My correspondent, on the strength of certain irrelevant facts of which I was perfectly well aware and which I never contradicted, offers me grievous incivilities, such as that I am an idle babbler, steeped in manifest ignorance and entire and absurd error, and that I have "little in common" with the charities of Norwich.

Now if this gentleman were a hospital governor to whom a concert is nothing but a dodge for raising the wind of charity, I should pass his assault over indulgently. But he is a musical critic, and a young one—exactly, that is, the sort of person whose vigorous support I should have for my efforts to knock into the provincial mind the idea that Music is worth cultivating for its own sake, and that the man who is brought up in a town where there are exchanges and chambers of commerce, but no orchestra and no opera, will never be a cultivated citizen of the world, though he were rich as Crœsus. I believe the provincials feel this themselves; for they buy innumerable books about Art, and pore reverentially over my articles, heedless of the fact that you may read all the writers on Art from Ruskin and Wagner downwards until you know their opinions by heart and are aglow (as you imagine) with their enthusiasms, yet at the end you will not be able to distinguish a Teniers from a Burne-Jones without looking at your catalogue, or a Beethoven symphony from a selection from The Mikado without looking at your program.

How then can a movement for the culture of the provinces best be opened on the side of Music? Obviously, to my mind, by beginning with the Festival, which is our leading musical institution, and making a vigorous protest against its present footing of a mere pretext for sending round the hat for the local hospitals under cover of my correspondent's eloquent flummeries about "an innocent cause," "splendid usefulness," "a city famous for its charity," and so forth. Let me make the issue clear. Norwich has to provide for a certain number of accidents and illnesses occurring to people who are too poor to pay for proper treatment for themselves, but whose labor Norwich is not in a position to do without. This provision, which is now regarded by sensible people as part of the working expenses of our civilization, can be met either by the private subscriptions of those who have money to spare, or by hospitals' rate, or, of course, by a combination of the two. The Norwich people can settle the method among themselves: all I need insist on here is that the expense has to be met somehow, willy-nilly, whether the inhabitants are the most generous or the stingiest in England.

Now any adventitious aid will relieve the people who pay for the hospitals, whether they are subscribers or ratepayers. Accordingly, such adventitious aid is always welcome. For instance, there is the bazaar, where the moral law is suspended for a day in the name of charity, and gambling, overcharging, and sale of innocent favors by the ladies are tolerated and encouraged. You have also the sermon on Hospital Sunday, and the street collection on Hospital Saturday. Now it happens that in some cathedrals the simple, oldfashioned charity sermon, in which the plate started its round with a few decoy banknotes and sovereigns on it, developed in the course of time into an annual oratorio performance, which later on developed into the Festival as we know it. The charitable institution thus became a musical institution; and yet charity, as represented by subscribers and ratepayers on the alert for a grant in aid of hospital expenses, continued to pocket the proceeds as a matter of course.

I now, as a musical critic, raise a protest against this, on the plain ground that as Music has earned the money it should go to her own support, and that a good orchestra is every whit as important to a town as a good hospital. Even a Philistine will admit that the absence of high-class recreation means a resort to low-class recreation, which runs up a heavy police bill and hospitals bill. I therefore denounced, and do here again denounce, the proposal to devote the proceeds of the surplus from the Norwich Festival to the Norwich hospitals, as a device on the part of the general committee to lighten the burden of their charities at the expense of the starving Art of Music and of the culture of the townsfolk.

If I, or anyone with the interests of Music at heart, had been upon that general committee, an attempt would have been made to have the surplus (if any) devoted to the bringing down to Norwich of Richter and his band for a few concerts, or of Jean de Reszke, Lassalle, and the rest, for a performance of Die Meistersinger, or for such other demonstration of the best that can be done in music as the money might run to. But no: the musicians are relegated to the managing committee, which has to look after all the work connected with the performance, but has no voice in the disposition of the proceeds—a vital distinction which my irate correspondent has overlooked to the extent of actually abusing me heartily for not overlooking it.

If a vigorous agitation on these lines were made by the critics and musicians at every Festival, it would very soon produce practical results; and in the end it is not inconceivable that all the Festivals might be rescued from the clutches of the hospital governors, and begin mightily to nourish and propagate artistic life in this, at present, barren and boorish country. I am well pleased to find that my sally has elicited a vehement protest on the ground that "since The World is perhaps the most widely-read newspaper in the Eastern Counties, a great deal of harm may be inflicted upon an innocent cause." When that sort of thing begins, I feel that I am making way.

Besides, the "innocent cause"—the hospitals—may surely be left to those charitable instincts which the author of the protest so enthusiastically extols; whereas the cause of music, which appears to me quite as innocent as the other, must depend on what it can earn. Why it should be saddled with more than its share of the cost of the hospitals does not appear in the letter of my correspondent, who on thinking the matter over a little further will, I hope, see the advisability of backing his own side in this matter, and leaving the hospital governors to take care of their pockets for themselves.

MUSIC IN LONDON 1890-94

PASSING through town from Switzerland to some deserted corner of England in which to lie down and recover from a holiday, I find promenade concerts in full swing at Covent Garden. It is the custom to disparage promenade concerts as involving "Beethoven to an accompaniment of popping corks." That is the epigrammatic formula which crops up autumn after autumn. No doubt in weather like this the whole life of London may be said to proceed to an accompaniment of cork popping; but one should not, in dealing with the effect of this small artillery on particular incidents, quite overlook the question of how far off the corks are. As a matter of fact a great artist can obtain as complete a silence at Covent Garden on a "classical night" as in St James's Hall; and the shilling public can watch the performance much more closely, since it can get right up to the platform instead of having to observe the pianist's fingers or "the marvellous fiddle bow" from afar across a vast space of half-guinea and five-shilling stalls.

The facility with which you can change your place, stroll about, hold a conversation, avoid a tedious item in the program, have a cork popped on your own account, or go to a corridor window for a draught of such fresh air as may be available in Bow Street, are points of superiority secured to the promenader by that great advantage, a uniform price. For though you can get any sort of privilege of place, from a two-guinea box to an eighteenpenny amphitheatre stall, still, the general freedom of circulation round the orchestra and from the gallery to the floor practically gives the shilling the run of the house. Further, the arrangements admit of two concerts every evening. From a quarter to eight till about half-past nine you get an overture, a concerto, a symphony, and a couple of songs, just as at any first-rate orchestral concert. For the rest of the time you have your "grand selections" and vocal waltzes and ballads, and so on—in short, the promenade concert in the ordinary sense.

The orchestra, except perhaps whilst a provincial festival is in progress, is always potentially as good as any in the world. Consequently it only needs the engagement of a conductor of high standing and virtuosos of the first rank to make the promenade season as important artistically as that of the Philharmonic, the Richter, the London Symphony, or the Crystal Palace Saturday concerts. It is, of course, equally easy, by engaging a seaside bandmaster whose highest flight is a comfortable jaunt through "the world-renowned masterpiece, Mozart's Jupiter Symphony," to reduce promenade concerts to the artistic insignificance of an entertainment at a Hall-by-the-Sea.

There have been seasons when I have never dreamt of the promenade concerts as concerning me more closely than the street pianos (on which, nevertheless, as on everything else that is a part of our musical life, I keep an observant ear). And there have been seasons which have marked important stages in the development of popular taste, on the one hand, and of the conquest of London by notable artists on the other.

I am sorry to say that I do not know which of these two policies pays the *entrepreneur* best. The high art policy is never persevered in, and yet never finally abandoned. After one or two first-rate years, the rule appears to be three or four second-rate years, after which rapid decay sets in until another first-rate year or so is administered by way of tonic. This year, fortunately, there can be no doubt that the turn of the tonic has come round. Mr Farley Sinkins has done the very handsomest thing in his power by engaging Isaÿe, who divides with Sarasate the position of greatest living violinist, and Slivinski, who, among pianists of the Leschetitzky school, is second only to Paderewski, and who, within a certain range of very brilliant and popular qualities, is second to none.

The other day, glancing through the last number of The Meister, I came across the following passage from one of the articles written by Wagner from Paris in 1841, about a concert given by Liszt, under the conductorship of Berlioz, to raise funds for a memorial to Beethoven:

"The Parisian public demands from Liszt at all costs wonders and foolish tricks: he gives it what it wants, lets himself be carried away at its hands—actually plays, in a concert for Beethoven's memorial, a fantasia on Robert the Devil! This happened, however, against his will. The program consisted solely of Beethoven's compositions. Nevertheless, the fatal public demanded with a voice of thunder Liszt's *tour de force par excellence*, that Fantaisie. For the gifted man there was no help. With words hastily extorted from his chagrin, '*Je suis le serviteur du public: cela va sans dire*,' he sat down to the piano, and played with crashing brilliancy the favored piece. Thus avenges itself each crime on earth. One day in heaven, before the assembled angel public, will Liszt have to perform that fantasia on the devil."

Now, as it happens, I never heard that fantasia performed until, not very long ago, Slivinski revived it as a sample of his extraordinary powers in that sort of "transcendent" execution. And nobody seemed particularly amazed by it, although not long before Paderewski had thrown his audience into ecstasies by a performance of Liszt's transcription of Schubert's Erl King, of which, as it happened, he made a laughable mess through a slip of his hand or memory at a critical moment. As far as this shews that everybody knows and delights in The Erl King, whereas only a few obsolete survivors from the Meyerbeerian age know Robert the Devil by heart, or care two straws about its *valse infernale*, it is an incident to rejoice in; but it bore hardly on Slivinski, who should try his hand on the Don Juan fantasia, and find whether he cannot get the same intoxicating effect as Paderewski did out of its final apotheosis of Finch' han dal vino.

I heard Slivinski, on Tuesday last week, play Tchaikowsky's concerto, which was last heard here at the Crystal Palace, where Mr Lamond played it with a rough Cyclopean force and somewhat smoky fire, which by no means anticipated the version given by the refined strength and feathery

54

swiftness of Slivinski. He had some trouble in the last movement to avoid being baulked by Mr Cowen, who is seldom
equal to the occasion when a movement has to be saved by
pure *entrain*, and who was himself probably baulked by his
consciousness of the artificiality with which the concerto is
pieced together from independent and discontinuous conceits.

On Wednesday Isaÿe played Bruch's Scotch Fantasia,
a work so easily within his power that he played it better
than one would have supposed it capable of being played,
and set a rather diffident audience cheering at the end. Decidedly, if Isaÿe only perseveres in playing splendidly to us
for twenty-five years more or so, it will dawn on us at last
that he is one of the greatest of living artists; and then he
may play how he pleases until he turns ninety without the
least risk of ever hearing a word of disparagement or faint
praise.

The orchestra is on its good behavior with Mr Cowen.
It reflects his qualities, and, with the help of an occasional
spur from Slivinski and Isaÿe, covers some of his faults. To
me it sounded wonderfully distinguished; but after a fortnight of Swiss art, musical and pictorial, anything would
have produced that impression on me; so I had better reserve my opinion until I have recovered my critical balance.
By the bye, since I have mentioned pictorial and musical art
together, may I appeal to Madame Belle Cole not to sing that
old-fashioned piece of secondhand Rossini about Judith
(not Dr Parry's, but Concone's) in a dress evidently designed—very successfully—by the colorists of the Glasgow
school? The anachronism is too violent.

If anyone is curious about the poem (by Count Sporck)
of Cyrill Kistler's Wagnerian music-drama Kunihild, which
we shall hear some of these days, I suppose, he can now
procure for eighteenpence an English metrical translation
by Mr Ashton Ellis. I may also remind Wagnerians that by
making a dash for Munich at once on seeing this, they may
arrive in time for some of the Wagner performances there,

though some of the Ring nights will have already passed before the day of publication.

4 October 1893

I CANNOT imagine why the Paris Grand Opera should fascinate English impresarios as it does. Here is Mr Farley Sinkins putting himself out of his way and charging double prices to produce a concert recital of Samson et Dalila. Who wants to hear Samson et Dalila? I respectfully suggest, Nobody. In Paris that is not a reason for not producing it, because Saint-Saëns is an illustrious French composer, and the Opera a national institution; consequently, Saint-Saëns must occasionally compose an opera, and the director produce it, for the satisfaction of the taxpayers. In the same way, we produce specially composed oratorios at our English festivals. We cannot sit them out without wishing we had never been born; but we do sit them out for all that; and though the English school does not immediately become famous over the earth, at least Messrs Novello sell a great many copies of the new work to provincial choral societies.

Now I am strongly of opinion that each nation should bear its own burden in this department of life. We do not ask the Parisians to share the weight of Job with us; then let them not foist on to us the load of Samson. However, on reflection, this is hardly reasonable; for it is our English Mr Sinkins who has insisted on our listening to Samson; whilst the composer and the tenor, representing the French nation, have done their best to save us by bolting at the last moment. The story of their flight; of Mr Sinkins's diplomatic masterstroke of sending the soprano to win them back; and of the fugitives rising to the height of the occasion by capturing the soprano, has already been told, though not explained. The sequel, shewing how Mr Bernard Lane came to the rescue by taking the part of Samson, is, I suppose, for me to tell; but I propose to shirk that duty, out of regard for Mr Lane's feelings.

Samson with the part of Samson read at sight, is perhaps better than Samson with the part of Samson left out: anyhow Mr Lane thought so; and no doubt in acting on that opinion he did his best under the circumstances. Miss Edith Miller, who undertook Dalila at equally short notice, was less at a disadvantage. Lyrical expression, to a musician, is much more obvious at first sight than dramatic expression, which can be planned only by careful study; and as Dalila's music is much more lyrical than Samson's, not to mention the fact that the most important number in it is already hackneyed by concert use, Miss Miller was able to make the most of her opportunity and to come off handsomely, all things considered.

The other parts, in the hands of Messrs Oudin, Barlow, Magrath, and Gawthrop, would no doubt have been well done if they had possessed any artistic substance for these gentlemen to bite on, so to speak. But the impossible Meyerbeerian Abimelech, with his brusque measures and his grim orchestral clinkings and whistlings, could have come from no place in the world but Paris, where they still regard Meyerbeer as a sort of musical Michael Angelo, and gravely offer to the wondering world commonplace imitations of the petty monstrosities and abortions of Le Prophète as sublime *hardiesses*, and pages of history read by flashes of lightning. No doubt Saint-Saëns had to copy Meyerbeer, just as poor Meyerbeer had to copy himself from the day when he made a specialty of religious fanaticism in Les Huguenots.

After the Huguenots and Catholics came the Anabaptists; and now, the Philistines and the Israelites being in question, we have Abimelech clinking and whistling as aforesaid; Samson calling his sect to arms to a trumpet motive in the best style of Raoul de Nangis at the ball given by Marguerite de Valois; stage rushes of the two factions at each other's throats, with every eye, aflame with bigotry, flashing on the conductor; and the inevitable love-duet, in which the tenor is torn by the conflicting calls of passion and party in a key with several flats in it. I did not wait for the

57

third act of Samson; but I assume that the hero attempted to bring the house down by a drinking-song before resorting to the pillars.

If Saint-Saëns were to be commissioned to write a new "historical opera" entitled Ulster, we should have the zealous Protestants of that region devoting the Pope to perdition in a Rataplan chorus, and confining themselves to ascetic accompaniments of double bass and piccolo; whilst their opponents would pay the same compliment to King William of glorious, pious, and immortal memory, in crisp waltzes and galops, whipped along into movements of popular fury by flicks on the side-drum, *strettos*, sham *fugatos*, and *pas redoublés*, with a grand climax of all the national airs of Ireland worked in double counterpoint with suitable extracts from the Church music of the rivals' creeds, played simultaneously on several military bands and a pair of organs. This is the sort of thing a French composer dreams of as the summit of operatic achievement. I feel that my own view of it cuts off my artistic sympathy with Paris at the musical main. But I cannot help that. It is not good sense to expect me to sacrifice my reputation as a serious critic for the sake of such tinpot stage history. Besides, I long ago gave up Paris as impossible from the artistic point of view. London I do not so much mind.

Your average Londoner is, no doubt, as void of feeling for the fine arts as a man can be without collapsing bodily; but then he is not at all ashamed of his condition. On the contrary, he is rather proud of it, and never feels obliged to pretend that he is an artist to the tips of his fingers. His pretences are confined to piety and politics, in both of which he is an unspeakable impostor. It is your Parisian who concentrates his ignorance and hypocrisy, not on politics and religion, but on art. He believes that Europe expects him to be, before everything, artistic. In this unwholesome state of self-consciousness he demands statues and pictures and operas in all directions, long before any appetite for beauty has set his eyes or ears aching; so that he at once becomes the prey of pedants who undertake to supply him with classical works, and swaggerers who set up in the romantic department. Hence, as the Parisian, like other people, likes to enjoy himself, and as pure pedantry is tedious and pure swaggering tiresome, what Paris chiefly loves is a genius who can make the classic voluptuous and the romantic amusing.

And so, though you cannot walk through Paris without coming at every corner upon some fountain or trophy or monument for which the only possible remedy is dynamite, you can always count upon the design including a female figure free from the defect known to photographers as under-exposure; and if you go to the Opera—which is, happily, an easily avoidable fate—you may wonder at the expensive trifling that passes as musical poetry and drama, but you will be compelled to admit that the composer has moments, carried as far as academic propriety permits, in which he rises from sham history and tragedy to genuine polka and barcarolle; whilst there is, to boot, always one happy half-hour when the opera-singers vanish, and capable, thoroughly trained, hardworking, technically skilled executants entertain you with a ballet. Of course the ballet, like everything else in Paris, is a provincial survival, fifty years behind English time; but still it is generally complete, and well done by people who understand ballet, whereas the opera is generally mutilated, and ill-done by people who dont understand opera.

Such being my prejudices against Paris, it is vain to expect enthusiasm from me on the subject of Samson et Dalila. Saint-Saëns would feel sufficiently flattered, perhaps, if I were to pronounce it as good as Les Huguenots; but I cannot do that, for a variety of reasons, among which I may mention that if Saint-Saëns had successfully imitated Meyerbeer's masterpiece, the effect would have been, not to establish the merit of the imitation, but rather to destroy one of the chief merits of the original—its uniqueness. Besides, Les Huguenots made the Paris Opera what it is; whereas the Paris Opera has made Samson what *it* is, unluckily for

Saint-Saëns.

Some of the improvements on Meyerbeer are question-able: for instance, in the instrumental prelude to Les Hugue-nots Meyerbeer borrowed the tune and invented only the accompaniment; but Saint-Saëns, scorning to borrow, has written a prelude consisting of an accompaniment without any tune at all, and not a very original accompaniment at that. I own I like Meyerbeer's plan better. I have already confessed to a preference for Raoul over Samson; and I defy anyone to blame me for thinking Valentine and Marcel in the Pré-aux-Clercs worth a dozen of Dalila and the High Priest of Dagon in a place described by the program, in the manner of a postal address, as "The Valley of Soreck, Palestine."

As to the orchestral part of the performance, those who heard Saint-Saëns' Rouet d'Omphale conducted by him-self at the Philharmonic last season, may possibly have been able to judge how the score of Samson would have come out under the composer's baton. Mr Cowen is quite a hopeless conductor for this sort of music. It requires a continual *en-train*, even at its quietest; and from this normal activity it has to be repeatedly worked up to the utmost vivacity and impetuosity. Mr Cowen's worst enemies have never ac-cused him of impetuosity or vivacity in conducting; and as to *entrain*, he has cultivated to perfection a habit entirely fatal to it: that is to say, he checks the band in every bar be-tween the first and second beat. I do not say that the inter-val is long enough to eat a sandwich in; but sometimes, when I am in my best critical condition, with my rhythmical sen-sitiveness highly exalted, it seems to me, even during a *presto*, that Mr Cowen always allows time somewhere in the bar for all ordinary exigencies of turning over, using one's handkerchief, nodding to an acquaintance, or the like.

If Mr Cowen were to equip Saint-Saëns with a long pair of spurs, and carry him pick-a-back during the perform-ance, he might possibly get through Samson with some effect, albeit with much loss of blood; but I doubt if any less heroic measure would meet the occasion; and even then it would be easier to let Saint-Saëns conduct himself. All sorts of excellent qualities in Mr Cowen are thrown away when it comes to dealing with French operatic music, for want of the vulgar little gift—contemptible enough by itself—called "go."

In conclusion, lest anything that I have said about the Parisians should unduly strain international relations, let me add that we already have in this country a class—and a growing class—of amateurs who have totally discarded our national hobbies of politics and piety, and taken on the Parisian hobby of art. As like causes produce like effects in both countries, will these ladies and gentlemen kindly apply to themselves everything that I have said about their neighbors across the water.

11 *October* 1893

PLEASANT it is to see Mr Gilbert and Sir Arthur Sullivan working together again full brotherly. They should be on the best of terms; for henceforth Sir Arthur can always say, "Any other librettist would do just as well: look at Haddon Hall"; whilst Mr Gilbert can retort, "Any other musician would do just as well: look at The Mountebanks." Thus have the years of divorce cemented the happy reunion at which we all assisted last Saturday. The twain still excite the expectations of the public as much as ever. How Trial by Jury and The Sorcerer surprised the public, and how Pinafore, The Pirates, and Patience kept the sensation fresh, can be guessed by the youngest man from the fact that the announcement of a new Savoy opera always throws the middle-aged playgoer into the attitude of expecting a surprise. As for me, I avoid this attitude, if only because it is a middle-aged one. Still, I expect a good deal that I could not have hoped for when I first made the acquaintance of comic opera.

Those who are old enough to compare the Savoy performances with those of the dark ages, taking into account the pictorial treatment of the fabrics and colors on the stage, the cultivation and intelligence of the choristers, the quality of the orchestra, and the degree of artistic good breeding, so to speak, expected from the principals, best know how great an advance has been made by Mr D'Oyly Carte in organizing and harmonizing that complex co-operation of artists of all kinds which goes to make up a satisfactory operatic performance. Long before the run of a successful Savoy opera is over Sir Arthur's melodies are dinned into our ears by every promenade band and street piano, and Mr Gilbert's sallies are quoted threadbare by conversationalists and journalists; but the whole work as presented to eye and ear on the Savoy stage remains unhackneyed.

Further, no theatre in London is more independent of those executants whose personal popularity enables them to demand ruinous salaries; and this is not the least advantageous of the differences between opera as the work of a combination of manager, poet, and musician, all three making the most of one another in their concerted striving for the common object of a completely successful representation, and opera as the result of a speculator picking up a libretto, getting somebody with a name to set it to music, ordering a few tradesmen to "mount" it, and then, with a stage manager hired here, an acting manager hired there, and a popular prima donna, comedian, and serpentine dancer stuck in at reckless salaries like almonds into an underdone dumpling, engaging some empty theatre on the chance of the affair "catching on."

If any capitalist wants to succeed with comic opera, I can assure him that he can do so with tolerable security if he only possesses the requisite managerial ability. There is no lack of artistic material for him to set to work on: London is overstocked with artistic talent ready to the hand of anyone who can recognize it and select from it. The difficulty is to find the man with this power of recognition and selection. The effect of the finer artistic temperaments and talents on the ordinary speculator is not merely nil (for in that case he

62

might give them an engagement by accident), but anti-pathetic. People sometimes complain of the indifference of the public and the managers to the highest elements in fine art. There never was a greater mistake. The Philistine is not indifferent to fine art: he *hates* it.

The relevance of these observations will be apparent when I say that, though I enjoyed the score of Utopia more than that of any of the previous Savoy operas, I am quite prepared to hear that it is not as palatable to the majority of the human race—otherwise the mob—as it was to me. It is written with an artistic absorption and enjoyment of which Sir Arthur Sullivan always had moments, but which seem to have become constant with him only since he was knighted, though I do not suggest that the two things stand in the relation of cause and effect. The orchestral work is charmingly humorous; and as I happen to mean by this only what I say, perhaps I had better warn my readers not to infer that Utopia is full of buffooneries with the bassoon and piccolo, or of patter and tum-tum.

Whoever can listen to such caressing wind parts—zephyr parts, in fact—as those in the trio for the King and the two Judges in the first act, without being coaxed to feel pleased and amused, is not fit even for treasons, stratagems, and spoils; whilst anyone whose ears are capable of taking in more than one thing at a time must be tickled by the sudden busyness of the orchestra as the city man takes up the parable. I also confidently recommend those who go into solemn academic raptures over themes "in diminution" to go and hear how prettily the chorus of the Christy Minstrel song (borrowed from the plantation dance Johnnie, get a gun) is used, very much in diminution, to make an exquisite mock-banjo accompaniment. In these examples we are on the plane, not of the bones and tambourine, but of Mozart's accompaniments to Soave sia il vento in Cosi fan tutte and the entry of the gardener in Le Nozze di Figaro. Of course these things are as much thrown away on people who are not musicians as a copy of Fliegende Blätter on people who do

63

not read German, whereas anyone can understand mere horseplay with the instruments.

But people who are not musicians should not intrude into opera-houses: indeed, it is to me an open question whether they ought to be allowed to exist at all. As to the score generally, I have only one fault to find with Sir Arthur's luxurious ingenuity in finding pretty timbres of all sorts, and that is that it still leads him to abuse the human voice most unmercifully. I will say nothing about the part he has written for the unfortunate soprano, who might as well leave her lower octave at home for all the relief she gets from the use of her upper one. But take the case of Mr Scott Fishe, one of Mr Carte's most promising discoveries, who did so much to make the ill-fated Jane Annie endurable.

What made Mr Fishe's voice so welcome was that it was neither the eternal callow baritone nor the growling bass: it rang like a genuine "singing bass"; and one felt that here at last was a chance of an English dramatic *basso cantante*, able to "sing both high and low," and to contrast his high D with an equally fine one an octave below. Unfortunately, the upper fifth of Mr Fishe's voice, being flexible and of excellent quality, gives him easy command (on occasion) of high passages; and Sir Arthur has ruthlessly seized on this to write for him an excessively specialized baritone part, in which we get not one of those deep, ringing tones which relieved the Jane Annie music so attractively. I have in my time heard so many singers reduced by parts of this sort, in the operas of Verdi and Gounod, to a condition in which they could bawl F sharps *ad lib.* at high pressure, but could neither place a note accurately nor produce any tolerable tone from B flat downwards, that I always protest against vocal parts, no matter what voice they are written for, if they do not employ the voice all over its range, though lying mainly where the singer can sing continuously without fatigue.

A composer who uses up young voices by harping on the prettiest notes in them is an ogreish voluptuary; and if Sir

Arthur does not wish posterity either to see the stage
whitened with the bones of his victims or else to hear his
music transposed wholesale, as Lassalle transposes Rigoletto, he should make up his mind whether he means to
write for a tenor or a baritone, and place the part accordingly.
Considering that since Santley retired from the stage and
Jean de Reszke turned tenor all the big reputations have
been made by *bassi cantanti* like Edouard de Reszke and
Lassalle, and that all the great Wagner parts in which
reputations of the same calibre will be made for some time
to come are impossible to completely specialized baritones,
I venture, as a critic who greatly enjoys Mr Fishe's performance, to recommend him to ask the composer politely
not to treat him worse than Mozart treated Don Giovanni,
than Wagner treated Wolfram, or than Sir Arthur himself
would treat a clarinet. Miss Nancy McIntosh, who was
introduced to us, it will be remembered, by Mr Henschel
at the London Symphony Concerts, where she sang in a
selection from Die Meistersinger and in the Choral Symphony, came through the trials of a most inconsiderate
vocal part very cleverly, evading the worst of the strain by a
treatment which, if a little flimsy, was always pretty. She
spoke her part admirably, and, by dint of natural tact,
managed to make a positive advantage of her stage in-
experience, so that she won over the audience in no time. As
to Miss Brandram, Mr Barrington (who by means of a
remarkable pair of eyebrows transformed himself into a
surprising compound of Mr Goschen and the late Sir
William Cusins), Messrs Denny, Kenningham, Le Hay,
Gridley, and the rest, everybody knows what they can do;
and I need only particularize as to Miss Owen and Miss
Florence Perry, who gave us some excellent pantomime in
the very amusing lecture scene, contrived by Mr Gilbert,
and set to perfection by Sir Arthur, in the first act.

The book has Mr Gilbert's lighter qualities without his
faults. Its main idea, the Anglicization of Utopia by a
people boundlessly credulous as to the superiority of the

English race, is as certain of popularity as that reference to England by the Gravedigger in Hamlet, which never yet failed to make the house laugh. There is, happily, no plot; and the stage business is fresh and well invented—for instance, the lecture already alluded to, the adoration of the troopers by the female Utopians, the Cabinet Council "as held at the Court of St James's Hall," and the quadrille, are capital strokes. As to the "Drawing Room," with *débutantes*, cards, trains, and presentations all complete, and the little innovation of a cup of tea and a plate of cheap biscuits, I cannot vouch for its verisimilitude, as I have never, strange as it may appear, been present at a Drawing Room; but that is exactly why I enjoyed it, and why the majority of the Savoyards will share my appreciation of it.

18 October 1893

THE historian Robertson, in his history of Mary Queen of Scots, approaches the delicate subject of Rizzio with an elaborate apology for mentioning a person so entirely beneath the dignity of history as a professional musician, and an Italian one at that. For obvious reasons, I am compelled in this column to be more tolerant than Robertson; but there are moments when I, too, feel that the art I profess has no concern with some of the entertainments upon which I am invited to exercise it. This superior mood came strongly upon me at the first performance of Little Christopher Columbus at the Lyric Theatre. I thought it utterly beneath serious criticism; and on thinking it over since, my sense of indignity has grown rather than abated. As far as I could understand the situation, Mr Sedger had made expensive provision for the production of an opera. He had engaged Mr Caryll to furnish the score, Miss Yohé and Mr Lonnen to draw the audience, Messrs Sims and Raleigh to provide Miss Yohé and Mr Lonnen with something to say, Mr D'Auban to invent dances, and various other artists to provide costumes, scenery, limelight, and so forth.

The only thing omitted was the opera itself. There was no opera; and nobody pretended that there was—not even the author of the playbill, in which the *genre* of Little Christopher was left carefully unspecified. Most of the lines spoken by the two principals were frankly written for them in what would ordinarily be called their private capacities. They had no parts, only dialogue; and when this dialogue ran into puns on the name Yohé, or references to Mr Lonnen's old Gaiety success, The Bogie Man, the effect was not incongruous, as it would have been in a real opera, but simply tedious, as if the two artists were neglecting their business to indulge in some private chaff between themselves. The other characters, having neither parts nor personalities, attained to perfect nothingness.

The cardinal flaw in the planning of Little Christopher was a mistaken estimate of Miss Yohé's talent. If she had comic genius, if her high spirits and love of fun had any artistic character whatever, she might have turned this bodiless spook of a comic opera into a passable burlesque by the style of play which made Miss Farren famous at the Gaiety. As it was, Miss Yohé caught nothing of the trick of burlesque except some of its vulgarity; and vulgarity, racy as it may be in the true street-Arab breed, is not enjoyable in a pathetically pretty young woman who, though touched with something of the rudeness as well as the *naïveté* of—let us say a wilder civilization, only requires a little refining and softening to be a charming artist.

Miss Yohé had only two really successful moments on Tuesday in Little Christopher: to wit, the siesta song, Lazily, lazily; drowsily, drowsily, and the plantation melody, Listen to the music far away, both of which took her completely out of her forced rôle of burlesque actress, and gave her an opportunity of appealing to the audience on the imaginative and sentimental side. For the rest, she had to rely on the general indulgent disposition to spoil her for the sake of her prettiness and the fascination of the few effective notes of that extraordinary *chalumeau* register to which she confines

67

herself, and which is, perhaps, the whole of her voice. Mr Lonnen, less gifted with personal beauty than Miss Yohé, had much the same class of task to perform; but he, being a born droll, was at no very great loss, though even he could do no more for me than help to make my heavy boredom just bearable.

However, let it be remembered that I am a superior person, and that what seemed incoherent and wearisome fooling to me may have seemed an exhilarating pastime to others. My heart knows only its own bitterness; and I do not desire to intermeddle with the joys of those among whom I am a stranger. I assert my intellectual superiority to those who enjoyed Little Christopher Columbus—that is all.

The composer, Mr Caryll, comes off with a certain consideration, because he has taken his work seriously and done his utmost to put at least some bounce, if not some life and substance, into the—I was about to call it the opera, but, as I have said, Mr Sedger did not commit himself to that description of the entertainment. But the harder Mr Caryll works, the more it becomes apparent that he is not naturally frolicsome. He has energy and determination, which he puts into his composition in an intelligent, mechanical way; but even the most impetuous pages in his score have not a smile in them. His orchestration is clever, active, full of traits and points, but certainly not normally smooth and beautiful, and often uneasy, self-conscious, and obtrusive. There is no pretence of novelty in the melodies and rhythms. I should imagine that Mr Caryll would find romantic opera of the tragic cast more congenial to him than the buffooneries of Little Christopher, which I may now dismiss with a word of remonstrance against the feeble *pas de quatre* in which four ladies, attired in what I really must denounce as stupidly ugly costumes, make a bid for the most worthless sort of applause by turning cartwheels. After this Miss St Cyr's plastic display in the second act is at least artistically respectable. It is difficult, original, and could not have been invented without some imagination and forethought, qualities which give it eminence in an entertainment otherwise rather stinted in them.

But Miss St Cyr is still a fascinating woman who dances, rather than a fascinating dancer. If she had no more beauty than the dance has grace, its ingenuity would hardly save it. The art of being a handsome woman is not the same thing as the art of dancing; and many passages in Miss St Cyr's feats are curious exhibitions of success in the one discounted by comparative failure in the other.

The serious business of the winter season began with the Crystal Palace Saturday Concerts last week. It will be remembered that last year a considerable advance was made in the accommodation of regular attendants from London, by issuing in a single batch for twenty-one shillings the twenty first-class railway tickets which used to cost two pounds. This year the occasional visitor, who did not benefit by the railway arrangement, has his expenses reduced eighteen-pence per concert by the abolition of the special charge for admission to the Palace on Saturdays, which is now a shilling day like the rest. At the same time, the numbered stalls, which were formerly half-a-crown, are now divided into two sets at four shillings and two shillings, the usual shilling admission to an unnumbered seat remaining as before; and the ordinary two-guinea serial stall-ticket is supplemented by a three-guinea one, which includes admission to the Palace on concert days only—though, as the same money will buy a two-guinea serial stall-ticket and a season ticket admitting to the Palace every day, no commercially sane human being will take a three-guinea ticket unless he wishes his admission, like his stall, to be transferable. It is now at last possible for the third-class traveller, by contenting himself with an unnumbered seat (no great disadvantage if he knows how to select it) and dispensing with an analytic program, to come from the City or West End and hear a Saturday concert for half-a-crown; whilst a regular attendant can travel first-class, sit in a reserved stall, buy a program, and indulge in two-penn'orth of refreshment for double that sum. These matters are worth noting; for the cost of attending the Crystal Palace concerts has hitherto greatly diminished their social utility. It now appears that the directors are sufficiently doubtful as to its having increased the total profit on each Saturday to make the reductions I have described. The immediate reason given is that "Saturday afternoon has now become a general holiday in London"; but this, though new in comparison with the death of Queen Anne, must surely have come to the notice of the directors before the present year. However, better late than never. I hope the public, however scarce its half-crowns may be, will bear in mind that it is a poor heart that never rejoices, and that except when there is something specially dismal on in the way of an oratorio, or specially attractive to star-gazers in the way of a soloist, there is generally plenty of room in the huge concert-hall for a few hundred more unreserved shillings.

The opening concert last Saturday, which was, as usual, too long, brought forward a new work by a young English composer. Similar items are set down for most of the other concerts. It cannot be said that Mr Manns does not give young England its chance. Young England, I am sorry to say, does not always make much of it, being for the most part able to do nothing but take some ballad for a program, and orchestrate away to its young heart's content upon a couple of well-worn themes, a climax or two, and a sentimental *pianissimo* to finish with. Still, these compositions are genuine as far as they go: they are not regulation exercises in sonata form: they represent the best the composer is able to do. Mr Godfrey Pringle's Ballad for Orchestra, supposed to illustrate Uhland's Durand, is in no way a specially remarkable example of its kind. It shews the influence of young Italy—that is to say, of Cavalleria—here and there. The scoring needs some revision; for the wood-wind parts in the serenade are ineffective, and an attempt to bring out a melody by reinforcing it with two trombones in unison is as disagreeable as Mr Pringle, one would think, might have

expected. Slivinski threw away an opportunity by playing
Saint-Saëns' concerto in G minor, of which we have had
more than enough lately. He made an attempt to treat it
seriously, with the result that it became very dull, whereas
in the hands of the composer it is at least gay. The only really
good bit in it is borrowed from the prelude to Bach's organ
fugue in A minor, a favorite of Saint-Saëns, as I guess from
having heard him play it. The overture was Sullivan's Macbeth, with its funny lapses from drama into drawing-room
decoration. It was played with perfect neatness, and with
great spirit, which latter compliment I cannot extend to what
I heard of Beethoven's fourth symphony, though I will not
undertake to say whether it was I, or the band, or both of us
who were demoralized and bored by the long interval of
Saint-Saëns, etc., that came between it and a transcription of
the Apostrophe to Night from the second act of Tristan, in
which the two vocal parts were given to a cornet and a tenor
trombone. These were obviously the right instruments to
use for the purpose, since they alone were able to maintain
the necessary distinction and power against the accompaniment; and the display by Mr Hadfield and his colleague of
what can be done in the way of expressive execution and
sensitive vocal touch with the brass was interesting; but the
makeshift produced an effect of solemn burlesque which
forced one to smile in spite of the fascination of a wonderful
page of music. If a couple of singers had been substituted
for the cornet and trombone, and the solos and pianoforte
concerto omitted from the program, we should have had a
thoroughly enjoyable concert of just the right length.

25 October 1893

COMIC opera is still trying to mend its luck, apparently with some success. The Mascotte has been
transferred from the Gaiety to the Criterion, where
Miss St John still keeps it going with ease, though from the
middle of the last act onwards it is certainly as crazy a piece
of dramatic botchwork as the worst enemy of the human in-

71

telligence could desire. What it would be without the prima donna I dare not imagine; rather let me sit quietly in my stall and wonder whether Miss St John's next speech will be delivered in the prettiest serious manner of Miss Ellen Terry, or in cockney, Irish, or Yankee, as the mood of the moment may suggest. But, however it comes, it comes with genuine comic force; and the opera does not flag for a moment while Miss St John is on the stage. Her singing is as good as ever; and though her voice is a shade less fresh than it was twenty years ago, it is in much better condition than most voices are after twenty months' stage wear. Mr Wallace Brownlow is unfortunate in having to impersonate a youth who is accepted by a travelling dramatic company as a nimble comedian, which is exactly what he is not; but his singing pulls him through. Mr Conyers, the tenor, does not improve, the fault being, not his, but his method's. Mr Fred Emney is condemned to enact one of those zany kings of opera bouffe whose tyranny, I hope, must be as heavy on the player as on the audience. Miss Phyllis Broughton, rather at a discount in the earlier scenes, brought off her song and dance in the last act triumphantly; and Miss Mabel Love, who with the natural expansion of her view of life has quite relaxed the tragic aspect which distinguished her in her teens, was left breathless by a double encore for a tarantella which was really a dance, and not one of the arrant impostures which have lately got into currency under the pretext of "skirt-dancing."

Mr Hollingshead's venture at the Princess's is chiefly notable for the new departure downward in prices. Whether Miami succeeds or not, Mr Hollingshead is certainly sound in his economic reasoning. The notion that you can keep on increasing the supply of places of entertainment in London without affecting prices can only be defended on the hypothesis that the demand at the old prices far exceeded the supply. Considering that theatrical business has been falling off in all directions for some time past at the old prices, whilst the music-halls, at lower prices, hold their own, the hypothesis seems contradicted by the facts. Obstinately high prices and obstinately high salaries on the one hand, with closing theatres and the most desperate precariousness of employment on the other, have been the rule for the last few years. It is not certain even that the theatres which have kept open have paid.

Actor-managers find "backers" to subsidize experiments with expensively mounted plays which are assumed to be successful because they are persisted in for some months; but in such cases there is no satisfactory evidence to shew that the backer has escaped a loss, much less come out with his capital intact, plus the ordinary interest on it. Meanwhile hundreds of half-crowns are paid every night at the pit-door by men who would pay five shillings for an orchestra or balcony stall if it were to be had so cheap; whilst hundreds of others stay at home or go to the music-halls because theatre managers will not make them comfortable at a reasonable rate. Whether the stalls are always filled by persons who pay half a guinea apiece is best known to the managers.

My own observation leads me to suspect that, under circumstances of no more than ordinary attractiveness, it is difficult to fill even three rows of stalls without the assistance of deadheads—and as I am a professional deadhead myself, I may perhaps be excused for hinting a doubt as to whether the tone given to the stalls by the courtiers of the box-office is so very much more elevated from the fashionable point of view than that which might be expected to prevail among plain persons good for hard cash to the extent of five shillings. On the whole, I agree cordially with Mr Hollingshead that there is room for his Volkstheater in London, and can testify, having tried the experiment, to the sense of economic satisfaction produced by a comfortable balcony-stall costing a modest extravagance of three shillings.

At the same time, I must confess I do not in the least believe in the success of Mr Hollingshead's extraordinary freak of combining the most advanced arrangements before

73

the curtain with an attempt to revive the Crummles repertory behind it. I daresay Miami will draw a certain number of veteran playgoers who will go to see Green Bushes again just as they might go to see their birthplace, or their old school, or anything else likely to recall the sensations of "auld lang syne." Such gnawing pleasures reassure and freshen the man who fears that he has lost his youthful power of feeling thoroughly maudlin. The veterans, combined with the devotees of Miss Violet Cameron and Mr Courtice Pounds, will, no doubt, keep Miami going for a time; but I am sceptical as to its enjoying any great vogue on the strength of its artistic merits. The fact is, it has no such merits, and never had.

I do not speak altogether as a modern: these eyes have seen the great Celeste as Miami, and also as the heroine of a melodrama in which she was eighteen in the first act, thirty in the second, forty in the third, sixty in the fourth, and eighty in the fifth; after which I came away wondering how old Madame really was, as she had looked like a made-up old woman in the early stages, and like a made-up young woman in the later ones, never by any chance presenting a convincing appearance of being near the age indicated by the dramatist. She was, I took it, a clever lady who had taken the measure of that huge section of the playgoing public which is enormously credulous of everything except the truth, highly susceptible to the instinctive emotions, entirely uncritical as to the reasonableness of what it is used to, and mutinously indisposed to face the painful and unaccustomed exertion of thought or artistic perception, though not without a certain practical shrewdness as to the worth of its money, which makes it very necessary to give good value for it in amusement, excitement, and, above all, in that moral satisfaction produced by the spectacle of punishment spread over crime like jam over butter.

The melodramas of Buckstone and the acting of Celeste had no other purpose in the world that I could ever discover beyond the exploitation of this stratum of the playgoing

74

world to the uttermost farthing. Considered in relation to
any other purpose, Green Bushes is foolish and Miami-
Celeste impossible. This is apparent to everybody now that
the purpose is no longer fulfilled, the falling-off in the efficiency of the play being due, not, I regret to say, to any elevation of the taste of its audience, but simply to a change of
fashion in stage folly. Green Bushes now looks dowdy, and
it is accordingly found out and cut by the very people who
would seduously chatter its praises in order to prove their
culture if it were up to date in externals. This, I apprehend,
is why Mr Hollingshead has not ventured to revive it as
it originally stood. Instead, he has, by a happy thought,
changed it into an opera, thereby securing for its absurdities
the benefit of the unwritten law by which the drama which is
sung is allowed to lag half a century behind that which is
spoken.

If the experiment succeeds, we shall perhaps have The
Wreck Ashore set to music by Mr Haydn Parry and revived. I shall not object, for Miami entertained me more
than most comic operas do, the obvious reason being that
Buckstone was a playwright without genius trying to be
popularly sentimental, an attempt in which a man of ordinary sense and sympathy may attain a tolerable measure of
success, whereas your modern comic-opera librettist is
mostly a man without brains trying to be clever, which is
out of the question. This is the most that can be said for the
Green Bushes basis of Miami; and I think that if Mr Hollingshead will rub the glamor of old times out of his eyes,
and contemplate that last act gravely from the point of view
of the rational stranger who never heard of Madame Celeste
or Paul Bedford, he will agree with me that its day is happily
past.

And before he changes that attitude, he might as well
take the opportunity to forget that Grinnidge is a notoriously funny part, and Mr George Barrett a notoriously
funny actor; so that, escaping for a moment from the fore-
gone conclusion that Mr Barrett's Grinnidge is a scream-

ingly funny performance, he may be able to give him a
friendly hint that it is a noisy, slovenly business, unworthy
of a comedian of Mr Barrett's standing. Mr Barrett himself,
indeed, continues to intimate, by an expressive gag, that he
considers the part an impossible one. All the more reason
why he should take it quietly.

The cast does credit to Mr Hollingshead's judgment.
Miss Jessie Bond did not appear on the night of my visit;
but the lady who took her place sang pleasantly, and would
no doubt have spoken equally well if she had frankly given
up her hopeless attempt at a brogue. Miss Violet Cameron
played Miami with a whole-hearted loyalty to the management, which stopped at nothing·but the firing off of a Mar-
tini rifle, a weapon unknown to Celeste and Fenimore
Cooper. Her voice is in excellent preservation, sound and
sympathetic in the middle, as a properly used voice of its age
ought to be. Miami's songs are all encored; and the audience
does not laugh at her when she is not singing, a fact which
speaks volumes for Miss Cameron's earnestness. Miss Isa-
bella Girardot celebrates the virtues and misfortunes of Ger-
aldine in song; and Mr Courtice Pounds struggles bravely
to avoid the throaty habits which seemed at one time likely
to cost him his voice. The score, which was probably composed originally to some other libretto, is pretty in a well-
established way, with plenty of bright and tender orchestral
color; but it has been considerably shorn on the comic side,
the numbers for Jack Gong and Grinnidge appearing only
in the program—which, by the way, costs nothing, and is
full of instruction and amusement. Miss Clara Jecks enters
into the humors of the Mrs Gong, *née* Tigertail, much
further than I could; but the opera is certainly none the
heavier for her. Each act contains at least one effective *coup
de théâtre* in the way of a finale or a dance. *Matinées* are promised of Cavalleria, Suppé's Galatea, Handel's Rinaldo (!),
Dr Arne's Artaxerxes (good heavens!), and an original operetta by Mr Squiers, not to mention a Christmas play for
children. I am sure I wish Mr Hollingshead every success.

76

I have said my say so often about Gounod, our nineteenth-century Fra Angelico, that I need not add to the burden of the obituary notices that have been laid upon us since his death on Wednesday last. In his honor the program of the Saturday concert at the Crystal Palace was altered so as to include his Religious March and the overture to Mireille. The march was only nominally appropriate: it is, in truth, an uninspired affair, with a trio that would not surprise anyone in a second-rate comic opera. That exquisite little funeral march from Roméo, called Juliet's Last Sleep, would have been far better. Mireille was altogether charming: the beautiful smoothness of its lines and the transparent richness and breadth of its orchestral coloration were admirably reproduced by the Crystal Palace band. In the sixties the Parisian critics found it Wagnerian: nowadays the abyss of erroneousness—not to say downright ignorance—revealed by such an opinion makes one giddy.

After the Gounod numbers came an orchestral prelude to The Eumenides of Æschylus, by Mr W. Wallace, whose Passing of Beatrice made some mark last year. Like that work, it shewed that Mr Wallace knows how to use every instrument except the scissors. It is all that a young man's work ought to be, imaginative, ambitious, impetuous, romantic, prodigal, and most horribly indiscriminate. Mr Wallace's imagination is so susceptible, and his critical faculty so unsuspicious, that when he once gets exalted he will keep pegging away at a figure long after it has been worn threadbare, or he will remind you, in the thick of The Eumenides, of the bathers' chorus in Les Huguenots, because he cannot resist a few rushing bassoon scales. If every bar in the overture were as good as the best, it would be very good; and if every bar were as bad as the worst, it would be very bad: further than that I decline to go, as there is no saying what Mr Wallace would be at next if he were rashly encouraged. Mr Manns and the band covered themselves with glory in Schumann's first symphony, which was very welcome after Saint-Saëns' violin concerto in B minor, with its trivially pretty scraps of serenade music sandwiched between pages from the great masters. Miss Frida Scotta failed to interest me either in the concerto or in her own certainly very surprising technical skill. The vocal part of the concert was unusually strong, Miss Emma Juch very nearly vanquishing the difficulties of Softly Sighs, and shewing herself at any rate a highly cultivated singer; whilst Mr David Bispham attacked a still more difficult song—Purcell's Mad Tom—and was completely victorious.

1 *November* 1893

THOSE who are interested in everything concerning Beethoven, even in his music, will perhaps be interested by Mariam Tenger's Recollections of Countess Theresa Brunswick, translated by Gertrude Russell, and just published by Fisher Unwin. Theresa was one of the noble Viennese ladies with whom Beethoven fell in love. According to Frau Tenger the two were engaged for four years, and the countess was the "unsterbliche Geliebte" to whom he wrote the famous letter of July 6th, 1806, which was found among his papers after his death, having been presumably returned when the "All is over between us" stage of the adventure was reached—unless, indeed, we are to suppose that Beethoven, like Mr Toots, amused himself by imaginary correspondences. For my part, I find the letter too idiotic to be other than a genuine love letter. The prodigious literary vogue which these tender episodes enjoy is due to the fact that very few people in the world have ever had a love affair.

Larochefoucauld was of opinion that most of us would never fall in love if we had never read anything about it; but I go further: I affirm that in spite of our reading, and the ambition it gives us to have an affair of the heart, the great majority never realize that ambition, and have to marry with a guilty consciousness of falling considerably short of the ardent condition in which the other party seems an *unsterbliche Geliebte*. We take an interest in love stories by the law

of nature which Richelieu turned to account when he hung
one side of his ante-room with battle pictures and the other
with domestic subjects in order to keep the soldier apart
from the bourgeois, each, of course, crowding to the side
which shewed him the romance of his life, and turning his
back on the reality.

Let no one, then, rashly set me down as unsympathetic
because I cannot gush with Frau Tenger over the Countess
Theresa. You have only to think for a moment to see that
the first qualification of a good art critic is extreme susceptibility to beauty, a fatal gift which exposes its possessor
professionally to actions for libel, and privately to suits for
breach of promise. Unlike the general reader, I have been
in love, like Beethoven, and have written idiotic love letters,
many of which, I regret to say, have *not* been returned; so
that instead of turning up among my papers after my death,
they will probably be published by inconsiderate admirers
during my lifetime, to my utter confusion. My one comfort
is, that whatever they may contain—and no man is more
oblivious of their contents than I am—they cannot be more
fatuous than Beethoven's. I have a modest confidence that
at the worst I shall not fall below the standard of punctua-
tion set by that great man in the following:

"My angel, my all, my soul!—a few words only today,
and those with pencil (with THINE!). After tomorrow it is
uncertain where I shall be, what a wretched waste of time
this is—why this deep sorrow when necessity speaks—can
our love live except by sacrifices, in not asking for all, is
thine the power to change it, that thou art not wholly mine,
I not wholly thine—O God, behold the beauty of Nature,
and let that calm thy mind concerning the inevitable—love
rightly demands all, so it is with *me and thee*, with *thee and
me*—but thou forgettest so easily that I must live for *myself*
and for *thee*—were we not wholly united in heart the pain
of this would affect thee as little as it would me—my journey
was fearful—I only arrived here yesterday morning at four
o'clock," etc., etc.

79

This is foolish enough; but it is worth quoting as an attempt to *compose* in letters. All Beethoven's music is an expression of his mood; and here he tries to make words do for him what he was accustomed to make notes and chords do.

I must confess to having read the little book from beginning to end with insurmountable scepticism. Not that I doubt the good faith of Frau Tenger; but the fact is, she has such a fifty-Ophelia power of turning everything to favor and to prettiness that to accept everything she says *au pied de la lettre* would amount to an abdication of reason. Here, for instance, is a passage of rapt sweetness which will make the hardiest reader shiver:

"Countess Theresa died in the year 1861. In the place where she loved most to live, and where she had been most deeply beloved, there, *in a cool vault*, she was buried."

A lady whose imagination can set a family vault to the tune of As In Cool Grot is to be envied; but I positively decline to accept her statements at par. Even when she tries to report Cornelius, Baron Spaun, and the Countess herself verbatim, there is a suspicious resemblance in their styles. The following specimen is from the Baron:

"I once went to see Beethoven at an unusual hour. He could not hear me, nor could he see me this time, for he was seated with his back towards me. The light from the window fell on the picture which he held in his hands and was kissing tearfully. He was talking to himself, as he often did when he was alone. I did not wish to be an unbidden listener, and drew back at the words: 'Thou wast too great—too like an angel.' When after a time I returned, I found him at the piano, extemporizing gloriously."

I am willing to believe that the Countess was engaged to Beethoven for four years, and that they then had sense enough not to bring the romance to the test of a marriage. Also, that when the Countess had turned fifty, and it was becoming apparent that to have been Beethoven's *Geliebte* was going to be a very big thing, not lightly to be left altogether to frivolous Guicciardi-Gallenbergs and the like, she may, on coming across such a very sympathetic listener as Frau Tenger, have—shall I say played up? However that may be, Frau Tenger's Theresa and Beethoven are clearly ideal figures, and not portraits. Real people are not made that way.

The speech in the book that carries most conviction is Guicciardi's "I do so long to throw over Gallenberg and marry that beautiful, horrible Beethoven—if only it were not such a come-down." The authoress is, apparently, not a musician; but nothing worse comes of this than a confusion between Beethoven's two Masses. The book is easy to read, and the facts stated come out clearly enough through the sentimentalizing, which need not impose on any ordinarily hardheaded reader.

Another book which is in evidence just now is Wagner's famous Opera and Drama. Mr Ashton Ellis has doubled the pace of his translation of Wagner's prose works, which is now coming out in sixty-four-page two-shilling parts, so as to complete a volume every year. The last few parts have been occupied with the translation of the book which did more than any other writing of Wagner's to change people's minds on the subject of opera.

Like all the books which have this mind-changing property—Buckle's History of Civilization, Marx's Capital, and Ruskin's Modern Painters are the first instances that occur to me—it professes to be an extraordinarily erudite criticism of contemporary institutions, and is really a work of pure imagination, in which a great mass of facts is so arranged as to reflect vividly the historical and philosophical generalizations of the author, the said generalizations being nothing more than an eminently thinkable arrangement of his own way of looking at things, having no objective validity at all, and owing its subjective validity and apparent persuasiveness to the fact that the rest of the world is coming round by mere natural growth to the author's feeling, and therefore wants "proof," historical, philosophical, moral, and so on, that it is "right" in its new view. People who are still in a state of perfect satisfaction with Faust and Les Huguenots, and perfectly bored by Tristan and puzzled by Parsifal, will never be persuaded by Opera and Drama that opera is a flimsy sham, standing as an inevitable refuse product at the end of a historic evolution in which the rise of Christianity is but an incident.

Wagner's *aperçus* of the whole history of human thought and aspiration, culminating in the double world-catastrophe of Meyerbeer being mistaken for a great composer and Mendelssohn for a model conductor of Beethoven's symphonies, are enormously suggestive to me, clearing my perception of the whole situation as regards modern music, and entertaining me beyond measure by the author's display of transcendent inventiveness and intellectual power. But I can shift my point of view back to that of the elderly gentlemen who still ask for nothing better than another Mario to sing Spirto gentil or Di pescator for them, or a quartet of Italian singers capable of doing justice to A te O cara. To recommend them to join the ranks of Mr Ashton Ellis's subscribers would be to mock them.

I can remember when I was a boy being introduced to Wagner's music for the first time by hearing a second-rate military band play an arrangement of the Tannhäuser march. And do you suppose that it was a revelation to me? Not a bit of it: I thought it a rather commonplace plagiarism from the famous theme in Der Freischütz; and this boyish impression was exactly the same as that recorded by the mature Berlioz, who was to me then the merest shadow of a name which I had read once or twice. At that time I was in a continual state of disappointment because the operatic music which had so delighted and stirred me as a child seemed no longer to inspire singers.

I will hardly be believed now when I say that Donizetti's Lucrezia was once really tragic and romantic, and the

Inflammatus in Rossini's Stabat Mater really grand; but it was so. What is now known only as the spavined *cheval de bataille* of obsolete Italian prima donnas and *parvenu* Italian tenors was formerly a true Pegasus, which carried fine artists aloft as Gounod's music carries Jean de Reszke—or did until it was superseded in his worship by the music of Wagner (I see by the latest interviews that Jean now declares that Siegfried is his favorite part. I have hardly recovered my breath since).

I have no doubt that if Rossini had had Wagner's brains, he too would have produced magnificent generalizations and proved his William Tell the heir of all the ages; but as he would also in that case have written much better music, I, for one, should not have objected. He would have been quoted with the utmost reverence in the days when people could not hear any melody in Die Meistersinger, and when the Philharmonic Society used to think Spohr's Power of Sound, as it was called, one of the greatest of instrumental masterpieces. Nowadays everybody under forty sees that all the composers that have lived since Beethoven would not, if rolled into one, make a single Wagner; and I am obliged to conceal the fact that I know every bar of Lucrezia as well as I know Pop Goes the Weasel, lest I should be stripped of my critical authority as a hopeless old fogey. Let me then rather pose as a cynical survivor of reputations. It was only last Saturday, at the Popular Concert, that I was compelled to confess that some of the first movement of Haydn's quartet in G minor (Op. 76, No. 2) shewed signs of infirmity, one or two passages being positively decrepit. Perhaps in a few years more the whole movement will sound very nearly as old as the next new comic opera. And yet Haydn was all but an immortal once. Brahms' quartet in the same key was quite clearly far in advance of it in harmonic structure and richness of color. That does not seem half so odd as the fact that the newer work is already thirty years old, dating, happily, from those early days when the composer eschewed the intellectual, and did not feel called on to

83

write Requiems. As to Chopin's Funeral March sonata, played very well by Mr Borwick on a magnificent Steinway, nothing was clearer about it than that it beat Haydn's work in point of form. Yes, I quite mean it: it was as if Haydn had put his bricks into a hod in a set pattern, whilst Chopin had built something with his.

Miss Wietrowetz led the quartet admirably. The gentlemen who declare that she plays out of tune do not know the difference between German intonation and Spanish. She is in every way a worthy successor of Neruda. I have been a great admirer of Lady Hallé in her day, and am so still; but she missed the highest excellence as a quartet player by depending too much on her genius and too little on the devotion which expresses itself in careful rehearsal. On that point I think Fräulein Wietrowetz will beat her, as it is fit that the younger artist, standing on the older one's shoulders, should.

8 November 1893

WHEN the fierce strain put by my critical work on my powers of attention makes it necessary for me to allow my mind to ramble a little by way of relief, I like to go to the Albert Hall to hear one of the performances of the Royal Choral Society. I know nothing more interesting in its way than to wake up occasionally from a nap in the amphitheatre stalls, or to come out of a train of political or philosophic speculation, to listen for a few moments to an adaptation of some masterpiece of music to the tastes of what is called "the oratorio public." Berlioz' Faust is a particularly stiff subject for Albert Hall treatment. To comb that wild composer's hair, stuff him into a frock-coat and tall hat, stick a hymn-book in his hand, and obtain reverent applause for his ribald burlesque of an Amen chorus as if it were a genuine Handelian solemnity, is really a remarkable feat, and one which few conductors except Sir Joseph Barnby could achieve. Instead of the brimstonish orgy in Auerbach's cellar we have a *soirée* of the Young Men's

Christian Association; the drunken blackguardism of Brander is replaced by the decorous conviviality of a respectable young bank clerk obliging with a display of his baritone voice (pronounced by the local pianoforte tuner equal to Hayden Coffin's); Faust reminds one of the gentleman in Sullivan's Sweethearts; the whiskered pandoors and the fierce hussars on the banks of the Danube become a Volunteer corps on the banks of the Serpentine; and all Brixton votes Berlioz a great composer, and finds a sulphurous sublimity in the whistles on the piccolo and clashes of the cymbals which bring Mr Henschel, as Mephistopheles, out of his chair. This does not mean that Berlioz has converted Brixton: it means that Brixton has converted Berlioz. Such conversions are always going on. The African heathen "embrace" the Christian religion by singing a Te Deum instead of dancing a war-dance after "wetting their spears" in the blood of the tribe next door; the English heathen (a much more numerous body) take to reading the Bible when it is edited for them by Miss Marie Corelli; the masses, sceptical as to Scott and Dumas, are converted to an appreciation of romantic literature by Mr Rider Haggard; Shakespear and Goethe become world-famous on the strength of "acting versions" that must have set them fairly spinning in their graves; and there is a general appearance of tempering the wind to the shorn lamb, which turns out, on closer examination, to be really effected by building a badly ventilated suburban villa round the silly animal, and telling him that the frowsy warmth he begins to feel is that of the sunbeam playing on Parnassus, or the peace of mind that passeth all understanding, according to circumstances. When I was young, I was like all immature critics: I used to throw stones at the windows of the villa, and thrust in my head and bawl at the lamb that he was a fool, and that the villa builders—honest people enough, according to their lights—were swindlers and hypocrites, and nincompoops and sixth-raters. But the lamb got on better with them than with me; and at last it struck me that he was happier and more civilized in his villa than shivering in the keen Parnassian winds that delighted my hardier bones; so that now I have become quite fond of him, and love to lead him out when the weather is exceptionally mild (the wind being in the Festival cantata quarter perhaps) and talk to him a bit without letting him see too plainly what a deplorable mutton-head he is. Dropping the metaphor, which is becoming unmanageable, let me point out that the title of Berlioz' work is The Damnation of Faust, and that the most natural abbreviation would be, not Berlioz' Faust, but Berlioz' Damnation. Now the Albert Hall audience would certainly not feel easy with such a phrase in their mouths. I have even noticed a certain reluctance on the part of mixed assemblies of ladies and gentlemen unfamiliar with the German language to tolerate discussions of Wagner's Götterdämmerung, unless it were mentioned only as The Dusk of the Gods. Well, the sole criticism I have to make of the Albert Hall performance is that the damnation has been lifted from the work. It has been "saved," so to speak, and jogs along in a most respectable manner. The march, which suggests household troops cheered by enthusiastic nursemaids, is encored; and so is the dance of sylphs, which squeaks like a tune on the hurdy-gurdy. The students' Jam nox stellata sounds as though middle-aged commercial travellers were having a turn at it. On the whole, the performance, though all the materials and forces for a good one are at the conductor's disposal, is dull and suburban. The fact is, Berlioz is not Sir Joseph Barnby's affair. On Thursday last (note that the concert night is changed back again from Wednesday to Thursday) Gounod's Religious March was played, as at the Crystal Palace. A printed slip was circulated asking the audience to stand up. What value a demonstration manufactured in this way can have I do not see, especially when the performance of the march at the Crystal Palace had proved that it would not have occurred spontaneously. It jarred on me as a forced and flunkeyish manœuvre; and I took no part in it. I have sufficient feeling about Gounod not to permit myself to be instructed in the matter by impertinent persons communicating with me by anonymous slips of paper. Besides, I object to confer on a trumpery *pièce d'occasion* the distinction which is the traditional English appanage of Handel's Hallelujah Chorus.

My great difficulty in describing Mr Cowen's Norwich Festival Cantata, The Water Lily, is to find a point of view sufficiently remote from common sense to enable me to keep my countenance during the process. The most ordinary decencies of professional etiquette bind me to accept with enthusiasm the lines of my distinguished fellow-critic. For instance:

> Though I know not where thou art,
> Well I know thou hast my heart.
>
> . . . . . .
>
> Nor so long be coyly hiding,
> In my arms is thy abiding.
>
> . . . . . .
>
> He is thine, and o'er the tide
> Thou shalt go to be his bride,
> Yield thee to love's soft allure,
> Never lived a knight so pure.

If I am ever paid to write a libretto in this style, I will simply buy a bushel of Christmas-cards and fall to with scissors and paste. But then I have not the true poetic gift. The worst of it is that Mr Cowen evidently has not got it either; for he has found no inspiration in Mr Bennett's numbers. Perhaps he did not want it: it may be that as long as Mr Cowen has any sort of *locus standi* for his orchestrating and modulating he is happy. But in that case I beg to say emphatically that I am not. The English horn is a very pretty instrument; and when it has some real work to do, as in the third act of Tristan, I am delighted to hear it. But when, having nothing to do, it insists on shewing itself off to me instead of holding its tongue, I find it an impertinent bore. Similarly, that pet transition from one major common chord to another lying a semitone higher, is magical in the first scene of the third act of Siegfried, where it has some very momentous business to transact; but a mere row of samples of it does not seem to me a fair equivalent for a piece of original composition.

Mr Cowen is too old now to be allowed to play with chords as children do with scraps of colored paper, or even as Mozart and Rossini, in their nonage, played with the ordinary dominant cadence. Some of Mr Cowen's little harmonic sweetmeats are by no means to my taste. It seems a hopelessly obsolete thing to quarrel with a composer for "false relations" nowadays; but still there is reason in everything. Take the case of a phrase in the key of A flat major stepping off C to B flat in order to spring up immediately to E flat, and accompanied in simple two-part harmony by A flat, G, C. Is it good sense, or rather good sound, to make the G flat, unless you want to shew that the old prohibition of false relations and consecutive major intervals had something in it after all?

What matter if the G natural would make the phrase remind everyone of the love-duet in Gounod's Faust? Better that than the suggestion of a wrong note. However, I suppose Mr Cowen likes it. I can only repeat doggedly, bigotedly, irreconcilably, that I dont. Why should I? If it were expressive of the accompanying words I should accept it without question—without consciousness, probably. But it is set to the words "Sleep and dream." Who on earth dreams of "false relations"?

For the honor of the cloth I must point out how faithfully Mr Bennett gives his composer the full regulation set of chances—the vision, the pastoral, the storm, the tournament, the funeral march, and the love-duet all complete. The introduction of the storm is particularly ingenious. Merlin, taking a walk on the sands, sees Ina's ship in full sail, and falls in love with it. After various rapturous compliments, he continues:

Hither, my bird, that I may view thy crest,
Which now appears as though a flower
Had opened that a goddess might emerge.
What! Dost pass me by contemptuously,
With mock obeisance? Thou my power shalt know
In loss of all thy beauty and thy pride,
So soon love turns to hate when love is scorned.
Spirits of storm, awake, etc., etc.

A fearful tempest then rages in the orchestra, and the ship is annihilated. Merlin's conscience at once begins to act, and he says, with irresistible bathos:

The earth contains so much of beauty less,
And I despise myself.

Perhaps it will be better for me to say now, without further circumlocution, that the whole entertainment bored me. No doubt a great poet, writing at a period when fairy romances had for the moment fascinated the imagination of the world, might have made a real poem of The Water Lily, and inspired a composer to set it to music. But as that period is passed, and Mr Bennett is (as far as I can judge) no more a poet than I am, he has produced nothing that has any beauty in its own versification or any vitality in its matter for the composer to work on.

Mr Cowen has just managed, by an elaboration of his drawing room ballad style, to produce one or two really pretty and live bits for the soprano; but the rest is the merest playing with chords and instruments. This sort of trifling, in the hands of men in whom professional pedantry has extinguished all musical susceptibility, sometimes produces a technical experiment or two of a certain mechanical interest to experts. But Mr Cowen, being still a musician, trifles only with effects that have charmed his ear in the music of Wagner and Gounod. For instance, Norna's boat-song, Swiftest birds that ever flew (need I add that the next line is To your mission be ye true?), is a very pretty bit of harmonic

89

change-ringing; but Mr Cowen can hardly expect anyone who has heard those changes in the original compositions from which he has taken them to be much interested.

No doubt plenty of simple people who have never heard these original compositions will be charmed with The Water Lily. The same people will, as likely as not, find Mr Bennett's verses as poetic as Mr Stopford Brooke finds Wordsworth's. I do not quarrel with their opinion. I simply record my own. The Water Lily, like St John's Eve, Jubal's Dream, and all the other works which have been manufactured by the same process, altogether fail to please me. I do not say they are bad; I do not attempt to prove that they are "wrong"; I do not deny that choral societies sing them, and that audiences pay at least once to hear them sung; I do not question the genius of the composers or the impartiality of the librettist-analyst-critic; I do not assert, suggest, imply, or hint anything about anybody but myself; and of myself I only say—fully admitting that the fact may be entirely discreditable to me—that, if the whole collection of these works were in my power, I would unhesitatingly commit them to the nearest County Council "destructor."

15 November 1893

MR HENSCHEL opened his London Symphony campaign on Wednesday last. When I arrived at half-past eight I found the concert in full swing, and a bevy of belated persons shut out on the stairs and arguing that the concert did not and could not begin at eight because the time printed on their tickets was half-past —much in the vein of the lawyer who proved to the man in the stocks that he could not have been put there because his offence was not legally punishable in that way. You find ladies, in particular, disposed to treat a misunderstanding of this kind as a personal matter between themselves and the gentleman who takes their tickets at the door, and who is, of course, obviously quite innocent and quite helpless. For my part, I magnanimously made no fuss, feeling quite well able to put up with the loss of Tchaikowsky's elegy and of the first two movements of Max Bruch's violin concerto. I will take it for granted that Miss Frida Scotta played those two movements better than the third, which she attacked with a sort of muscular passion that seemed to make her insensible to every consideration except breaking the record for speed. She afterwards re-established herself in some degree by playing Svendsen's Romance with expression and even with refinement; but then Svendsen's Romance is not a very abstruse work. Probably as time goes on Miss Frida Scotta will begin to study her concertos poetically as well as physically, and to assert the feeling of the composition as earnestly as she now asserts her own execution of its technical difficulties. At present her concerto playing, though sometimes astonishing, is prosaic, and often insensitive and inelegant in decorative passages. Professor Villiers Stanford has broken out again with a very Irish song, Prince Madoc's Farewell, sung so patriotically by Mr Plunket Greene that he once or twice almost burst into the next key. Patriotism is, fundamentally, a conviction that a particular country is the best in the world because you were born in it; and it is therefore as well to keep it strictly in tune when you happen to be in some other country for the moment. Irish patriotism is a particularly trying variety, especially to the Englishman. It is intensely melancholy, for no reason whatever; whereas English patriotism, though equally unreasonable, is convivial.

Again, Irish patriotism has the subjectivity of pure feeling: it expresses itself in wailing melody, and, when forced to associate words with that melody, declines to pronounce them distinctly. But the patriotic Englishman, when sober, is highly articulate, and always knows his words—Britons never, never, etc., We always are ready: steady, boys, steady, We dont want to fight; *but*, etc., Who's afraid? Never say die, and so on—though he frequently breaks down most ingloriously when he tries to remember the tune. Now, in Ireland, nobody ever knows the words of anything;

91

though a native who does not know the tune of everything may safely be put down as having no musical faculty whatever.

It is for this reason that Italian opera is so much more genuinely popular in Ireland than in England, and why librettos sell so badly there. The Irishman is absolutely satisfied with the melody of Il balen, and encores it for the hundredth time without dreaming of asking what the words mean. If they were English words he would be equally ignorant; for he would never take the trouble to attach any ideas to them. Ask him the English for Il balen, and he will pull himself together; make a perceptible intellectual effort; and observe that his Italian is rather rusty, but that he supposes it means a piece of whalebone, or something of that sort. When he turns back to the music, his intellect will go to sleep again, and he will not think for a moment of the absurdity of the Count di Luna passionately apostrophizing a piece of whalebone. Mr Plunket Greene, in spite of all his English experience and training, no sooner got steeped in Stanford's Irish melody than his words began to lose all sharpness of definition, and at last, in one poignant moment, trailed off into an inarticulate cry.

If he would like to learn how that affects an Englishman, he should read Chorley's criticism on Catherine Hayes, with its complaint that all Irish singers deliver their words indistinctly and without meaning, and are monotonous and uninteresting in spite of their musical facility and charm of voice. It is the old English grievance against us: we are emotionally too barbarously excitable, and intellectually never in earnest. No doubt Mr Plunket Greene, as an Irishman, holds as I do that the real truth of the matter is that the English brain is so dense that it is only by a strenuous and most desperately serious effort that the Englishman can set his intellect in action, a feat so easy to the Irishman that he is constantly doing it merely to amuse himself, and so acquires a playful intellectual manner as naturally as the Englishman acquires a ponderous and solemn one.

MUSIC IN LONDON 1890–94

It has taken me nearly twenty years of studied self-restraint, aided by the natural decay of my faculties, to make myself dull enough to be accepted as a serious person by the British public; and I am not sure that I am not still regarded as a suspicious character in some quarters. But what I would put to Mr Greene is that since we are here, and dependent for our livelihoods on the sixpences and shillings of the British public, we must give them what they like and not what we like. And so, when next Prince Madoc's Farewell is in the program, let the words be delivered with an air of careful and persuasive intelligence, and never mind the melody. Above all, no patriotism.

Professor Stanford is naturally at his best in a piece of folk-music, since it is the one indulgence a professor is allowed by the etiquette of his profession. All the rest of the time the academic musician must write oratorios; search for some form of the plagal cadence that has not been anticipated by Dr Parry; compose canons nineteen-in-twenty-six *al rovescio*; teach students that the theme of the finale of Mozart's E flat symphony is "better avoided," because the quaver F, being a passing note, should not skip down to B flat; and generally waste his time, blaspheme against his art, abdicate his manhood, and dishonor his reason. Only, he is allowed occasionally to practise as he pleases on a little folk-music, lest he should commit suicide. And Professor Stanford does it with an infinite yearning and relief which enters into his music and gives it a searching pathos. He seems to cry out through all the instruments, "I have been starving on Festival fare for years: now at last I may have some music." Mr Joseph Bennett, strange to say, has entirely missed this aspect of Professor Stanford's composition; for not a word is said of it in the analytic program.

To make amends, however, there is a surprisingly eloquent description of Brahms' first symphony, not in inverted commas, and therefore presumably original. This symphony is a wonderful feat of the young Brahms—a mere heap of lumps of absolute music; but then, such magnificent

93

lumps! such color! such richness of substance! one is amazed to find the man who dug them out half smothering them with mere slag, and quite unable to construct anything with them. Mr Henschel, though neither he nor the band were at their best, brought off a vigorous performance which roused much enthusiasm. We also had an orchestral arrangement of the flower-maiden scene from Parsifal. It was rough and hurried, and must have sounded very glum without the girls' voices to those who did not know the work.

But the Bayreuth pilgrims no doubt enjoyed it, and saw in imagination all the naïve enchantments of the Festspielhaus—the pantomimic flowers, the damsels running away and returning decorated with monstrous tufts of red and blue paper, and the magical apparition of Kundry, in an antique ball-dress with ruchings, alluringly disposed on a sofa, and pulled out from the wing by a cable, presumably hauled by a pair of horses, the weight being not less than seventeen stone.

I must say I do not clearly see why we should be put off with these "arrangements" of Wagner. Mr Henschel has a choir with plenty of young ladies in it. He can find a tenor and soprano for Parsifal and Kundry just as easily as for Walther and Eva. Why not give us the music as it was written, instead of treating us to the accompaniments alone, with Kundry's call touched in on the cornet-à-piston? What would Mr Henschel say if Richter, instead of engaging him to sing Pogner's address and Wotan's farewell and summons to Loki, were to have them economically performed on the euphonium?

Madame Favart has been revived at the Criterion Theatre. Although it is one of Offenbach's late works, quite mild and domestic in comparison with La Belle Hélène or La Grande Duchesse, it is far less like itself at the Criterion than the works of Planquette, or even Lecocq. Of the true Offenbachianismus—the restless movement, the witty abandonment, the swift, light, wicked touch, the inimitable sly *élan* stealing into concerted pieces as light as puff paste—

there is not a trace left in Mr Wyndham's revival. The effervescent orchestration, with its Bohemian economy in the wood wind, and its devilish grace and swagger to make up for its poverty, no longer puts any sort of face on its own shorthandedness. Even the rowdy big drum, which always marked Offenbach out as a musical blackguard in spite of his cleverness, thumps away without any of the old enjoyment.

Of late years we have accustomed ourselves to a ponderous style of execution, sentimental or inane as the case may be, and to thicker scoring, heavier finales, and a larger assortment of discords—especially tonic discords—than would have been tolerated in Offenbach's time; and it says a great deal for the grace, gaiety, and intelligence of his work that it should hold its own still even when performed, as it most ruthlessly is at the Criterion, without any of the piquancies of style which he and his librettists had in contemplation. Occasionally, however, it gains by the change; for it is hardly necessary to remark that the old style had its vicious side. It was not only smart, lively, and cynical, but it was abjectly afraid to be anything else; and this cowardice made it irritating and contemptible as soon as it began to get a little stale. Since then a course of Dorothy and her imitators has made us infinitely tolerant of sentimental melodies and witless words; and now that we are turning back to Offenbach, our musical handling of him, though very clumsy, is not so heartless as it used to be, whilst the books of his operas appear quite intellectual to us.

As an operatic manager Mr Wyndham cannot be counted among the moderns. Since he has resorted to comic opera more or less as a stopgap, and is not counting on very long runs, or on the Criterion acquiring an operatic reputation, he is naturally content to fit up his revivals on readymade lines. Still, there is one matter in which he seems needlessly old-fashioned. Nothing marks off Mr D'Oyly Carte from his rivals more effectually and favorably than the fact that on the Savoy stage the women appear as women, and the men as men. The old rule was that the women should appear as men, and the men be hidden as much as possible behind the women. Every regiment of soldiers was a row of mincing, plump, self-conscious young women in satin uniforms, pinched at the waist and toes, and bulbous in the unpinched regions.

The founders of this tradition must have conceived it to be a seductive one; but I, who have seen whole armies of these female warriors from my credulous boyhood onward, am prepared to have my feelings towards them from first to last tested by the austerest canons of propriety. When I first saw them I thought them comically revolting; and what I now think of them is exactly what the Criterion audience thought last Thursday when two of them crossed the stage to reply to a question from Miss St John. As they marched off in the true opera-bouffe army manner Miss St John contemplated them for a moment with an inimitably dubious gravity, and then, in one of her favorite relapses into *gaminerie*, said slowly: "Thanks, gall'nt orficers." The whole house screamed with merriment; and if Mr Wyndham were wise, he would take the female man as laughed off the stage altogether in that outburst.

Madame Favart has, fortunately, a reasonably good book, though, like most of the books of its period, its merits do not hold out to the third act. Mr Wallace Brownlow plays with plenty of fun and spirit as Favart; and the part, however obviously planned for a more mercurial actor, adapts itself to him fairly well. Mr James can neither sing nor even plausibly pretend to sing, not from lack of ear, but because his trick of speech has made his voice useless for lyric purposes; but he manages to pull Pontsablé cleverly through. Mr Emney is perfectly fitted with the part of Biscotin, who is persistently called "Biscotemps" by the others. Miss St John, of course, carries the whole opera on her shoulders, and is not at all overburdened by it, though the music does not lie so easily for her voice in its present phase, and cannot be so conveniently transposed, as that of

MUSIC IN LONDON 1890–94

The Mascotte. Miss Ellis Jeffreys, who in Madame Angot shewed a certain talent which she might take a little more seriously, plays one or two passages in Suzanne very well; but her performance, on the whole, is still a little crude. The book, by the way, would be the better for an overhauling. The late H. B. Farnie was for an age, but not for all time.

22 November 1893

I CONTINUE to be amazed at the way in which the younger generation plays the fiddle. Formerly there were only two sorts of violinists: the Paganinis or Sivoris, and the bad amateurs whose highest flight was an execrable attempt to scrape through a variation or two on The Carnival of Venice. The orchestral players I leave out altogether; for the trade knack they picked up under stress of bread-winning had nothing to do with violin-playing, as one found out when they got promoted to the leader's desk, and had to play an obbligato occasionally. Nowadays all that is changed in the most bewildering manner. Europe appears to be full of young ladies between twenty and thirty who can play all the regulation concertos—Beethoven, Mendelssohn, Brahms, Bruch, and Saint-Saëns—and throw in Bach's chaconne in D minor as a solo piece at the end of the concert.

And yet they are not geniuses, though they do with apparent ease the things that only geniuses used to do. I should be tempted to put it all down to the terrific determination with which women are qualifying themselves in all branches for an independent career, were it not that the improvement is discoverable in the young men also—though, of course, no male can hope for such chances of shewing his mettle as are offered readily enough to young women. The fact is, people do not like concertos for their own sake. A concerto must have a hero or a heroine; and every plucky and passably pretty feminine violinist under thirty is a heroine in the imagination of the male audience; whereas a callow young man is not anybody's hero, having no touch of that art of

97

personal beauty and dignity at which every woman with grit enough to face the public at all is at least a passable amateur. He can only play the hero if he is a real genius, whereas his female rival will be heroine enough for the public if she has worked hard enough to be able to play the concerto as her master tells her to play it. Hence we have half a dozen young ladies getting first-rate chances every season, whilst young men who can play as well, or better, languish for years unheard.

Take the case of Mr August Manns, for instance. His generosity to young gentlemen with unperformed orchestral scores is the theme of all our praises at present; and he is a second father to Miss Mary Cardew, Miss Frida Scotta, Miss Beatrice Langley, and the rest of our young lady violinists. But may I suggest to him that as all young gentlemen compose very much alike, and all young ladies play very much alike, it would be a relief if he were to transpose the sexes next season, and treat us to a series of compositions by young women and violin concerto performances by young men.

The fact is, I am getting tired of ladylike versions of Bruch's concerto in G minor—very agreeable and skilful, certainly, but utterly unmemorable. I was greatly pleased with Miss Beatrice Langley's playing of it at the Crystal Palace the other day: her youth, her dexterity, and her quick and delicate musical feeling would have earned her a handsome tribute of praise and encouragement from me a few years ago; but today, somehow, my mind keeps going back to that note at the end of the program: "This concerto was last played at the Saturday Concerts on February 25th, 1893, by Miss Mary Cardew." I was at that concert; and I remember being "greatly pleased" by Miss Mary Cardew's performance—quite astonished, in fact, by her execution of the Bach chaconne.

But I had completely forgotten the concerto when the paragraph re-informed—not reminded—me of it. That may be my own fault, or Max Bruch's; and yet I do not forget Isaÿe's performances of Bruch. Anyhow, I plead for a chance for the young male fiddler. However unattractive his sex may be, it must at least produce some small percentage of the beginners who deserve a chance with a concerto at our leading orchestral concerts.

The concert at which Miss Langley made her success, and, let me add, shewed some spirit and common sense by giving the eternal Saint-Saëns a rest, and introducing a welcome novelty in the shape of a capriccio for violin and orchestra by Niels Gade, also gave a lift to Mr Granville Bantock, whose Caedmar, produced by Signor Lago, made us all curious about his overture, The Fire Worshippers. Unluckily, The Fire Worshippers turned out to be an earlier work than Caedmar, mainly occupied with a six-eight movement which was as pure Mendelssohn as Caedmar was pure Wagner. It explained why Mr Bantock got the Macfarren Scholarship at the R.A.M.; but it threw no new light on his development. The Mendelssohn Worshippers was followed by a performance of the Lohengrin prelude in A, finely executed by the wind, and very poorly indeed by the strings. The gem of the concert was Goetz' symphony, which has fallen into neglect because, I suppose, it is the only real symphony that has been composed since Beethoven died. Beside it Mendelssohn's Scotch symphony is no symphony at all, but only an enchanting *suite de pièces*; Schubert's symphonies seem mere debauches of exquisitely musical thoughtlessness; and Schumann's, though genuinely symphonic in ambition, fall short in actual composition. Goetz alone among the modern symphonists is easily and unaffectedly successful from beginning to end.

He has the charm of Schubert without his brainlessness, the refinement and inspiration of Mendelssohn without his limitation and timid gentility, Schumann's sense of harmonic expression without his laboriousness, shortcoming, and dependence on external poetic stimulus; while as to unembarrassed mastery of the material of music, shewing itself in the Mozartian grace and responsiveness of his polyphony, he leaves all three of them simply nowhere. Brahms, who alone touches him in mere brute musical faculty, is a dolt in comparison to him.

You have to go to Mozart's finest quartets and quintets on the one hand, and to Die Meistersinger on the other, for work of the quality we find, not here and there, but continuously, in the symphony in F and in The Taming of the Shrew, two masterpieces which place Goetz securely above all other German composers of the last hundred years, save only Mozart and Beethoven, Weber and Wagner. Of course, if Goetz were alive this would be an excellent reason for opposing him tooth and nail, for the same reasons that moved Salieri to oppose Mozart. A very little Goetz would certainly spoil the market for Festival symphonies; but now that the man is dead, why may we not have the symphony made a stock-piece at the London Symphony and Richter concerts, and performed oftener than once in four years at the Crystal Palace?

There is that beautiful Spring Overture, too, which the lamented Macfarren denounced as containing unlawful consecutive sevenths. Are we never to hear those consecutive sevenths again? Is it to be always Brahms and Bruch and Liszt, until our rising generation loses all sense of the subtle but immense difference between first-rate and second-rate in contemporary symphonic music?

From Goetz' symphony to the second edition of Morocco Bound is one of those violent transitions which steel the critic to all reverses of fortune. Morocco Bound is not bad fun: its success, as I shall presently shew, is by no means undeserved. But it has certain defects which must be as objectionable to nine out of ten of the people in the theatre as they are to me. Take the orchestration, for example. Does anybody really enjoy music of which every alternate four bars or so is played *fortissimo* on two cornets in unison, one trombone supplying a bass, two horns filling in the middle parts, and a side-drum rolling all the time *con tutta la forza*. The stridency and frequency of this exasperating noise at the

Shaftesbury would try the endurance of an agricultural laborer, much less a nervous Londoner. I am prepared to put up with it at a circus or a second-rate music-hall; but in a West End theatre, where a stall costs half a guinea, I protest against the marrowbones and cleaver. I find the same kind of fault in the performance of Mr Charles Danby as Higgins. He has plenty of fun in him; and he works hard and successfully to keep the piece going; but he makes an intolerable noise with that brazen voice of his, which at last begins to jar worse than the cornets, horns, trombone, and side-drum all together. Mr Danby may imagine that since he represents a retired costermonger he must bawl through his part as if he were crying the contents of a barrow; but I can assure him, as a critic with a wide and catholic circle of acquaintances, that costermongers do not talk like that, even when they are crying their wares. Persuasiveness is the note of the coster in private conversation; and though in addressing the public he may be stentorian, he is not necessarily unmusical even then. If Mr Danby were a real coster, and were to rasp his customers' ears as he rasped mine nearly all the evening except when he was singing the plantation song, he would go home a bankrupt. Mr Shine, with an equally prominent part, makes fun quietly and with a certain grace and handsomeness which, even in the thinnest parts of the play, protect the audience from being worried. Mr Danby should take the edge off his voice, and provide his grotesque humor with a background of human feeling and expression, however superficial. At present he discounts his fun and amusing feats of activity by that callousness to gratuitously harsh sounds and ugly sights which makes all the difference between the style of an opera comedian like Mr Rutland Barrington, for instance, and that of a music-hall "comic."

There is another feature common to Morocco Bound and most entertainments of its class against which I venture to protest. The authors of these works are nothing if not preternaturally smart. It is their boast that there is nothing heavy or Shakespearean about them. Why, then, are they licensed to bore us with elaborate plots and "expositions" thereof which would not be tolerated for a moment from Shakespear or Goethe? In Morocco Bound there is a plot involving the most complicated family relationships. It is of no use, of no interest: it is tedious, inept, unpardonable; and yet the characters stand there fruitlessly trying to explain it for five minutes at a time as if it were the most succulent dramatic poetry, or the most incandescent comedy. Even if the explanation were successful, and left me in complete command of the fictitious reasons for the presence of Miss Agnes Hewitt, Miss Jennie McNulty, and the rest, I could quite well dispense with them, as I am perfectly willing to accept the company of those ladies without asking any questions. But when the explanation is totally unintelligible, the last excuse for pestering me with it vanishes. If the management must have an "exposition," they had better employ Ibsen or some other reasonably lively person to contrive it for them.

The success of Morocco Bound centres round a single artist—Miss Letty Lind. Sarasate's playing is not more exquisite than her dancing: it is a delight to see her simply march across the stage in time to the music. She is no mere skirt-dancer: if she were invisible from the waist downwards the motion of her head and wrists would still persuade me to give her anybody's head on a charger—and this is the test of the perfect dancer as distinguished from the mere stepdancer. She gives us all the grace of classical dancing without its insufferable pedantry and its worn-out forms. Her caricatures of academic dancing and amateur dancing are most delicately touched; even the wrestling trick by which Mr Danby throws her heels over head does not disturb her grace and simplicity one jot.

I can quite understand that people go again and again to Morocco Bound to see her; and as she manages to sing very prettily and ingeniously without the formality of a voice, and acts humorously to boot, I do not think I need hesitate to credit her with practically the entire success of the piece, though I must duly allow that young Mr Grossmith, Mr Colin Coop, and the others kept matters at a very lively pitch between whiles, with Mr Templar Saxe and Miss Maggie Roberts to throw in an occasional drawing-room ballad as a concession to the claims of high art.

29 November 1893

PADEREWSKI'S Polish Fantasia for pianforte and orchestra, which he introduced to London at Mr Henschel's second Symphony Concert last Wednesday, shews a considerable advance in his power of composition. Formerly he was too young to be a good host to his own ideas: he used to contrive an orchestral reception room to assemble them in; but neither in his invitations nor his introductions did he consider how they would get on together, so they for the most part took one another into dinner under protest, and the entertainment was more or less a failure, in spite of the prime attraction of his own playing. He arranges things better now: in his latest fantasia there is harmony, congruity, reciprocity—in short, the wholeness which shews the hand of the master composer.

It is greatly to be desired, however, that some skilful surgeon should dexterously split Paderewski into two separate persons—Paderewski the composer and Paderewski the pianist. At present they interfere with one another constantly. The pianist no sooner gets excited by the orchestra than he says to the composer, "I understand, I'll do it for you. Leave it all to me," and takes the matter into his own itching fingers. At such moments the composer, if he were split off as I suggest, could say, "Do hold your noise. Do you suppose I am going to reduce my grand passages to a mere paroxysm of banging and clattering on your box of wires merely because you cant keep your hands quiet?"

The fact is, Paderewski, though he writes for the orchestra with excellent judgment, shews the deafest partiality when he comes to write for the pianoforte. He cannot deny it a lion's share in all the good things, whether they suit it or not; and the result is that in most of the big climaxes he is making such a thundering noise that he cannot hear the orchestra, whilst the orchestra is making such a thundering noise that the audience cannot hear him, and can only gaze raptly at the inspiring spectacle of his fists flying in the air as he trounces the keyboard. He had much better use a big drum for such emergencies: the sensation of playing it would be equally exhilarating; the fingering would be easier; and everybody would hear it. There is another technical consideration which I must urge if I am to concede the desirability of developing the capacity of the pianoforte as an orchestral instrument to the utmost.

In that case, I submit that one pianoforte is not enough to cover the ground. When Paderewski writes horn parts in his scores he not only employs four instruments, so as to be able to sound four horn-notes simultaneously if necessary: he also divides the four into two pairs, each of diverse range and quality of tone, so that his first horn-player can produce one set of notes and effects, and his fourth another. Now the pianoforte, as used by Paderewski, is an instrument highly specialized for his use so as to produce the utmost lightness, swiftness, and precision of action; and it so happens that an excess of these qualities can only be gained at the cost of richness and softness of tone-color. Paderewski's pianos are made by Erard; but the ordinary Erard grands used by people who are not Paderewskis are much more delightful instruments, though the mechanical difference is probably only a matter of a layer of felt on the hammer.

I suggest, then, that if Paderewski wishes to combine the orchestral effect of the piano as a very brilliant, steel-hard, and transcendently facile and florid instrument of percussion, with that of its richer and more majestic qualities, he should write his fantasias for two pianofortes, a virtuoso's hair-trigger Erard and a normal Erard. If the difference in tone-color between a clarionet in C and one in A, or between a horn in D and one in B flat basso, is worth considering in composition, I do not see why the equally remarkable difference between a Pleyel and a Steinway piano should be ignored. It would add a new sensation to the performance of that Polish Fantasia if there were two pianos on the platform, with the pianist rushing from one to the other according to the character of the passage he was about to play. I do not say that the effect of the multiplication of pianos would be worth what it would cost: what I do say is, that in Paderewski's fantasia not all his power of modifying the tone of the instrument by his touch conceals the fact that the supreme qualifications of the instrument for certain passages act as disqualifications for certain others, and that this could be got over by using two pianos.

At the same time, I had rather see Paderewski, in his next composition for orchestra, drop the piano altogether. It is the one instrument that he does not understand as a composer, exactly because he understands it so well as an executant. The fantasia was very well received, though the audience most certainly did not mean to encore the finale. What they were after was a solo; and Paderewski, in accepting their persistent acclamations as an encore of a full third of his fantasia, took a diabolical revenge on them, consciously or unconsciously, for their shameless mendicity. His performance of Schumann's concerto was enormously satisfactory. If the band had only been able to follow his gradations of tone and to make the little orchestral rejoinders to the pianoforte a little less stolidly, as much might be said for the whole performance. It was impossible not to rejoice in his complete comprehension of the work, and the certainty with which he found the right *tempo*, handling, and expression for every phrase, so that it came out as a living utterance and not as a mere finger trait committed to memory. I cannot speak with any confidence of the orchestral numbers in the program; for my seat was, except as to the piano, almost useless for critical purposes. As far as I could judge, the band was very rough, especially in the Kaisermarsch. As to the new overture by Emmanuel Moor, I could make nothing of it as a whole. One moment it was obviously decorative music: the next it seemed to be following some imaginative subject, as to which the program offered no clue. It was as if a number of bars from Das Rheingold had got mixed up with a Haydn allegro. This slipping from one kind of music to another is common enough with composers who merely echo the sound of the great masters, and are as likely as not to make their symphonies out of scraps of opera, and their operas out of scraps of symphony. Now Mr Moor is not a mere echo: his talent is a fairly strong and self-reliant one; but as far as I could judge from a first hearing under somewhat unfavorable conditions, his overture had been put together without any definite inspiration or intention; and so, having no point to keep to, it turned out neither flesh, fowl, nor good red herring.

At the Albert Hall on Thursday last the Royal Choral Society was much more at home with Handel than it had been at the previous concert with Berlioz. The crisp and vigorous stroke of Handel, and the strength and audacity of his style, were of course lacking, partly because these huge lumbering choirs of which we are so proud always seem to oppress conductors with a sense of their unwieldiness, partly because Sir Joseph Barnby's style is so measured and complacent. He evidently enjoys Handel's high spirits; but as he invariably stops to dwell on them, and, what is more, stops longer as the movement gathers momentum on the paper before him, its qualities remain hidden in his own imagination, and the actual performance gets slower and heavier.

But if the choir is not impetuously led it is certainly well trained. There is a certain vulgarity of speech about it, especially on the part of the men; but the tone is remarkably good and free from incidental noises; the soft passages are pretty and effective; and the execution is careful and precise. If only some spontaneity and forward spring could be substituted for the perpetual leaning back of both the conductor and the choir, the oratorio performances at the Albert Hall would become about as good as it is in the nature of such things to be. Israel in Egypt is an extraordinary example of the way in which a musical giant can carry off an enterprise which is in its own nature a monumental bore, consisting as it does, to a great extent, of passages of cold narrative which not only do not yearn for the intensity of musical expression, but positively make it impossible.

How can any composer set to music the statement that Egypt was glad when they departed? If the fact were exhibited dramatically, and the actual exclamations of gladness uttered by the Egyptians given, something might be done with them; but the mere bald narrative statement is musically out of the question. Handel therefore falls back here on a purely formal display of his professional skill in fugue writing, and in that sort of experimenting with the old modes which consists in writing in the key of E minor and leaving the sharp out of the signature and occasionally out of the music. The result is extremely interesting to deaf persons whose hobby is counterpoint and the ecclesiastical modes; but to the unsophisticated ear it is deadly dull; and it is hard to refrain from laughing outright at the thousands of people sitting decorously at the Albert Hall listening to the choir trudging through And believe-ed the Lord and his ser-vant Mo-oh-zez, and then through And! I! will exaw-aw-aw-aw-alt Him, as if the gross absurdity of these highly scholastic choruses, considered as an expression of the text, were any the less ridiculous because they were perpetrated by a great musician who could not do even an unmusical thing quite unmusically.

The situation was heightened on Thursday by the recollection that at the last concert the joke of the evening was a parody of just such choral writing. Indeed, Berlioz' burlesque Amen is far less laughable than He led them through the deep as through a wilderness, the insane contrapuntal vagaries of the last four words surpassing in irreverent grotesqueness anything that the boldest buffoon dare offer as professedly comic composition.

While the world lasts these choruses will make a complete performance of Israel a very mixed joy indeed, to be endured only for the sake of the moments in which Handel made a chance for his genius by forcing a vividly descriptive character on the narrative. He could do little with the frogs and flies, and nothing with the blotches and blains, the rinderpest, and the lice; but the thick darkness that might be felt, the hailstones and the fire mingled with the hail running along the ground, the waters overwhelming the enemy, the floods standing upright as a heap, and the depths congealed in the heart of the sea—these he worked up into tone-pictures that make it impossible to leave Israel unperformed, and that bribe us to sit out in patience the obsolete pedantries in which he took refuge when the narrative beat him. One likes, too, to be heartened with the indomitable affirmation that "there was not one—*not one* feeble person among their tribes," and to exult over the "chosen captains" drowned in the Red Sea.

I wish, by the bye, it were possible for Sir Joseph Barnby to find two singers capable of dealing with those chosen captains, instead of falling back on his four hundred tenors and basses, whom at such moments I am guilty of wishing in the Red Sea themselves, so prosaically do they let the great war-song down. On Thursday they broke my spirit so that I went home forthwith, and so heard hardly anything of the soloists except Miss Butt, who sang Their land brought forth frogs, with some little awkwardnesses and nervousnesses and misplaced breaths which she will some day learn to avoid. All the same, she sang it magnificently. The last fourteen bars came with the true musical and dramatic passion which reduces all purely technical criticism to a mere matter of detail—such detail, however, as Miss Butt would do well not to neglect. All those long phrases on single words *can* be sung in one breath if only you know how to do it.

EVERYBODY knows the story of "Have a piano, Thack"; although I believe "Atlas" alone ever tells it correctly. I prophesy that it will presently be grafted on to the biography of Paderewski, in the form of "Have a lecture, Paddy." For it is actually coming to this, that people are demanding lectures at recitals, to save them the trouble of reading analytic programs, and to relieve the tedium of the music. The plan, after all, has its advantages. In St. James's Hall, where you get not only a trained pianist, but—what is quite as necessary to a first-class recital—a trained audience, I doubt whether the lecturer would be tolerated; but for smaller semi-private recitals, where the little audience is not trained, but is quite willing to be if only someone will take it in hand, the musical lecture can be made a useful institution enough. I came to this conclusion at a "recital-lecture" given by Mrs Liebich, the subject being Chopin. It was clearly better for the audience, assuming them to have come in a quite uninstructed condition, to be told something about Chopin than to hear a string of his compositions played straight off without a notion of their bearings. At the same time, the arrangement created certain difficulties. For instance, Mrs Liebich delivered the lecture; and Mr Liebich played the "illustrations." Now Mr Liebich, though a perfectly presentable player, is not a Paderewski or a Rubinstein; therefore he was entitled to a certain forbearance on the lecturer's part in the matter of raising expectations. I regret to say that his claims in this direction were not deferred to by Mrs Liebich. She seemed to revel in prefacing each performance with a description which might conceivably have been realized by Paderewski, Rubinstein, Liszt, and Chopin himself all rolled into one, especially if powerfully aided by the electric atmosphere of a vast hall crowded with imaginative enthusiasts, but which was out of the question for the unaided skill of Mr Liebich in the select afternoon quietude of Mrs Richards's drawing room in Stanley Crescent. One passage struck me as particularly inconsiderate. A man may be a very solid musician and skilful pianist, and yet not be able to play a mazurka. That, as it happened, was Mr Liebich's predicament. In the heroic measure of the polonaise he was at his ease; but the mazurka eluded him: he could not make it dance a step. Yet Mrs Liebich, who must have known this, positively expatiated on the rarity of successful mazurka-playing among pianists, and the necessity of judging Chopin's mazurkas in particular only by the performances of those who catch the true genius of the dance. Then, instead of frankly adding, "As my husband is one of those players who cannot manage a mazurka, we had better pass on to those broader, stronger rhythms which appeal to his robust Germanic temperament," she sat down, leaving the audience under the impression that he was about to give an exhibition of the most highly specialized aptitude for the mazurka. What made it more cruel was that Mr Liebich seemed a perfectly quiet, well-bred, unostentatious musician —one who would never by himself dream of making such pretensions. But of course Mrs Liebich did not intend this: it arose out of her conscientious endeavor to say the correct thing about Chopin. What she does not see is, that this correct thing is an uninteresting abstraction, only to be resorted to on occasions when it happens to be convenient to say nothing at all in a few well-chosen words. Her lecture was carefully prepared and carefully delivered; but the care was the effect of a modesty as to the value of her own opinion which made her shrink from the audacity of sincerity. She did not presume to give us her personal view of Chopin, or to express the conventional view in the language she habitually uses herself in social intercourse. She has not yet discovered that in literature the ambition of the novice is to acquire the literary language: the struggle of the adept is to get rid of it. Though I would not dissuade her from cultivating the literary language until she has brought its logic and its economy to the utmost attainable perfection, she may take my word for it that her meaning will never be seized instantly in all its fullness by the instinct and feeling of her audience, unless she expresses it in vernacular language. In several passages her lecture was quite artificial: it did not rise above a carefully compiled biographical statement, interlined with an auctioneer's catalogue of Chopin's works, her own individuality being suppressed throughout in a thoroughly ladylike way. Now it is one thing to be a lady and quite another thing to be a lecturer. Lecturing is in its own nature a hopelessly unladylike pursuit. It is not ladylike to monopolize the whole conversation for an hour. I greatly doubt whether it is strictly ladylike to appear even remotely conscious of the existence of such a person as Madame Sand, much less of her relations with Chopin. Now, since it is impossible to lecture at all without committing such crimes as these, and since you may as well be hung for a sheep as a lamb, why hesitate to perpetrate the final outrage of letting loose your individuality, and saying just what you think in your own way as agreeably and frankly as you can? Of course you may have no opinion; but in that case, how much easier it would be to simply read aloud the article on Chopin from Grove's Dictionary, or some other standard work, instead of taking weary pains to produce a bad paraphrase of it?

I must apologize to Mrs Liebich for making her lecture the text of so ponderous a discourse on lecturing, for her discourse was far more entertaining than the ordinary private concert; but if the musical lecture is going to become an institution, it is my business to pounce on its weak points, with a view to its improvement, and, finally, to such perfection as it is capable of. By the way, I was reminded that it is not quite a new thing by a lecture in the same week at the London Institution by Mr Carl Armbruster, who has for a long time past been using the lecture platform as a means of propaganda for that great art development of modern times which may be described comprehensively as German music. He is, in fact, a Bayreuth Extension lecturer: that is, he does for Bayreuth what our University Extension lecturers do for Oxford and Cambridge. And I think he has solved the true educational use of the drawing room, as far as music is concerned, by holding classes there from which you can get turned out ready for a trip to Bayreuth, fully equipped with a knowledge of the motifs and their subjects in the dramas to be performed. At the London Institution he was lecturing, not on Wagner, but on Löwe, and on an admirable contemporary German song-composer, Hans Sommer, of whom we shall hear considerably more presently, though he is as yet but a youth of sixty or thereabouts. Miss Pauline Cramer sang the only song of Löwe that ever sends a real shiver down my spine, the grisly Edward; also The Goldsmith's Daughter, the most charming of all his cheerful songs, as far as my knowledge of them goes. Miss Cramer sang them both so well that I wondered for the fiftieth time why she has chosen to hide her talent in a country where her artistic seriousness simply makes the natives uncomfortable. Löwe, being by this time long enough dead, is coming into fashion, though the vogue of his songs will always be restricted by his disregard of the normal limits of the human voice. His own range seems to have been greater than that of any recorded vocalist, except, perhaps, Mr Corney Grain, who, I believe, does not sing his music. Archibald Douglas, which is not open to this reproach, was finely sung at a recent Monday Popular Concert by Mr David Bispham, accompanied by Mr Henry Bird. It was tremendously applauded, partly on its own account, partly because the public has at last discovered that the striking difference between Mr Bispham and most other concert-singers is altogether to his advantage. At the same concert I heard for the first time this season Lady Hallé, who gave an astonishingly able performance of Tartini's Trillo—quite equal in all essential qualities to Norman Neruda's best. Piatti was there too, unimpaired. At this and the next concert I heard two novelties: a pianoforte quintet by Goldmark, and a string quartet by Villiers Stanford. Goldmark is evidently a man of weak academic fibre: he aimed at nothing higher with his fiddles and piano than the production of some extremely pretty music. And he certainly hit his mark. Only for a moment did he awake to a sense of what was due to himself as a scientific musician, and that was in the last movement, when he indulged in a fugato. The sound was ludicrous; but artists and audience sat tight, without daring to look at one another, and it was soon over. The Stanford quartet was exceedingly clever: this I say in its praise; for if I am to have scientific music, I had rather have it cleverly scientific than stupidly so. And I maintain that Professor Tyndall himself could not have written a quartet more creditable to the Irish intellect. Still, there are blemishes in it. For example, though the scherzo, with its recurring trio, is, like the rest of the work, unquestionable in form—respectable precedents being discoverable in Beethoven and elsewhere—it condescends to be enjoyable. And the elaborately invented harmonies of the slow movement, by their very aloofness from the vulgarities of poetic purpose or voluptuous tone-weaving, accidentally acquire an unexpectedness of arrival and a vagueness of destination which might suggest to an ignorant and imaginative hearer that the composer was portraying the wanderings of a blind heroine in an Irish waste. It is in the first and last movements that the Professor is most completely himself, though even here there is an escapade or two. I must reserve my final judgment, however, until I have *seen* the quartet. Merely to hear music of this sort is to miss half its qualities.

13 December 1893

THE chief musical event of last week was the performance of Schumann's Genoveva for the first time on the English stage by the students of the Royal College of Music. The pit and galleries of Drury Lane (handsomely lent for the occasion) were crammed with students. Parents and uncles and aunts of students were everywhere, interrupting the performance in the wrongest possible places by untimely applause, and feeling that such incomprehensible and solemn music as Schumann's must be excellent training for young people. The stalls and boxes were full of critics and other distinguished persons. Speaking as one of them, may I suggest that when we are so numerous, and consequently so tightly packed, the management should have a steam crane on the site of the prompter's box between the acts, so that any critic desiring to leave his place during the intervals could hook himself by the waistband to the end of the chain and be hoisted out of his seat, swung round, and dropped at the door nearest the refreshment bar?

The orchestra, being nearly eighty strong, was responsible for some of the packing. It was quite the most brilliant part of the house, as thirty-four out of fifty of the strings were young women, most of them so attractive that for once the average of personal beauty was higher in the band than on the stage. The swarming and chattering when they assembled, and the irreverent waving of bows to friends in the house, put everybody into good humor—even those critics who were furious at having to begin their afternoon's work as early as half-past one.

Genoveva was an excellent selection for the College to make. Since it is commercially valueless as an opera, we should never have heard it at all if it had not been taken in hand by a purely academic institution; and yet, being by Schumann, it was certain that some interesting music lay buried in it. For Schumann had at least one gift which we have now come to rank very highly among the qualifications of a composer for the stage: to wit, a strong feeling for harmony as a means of emotional expression. There are passages in Genoveva which are in this respect genuinely Wagnerian—and I am not one of those incorrigible people who cry out Wagner whenever they hear an unprepared major "tonic discord."

Unfortunately, in the other qualifications of the music-dramatist, Schumann is as far behind Beethoven as Beethoven was behind Mozart and Wagner. To begin with, he gives away all pretension to seriousness in his enterprise by providing as its subject a book which is nakedly silly. He may have persuaded himself—such a folly would have been just like him—that he could make his heroine do for his opera what Beethoven made Leonora do for Fidelio. But Fidelio, though commonplace and homely, is not silly. Its few harmless stage conventions do not prevent it from being credible and human from beginning to end; whereas Genoveva, from the moment when the witch enters in the first act, degenerates into pure bosh, and remains mostly at that level to the end. The witch's music is frivolous and serio-comic, the orchestration sprouting at the top into an outrageous piccolo part which would hardly be let off with mere indulgent laughter if it came from any less well-beloved composer.

In one place, the villain being left with the heroine, who has fainted, he exclaims: "We are alone." Immediately—the witch being round the corner—the piccolo utters a prolonged and derisive squawk, as if a cockatoo were reminding him that it had its eye on him. Instrumentation, as we all know, was not Schumann's strong point; and there is plenty of his characteristic orchestral muddling in Genoveva; but I can remember no other instance of his scoring being foolish in its intention. The witch is perhaps not much worse in the early scenes than Sir Arthur Sullivan's Ulrica in Ivanhoe, or in the incantation scene than Verdi's Ulrica in Un Ballo; but one has only to think of Ortrud in Lohengrin to realize the distance that separates Schumann's second-hand ideas from those of a really creative genius.

Another of the failures of Genoveva is Golo, the villain. As he is, unfortunately, a sentimental villain, it would require a Mozartian subtlety of characterization to differentiate him from the other sentimental people in the opera —the hero and the heroine, for instance. This subtlety Schumann did not possess: accordingly, Siegfried or Genoveva might sing every bar of Golo's music without the smallest incongruity. Imagine the effect of Don Giovanni singing Leporello's music, Elvira Zerlina's, Wotan Loki's, or Alberich Mime's!

Even Beethoven, whose powers in this respect were so

blunt that, like a veritable Procrustes, he levelled four different characters in his Fidelio by writing a quartet in canon
for them (conceive Non ti fidar or Un di si ben in canon!),
not to mention that his prison porter and gaoler's daughter
are absolutely indistinguishable in kind from his Florestan
and Leonora—even Beethoven made Pizarro an unmistakeable scoundrel. He could not, like Wagner or Mozart, have
given us half a dozen scoundrels, each as distinct from the
other as Tartuffe from Harpagon or Rogue Riderhood from
Silas Wegg; but he could at least distinguish an amiable
person from an unamiable one. But this moderate feat has
baffled Schumann in Genoveva.

It is obvious, then, that we must fall back on the symphonic, descriptive, and lyrical pages of the score for such
merits as it possesses. In none of these can anything be found
that need be heard by anyone who knows Schumann's songs,
pianoforte pieces, and symphonies. In the nonsensical magic
mirror and ghost scenes of the third act, and the demented
business in the ravine in the fourth, Schumann, for the most
part, leaves the stage to get on as best it can, and retires into
pure symphony, with an effect which is only tolerable on
condition of dismissing as so much superfluous rubbish all
of the actual drama shewn on the boards, except, perhaps,
what may be barely necessary to motivate in the vaguest
manner the emotions of Genoveva and her husband.

The opera is at its best when Genoveva is on the stage;
and it is never absolutely vulgar and trivial except in the
witch music. The departure of the troops in the first act is
an effective piece of composition for the stage; and there are
one or two episodes in the second act, when Genoveva is
alone in her chamber, which are by no means unsuccessful.
But the work, as a whole, is a failure; and glad as I am that
I have heard it, I cannot blame the world for dropping its
acquaintance, though it has left a good many less worthy
names on its operatic visiting list.

The performance, conducted by Professor Stanford,
went without a hitch. It had been faithfully and thoroughly

rehearsed; and the performers, unpaid, and unspoiled by popularity or practical experience of the credulity of that harmless monster, the public, did their very best anxiously and eagerly, the result being, in spite of a hundred comical little accidents due to the nervousness and ineptitude of the performers, a certain satisfactoriness and even a degree of illusion which is the rarest thing in the world at regular professional performances.

The most obtrusively academic part of the affair was the posing, walking, and gesticulation. The unhappy students had been taught "plastique" until they dared not call their arms and legs their own. The plastique professor, with his principles of beauty, and his set of regulations for the attainment of absolute grace of attitude, is almost as fatal a person as the harmony professor with *his* set of regulations for the attainment of "correct" part writing. No attitude, unfortunately for professordom, is unconditionally beautiful. Apollo, eight heads high, and with his shoulders broader than his waist, may look like a god in an attitude in which Smith, seven heads high, and with his waist perhaps broader than his champagne-bottle shoulders, may look absurd.

It is all very well to compile principles of beauty from Greek statuary; but the sculptor can shape his man to suit his attitude, whereas the actor has to make the attitude suit the real human shape, which varies so infinitely from one person to another that methods of identifying criminals by their physical proportions are said to be infallible. As an alteration of an inch in the relation between the size of the body and legs or head may make all the difference in the world in the grace of a pose, it is not to be wondered at that people who copy the attitudes and gestures of others— especially of those famous for their grace—at once make themselves ridiculous. There are, in fact, no standard attitudes; and the utmost a teacher can do is to rouse the pupil's conscience on the subject of personal grace, and leave him, under the guidance of that conscience, to grow his own plastique.

117

This, of course, is not the view taken at the Royal College. The characters in Genoveva were always defying common sense, and even the law of gravitation, in standard attitudes. Golo, in particular, was most conscientious: his profile when he placed his right foot on the castle steps in the first act would have delighted Mr Wopsle's dresser. Later on, however, his efforts to fulfil the precept "Stand always on one leg" wore him out; and he repeatedly supported himself, in mere exhaustion, on two, very unclassically. Genoveva repulsing him with her right arm stretched out and the hand prettily pronated was also an elegant spectacle. But the attitudes, on the whole, lacked conviction.

The one or two which came off successfully were abstractly beautiful, perhaps; but they would have been the same in any other drama or with any other individuals. I confidently recommend the youthful posers of the College, whilst cultivating strength, grace, and a fine bodily tone to their heart's content, to carefully forget all the attitudes and rules they have been taught. A graceful attitude is an attitude taken spontaneously by a graceful person; and nothing is more hopeless than to attempt to begin with the attitude and work backwards to the person.

The singing was decidedly better than might have been expected. There was no great success like that of Miss Clara Butt last year in Orfeo, though the audience made a sort of attempt to manufacture one by making a heroine of the witch, who was clever, spirited, fluent, and ready, but whose voice and style were rather shallow. Mr Archdeacon (Siegfried) and Miss Bruckshaw (Genoveva) are to be heartily congratulated on the condition in which they have come out of the destructive process of being taught to sing. We shall certainly hear more of Mr Archdeacon, who has an agreeable baritone voice.

Mr Charles Green, unmercifully victimized by academic principles, both in singing and attitudinizing, did his best as Golo. His voice is stronger than it was; but he is still hampered by the bleating method with which he began. If he will earnestly set himself during the forthcoming year to do exactly the reverse of everything he is told, the favorable results of the new departure can be judged at next year's performance.

There was a great crowd at the Crystal Palace on Saturday to hear Paderewski. A young lady ventured on O zittre nicht (Non paventar) from Die Zauberflöte, leading us to expect either the noblest powers of dramatic expression in the *larghetto*, or else the extreme range up to F needed for the florid *allegro*—if not both qualifications. As it turned out, she had neither, her singing of the *larghetto* being exceedingly commonplace, whilst at the crucial point of the *allegro* she sang B C D instead of B D F, thus falling a minor third short of the range required. Under these circumstances what does the lady expect me to say about her choice? Her second selection, the well-worn song of Solveig, from Grieg's Peer Gynt music, was much more sensible, and won her an encore, though the hour was late and Paderewski next in the program.

20 December 1893

LIKE all intelligent people, I greatly dislike Christmas. It revolts me to see a whole nation refrain from music for weeks together in order that every man may rifle his neighbor's pockets under cover of a ghastly general pretence of festivity. It is really an atrocious institution, this Christmas. We must be gluttonous because it is Christmas. We must be drunken because it is Christmas. We must be insincerely generous; we must buy things that nobody wants, and give them to people we dont like; we must go to absurd entertainments that make even our little children satirical; we must writhe under venal officiousness from legions of freebooters, all because it is Christmas—that is, because the mass of the population, including the all-powerful middle-class tradesman, depends on a week of licence and brigandage, waste and intemperance, to clear off its outstanding liabilities at the end of the year. As for me, I shall fly from it all tomorrow or next day to some remote spot miles from a shop, where nothing worse can befall me than a serenade from a few peasants, or some equally harmless survival of medieval mummery, shyly proffered, not advertised, moderate in its expectations, and soon over. In town there is, for the moment, nothing for me or any honest man to do. There will be no London Symphony Concert until January 11th, no Crystal Palace Saturday Concert until February 17th, no Popular Concert until January 6th, and no new comic opera, I trust, until I am dead.

Mention of the London Symphony Concerts reminds me that I said nothing at the time about the last one, at which Mr Henschel revived Rubinstein's Ramsgate Symphony, sometimes described as The Ocean. In judging this work it should be borne in mind that Rubinstein is a Russian, and that in no country in Europe is it possible to keep so far away from the ocean as in Russia. Also that Rubinstein's rating as a composer is not high. He is only oceanic in respect of not being fresh, and of being drenchingly copious. His songs, duets, and pianoforte pieces are sincerely sentimental and sometimes pretty, though they are all compiled from the works of greater composers; but an ocean symphony—no, thank you.

If I cannot have Wagner's sea music, I can content myself with Mendelssohn's Hebrides, or even Grieg's scrap of storm music in Peer Gynt, or, if no better may be, with Strauss' North Sea waltz played in the true Strauss manner. I only draw the line at Rubinstein's attempt to stuff out the chords of C and G major with musical chaff to something like the bigness of the round pond in Kensington Gardens. It is no use: the thing, oceanically considered, is a failure. Leave the ocean out of the question, and you have a commonplace but bustling and passable third-hand Schubert symphony. Mr Henschel mercifully cut two movements out of it; and when he proceeds to cut out the other four my enjoyment of the work will be complete. By way of putting Rubinstein entirely out of countenance, his work was pre-

120

faced by Weber's Ocean, thou mighty monster, sung by Mrs Eaton, a lady of formidable physical powers, which she used with due discretion and artistic feeling.

Miss Beatrice Langley played Spohr's ninth concerto. She might have played its arabesques better; but then, in the modern school, which turns out such an amazing quantity of virtuosos, "better is the enemy of well." That principle is a good working one; and I am far from contending that Miss Langley should not play Spohr at all because she cannot play his allegros with ideal elegance: still, I must not imply that she has yet attained the combination of swiftness with perfect pitch and measure required by purely decorative passages which, having no dramatic interest whatever, are nothing if not exquisitely graceful. In the rondo the snapping of a string compelled her to borrow Mr Hollander's fiddle to finish with. I have seen that happen before; but I cannot recollect any other violinist whose first proceeding on borrowing a violin from the band was to hastily alter its tuning. Mr Hollander's chanterelle no doubt sounded flat to Miss Langley's sharp ear, though his and mine were satisfied; but it seemed ungrateful to criticize the tuning of the leader's fiddle before the audience. The performance of the concerto, on the whole, made a brilliant impression; but the famous adagio was the only movement which was as nearly up to the mark as the audience thought. The concert wound up with the Meistersinger overture, which was, perhaps, the most successful moment in Mr Henschel's winter campaign so far. The truth is that some such moment was rather badly wanted; for the recent London Symphony Concerts have fallen perceptibly short of the very high standard of excellence attained by them at the beginning of the year.

A miscellaneous concert of considerable pretension was given on Tuesday last week by Mr Fred Fawcett, a gentleman whose singing I had occasion to notice last season at Mr Maud Crament's concert. Such old stories as Madame Belle Cole's singing of Sognai, Mr Norman Salmond's of The Wanderer, and Mr Ben Davies' of Deeper and deeper still, need not here be re-told. Fresher in interest was the appearance of Miss Ella Russell, who has, I imagine, been triumphing exceedingly in the provinces. She has evidently discovered that it is not enough to sing well to a public which does not know good singing from bad. It is necessary to assert your qualities, throw your emotions at their heads, wake them up with strenuous tone-vibrations, and keep things going at a lively pace generally, as our music-hall artists are trained to do. Miss Russell has developed her style vigorously in this direction; and the audience was encoring her enthusiastically when I came away. This I did not do without hearing The Ladies' Amateur Harp, Mandoline, and Guitar Band, consisting of thirty-two damsels, of whom three played the harp, four the violin, six the guitar, and nineteen the mandoline. It is disquieting to find that there are nineteen people in England who can play the mandoline; and I sincerely hope the number may not increase. I know nothing more maddening than the sostenuto produced from a string by rapid repercussion or replectration (if there is such a word). Pianoforte-makers from time to time take out patents for diabolical contrivances to keep something whirring against the string whilst you hold the key down and work a treadle; and the effect of the mandoline band is not unlike that of a monster pianoforte with some such appliance in full blast. The effect is pretty at first; and certainly the band is thoroughly drilled, and makes the best of itself.

No doubt, if there were dancing and singing to divide one's attention a little, it might go on for a whole evening without turning anyone's hair white; but I confess that ten unrelieved minutes of it left me more than satiated. By the way, I am credibly informed that Chelmsford is happy in the possession of an amateur body called The English Ladies' Orchestral Society, in which the wind and percussion instruments are played by ladies as well as the strings. This is good news for ladies with undeveloped lungs. After all, the chief objection to playing wind instruments is that it prolongs the life of the player beyond all reasonable limits. If you want to become phthisis-proof, drink-proof, cholera-proof, and, in short, immortal, play the trombone well and play it constantly. I hope the Chelmsford ladies will visit London and shew how very unnecessary it is for their sex to waste itself on the mandoline.

The other evening I came upon an extraordinary instance of public insensibility to music. I seldom go to the theatre, partly because my evenings are otherwise engaged, partly because my theatrical sense is so blunt that in spite of my most earnest efforts to improve myself I hardly ever can see any difference between one modern play and another. On Monday last week I went, as I supposed, to a certain concert at Prince's Hall; but though my ticket was not challenged, I found myself, when I got inside, at quite another concert—an amateur orchestral one—to which I had not been invited. I had come a week too soon.

To remain, an unbidden guest, and listen to an amateur band, would have been an act of wantonness; so I hastily retreated by way of King Street, St. James's. Here, glancing at the bills on the St James's Theatre, I found that they were performing a play which has attained extraordinary celebrity, and which I had been strongly urged to see as a masterpiece of modern drama. So in I went, and conscientiously applied myself to my usual task of trying to persuade myself that I had never seen anything like it before. I was late, and only saw a scrap of the first act; but when the curtain rose on the second it revealed a pianoforte, at which the chief lady in the piece—a very attractive person—presently sat down and began to play. To my surprise, she played not only with sufficient skill, but with such convincingly right expression and feeling and so sympathetic a hand that I immediately forgot all about the comedy, and prepared to enjoy Schubert.

Will it be believed that the wretched people on the stage interrupted her after a few bars? The same thing happened at a subsequent and equally promising attempt. After that she never succeeded in even sitting down to the piano; and at last, worn out by repeated interruptions, she left the stage abruptly, and we were presently given to understand that she had committed suicide. No wonder! Now, is it not an extraordinary thing that though her performance has attracted more attention and been more written about than that of any other artist in London this year, nobody seems to have noticed the difference between her playing and the ordinary leading lady's stage strum over the half-dozen easiest bars of some half-forgotten relic of the schoolroom?

Everybody can act more or less—all the world's a stage, unfortunately. But all the world is not a pianoforte; and yet when the dramatic critics for once in their misspent lives hear someone who can touch a piano with a musician's hand, they can talk about nothing but her *acting*—as if she only pretended to play. If the St James's management will give a special performance for the musical critics, with the second act extended so as to allow of a recital of the lady's entire repertory, and the fourth act left out (the motive for the catastrophe being gone), then I think we musical critics, with all our faults, will rise to the occasion.

Everybody, I presume, knows Chappell's Popular Music of the Olden Time, issued in 1859. Perhaps some of my readers have a copy of the original 1840 Collection of National English Airs. A new edition has just been issued called Old English Popular Music, in two volumes, bound bravely in blue buckram, and edited by Mr H. Ellis Wooldridge. The first volume, as may be imagined by anyone who knows how much our eyes have been opened in historical matters during the last thirty years, is a vast improvement on the old edition. Macfarren, the former editor, never really succeeded in conceiving musical ideas as expressible otherwise than in terms of our modern major or minor mode. He believed in his heart that the old musicians, although they omitted the sharps and flats in writing music, modified the notes in performance, except when they simply blundered in their unconscious striving towards modern tonality. The result was, of course, that his editing of those works which date from before the triumph of the two modern modes is now quite unpresentable.

Mr Wooldridge has accordingly rejected the Macfarren versions and arrangements up to 1650; and though he himself is not altogether emancipated from Macfarrenism—for he offers King Henry VIII an occasional leading note or flattened sixth which would, I strongly suspect, have horribly offended that virtuous Prince's scruples as to our "lascivious" modern musical ways—and though, further, he fits the very oldest tunes with nineteenth-century imitations of late sixteenth-century harmonies which he admits to be anachronisms, yet, as he also gives the original descants, and makes the exact extent of his interference quite clear, no harm is done: indeed, the general public will be glad of such harmonizations of the tunes as are needed to make them acceptable and even intelligible to—shall I say the mob? Anyhow, there are the two volumes, full of tunes, invaluable to the musician, and highly interesting to anyone with the least historical instinct.

27 December 1893

WE seem never to get finally rid of the relics of the autumn festivals. The "specially composed" oratorio, cantata, or symphony, having been duly proclaimed a masterpiece, is set down for its first performance in London later on; and these first performances keep dropping in all the winter and stirring up our worst passions. The latest arrival in this department is the symphony composed by Mr Edward German for the Norwich Festival. It was played at the Crystal Palace on the 16th, and conducted, like the rest of the concert, by the composer, Mr Manns being absent at Glasgow, as he always is for the last concert of the year. One advantage of this arrangement was that we got a more exciting performance of Mendelssohn's Ruy Blas overture than Mr Manns would have indulged us with now that he is waxing grave in his *tempi*, and takes even a Beethoven scherzo at ninety-six bars per minute instead of the old hundred and ten or fifteen. Mr German raced the overture; and as Mendelssohn's allegros are built for speed, comparing with Beethoven's much as a yacht does with a three-decker, the result was brilliantly satisfactory.

The Norwich symphony struck me as a mass of clever composition wasted. It is dramatic music without any subject, emotional music without any mood, formal music without conspicuous beauty and symmetry of design, externally a symphony, really a fulfilment of a commission or seizure of a professional opportunity, otherwise purposeless. It is much as if the Festival committee had invited Mr Pinero to write an ode, arguing that since odes are literature, and plays literature, and since Mr Pinero, as a producer of plays, is a producer of literature, he must be the right man to produce odes. And no doubt Mr Pinero could string sentences into the form of an ode, just as Mr German has strung themes into the form of a symphony. But compare the symphony with the incidental music to Henry VIII by the same hand, which was played at the end of the concert; and note how Mr German, when he gets on his own ground, with definite dramatic business in hand, suddenly becomes intelligible, interesting, purposeful, and individual.

The fact is, symphony is no more Mr German's business than epic poetry is mine. Some years ago, when he composed his Richard III overture for Mr Mansfield, he wavered between descriptive and absolute music, the latter rather getting the better of Richard III. At that time he would probably have written a very creditable Mendelssohn student's symphony. Since then he has developed his descriptive and dramatic powers; and now Fate, maladroit as usual, offers him an opportunity of distinguishing himself in exactly the opposite direction. However, the Festival being happily over, and the first performance in London duly achieved, he can easily break up the symphony, and use the scraps—which are valuable—as material for future work in his own line.

Both the vocalist and the pianist failed to appear at this concert. We accordingly had Rubinstein's concerto in D minor from Herr Schönberger, an artist whose technical instinct would place him in the front rank if his artistic instincts were equally keen and delicate.

On Monday last week the students of Trinity College gave a concert at Prince's Hall. In the band they were helped out by experienced hands and by the careful conducting of Mr F. Corder to an extent which took the full orchestral responsibility off their shoulders; but so far as their share went, it was creditably discharged. In looking through the list of the College professors on the back of the program, I could not help being struck by the fact that the orchestral departments were in the hands of men like Radcliffe and Barrett, Lazarus and Clinton, Malsch, Mann, etc., all known as capable performers on the instruments they teach.

Not for a moment do I question that the gentlemen who teach singing are equally distinguished in private as vocalists; but I am certainly not so familiar with their triumphs; and, as a mere matter of taste, I do not like the results of their teaching so well. I heard a young lady with a contralto voice, the condition of which was a perfect example of the results of the method of teaching singing which has grown up in our musical academies; and I am therefore able to certify that this method seems to be thoroughly understood and carried out in Trinity College. To those who like the academic style of singing this should prove a high recommendation. The most interesting and important item in the program was Ferdinand Hiller's pianoforte concerto in F minor, played by Mr Arthur Lestrange. The selection was not a wise one. The concerto, which is very difficult, very able, very handsome, and quite heartless, requires a certain serene elegance of handling and mundane self-possession on the part of the player, as well as faultless dexterity of finger; whereas Mr Lestrange is, above all things, a feverish player—one who cannot play even a scale without a crisis in it somewhere: in short, just the wrong man for Hiller, and likely to become still more incompatible with him the more he develops his own style as a player; for the modest, conscientious formalism of his youth and pupilage trimmed him closer to the symmetrical propriety of Hiller's style than he will ever be trimmed again, probably. If Mr Lestrange could manage a run abroad—say, in Vienna—for a year or so, his return would be awaited with some interest, as he is well endowed musically, and has initiative and individuality.

Mr Robert Buchanan's opera, The Piper of Hamelin, produced last Wednesday afternoon at the Comedy, was a happy thought in every way. I have been for years wondering why Browning's poem was not snapped up by some English musician: in fact, I once planned a choral symphony on the Pied Piper myself, and the world has lost an interesting work through my lack of leisure to carry out my design. Mr Comyns Carr has shewn himself the right manager for a work of this sort. He knows what no other manager seems yet to have found out—that it is quite possible to fill up the stage with pleasant young people who can dance a little, act a little, sing a little, look educated and presentable, and wear pretty dresses naturally, if only you are sufficiently in touch with general society to know where to look for them, and if you can at the same time make them and their friends feel sure that your theatre is a nice place to be employed in.

I am not here hinting at the current objections to the morals of the rank and file of the comic-opera stage. Morals, in that sense, have not half so much to do with the question as manners. Young women of sensibility and refinement, natural or cultivated, know too little of stage morals to care much about them; but they object none the less to throw in their lot with a regiment of girls who are studiedly and purposely slangy of speech and brazen of bearing, absurdly conscious of being alluringly dressed and much stared at, and quite incapable of comprehending their artistic function and respecting themselves for discharging it. Now at the Comedy Theatre not only do the principals look like cultivated, decent people, but when they stand among the chorus they seem to be moving in their own set. This is a managerial feat to be proud of: it raises the standard of respectability for comic opera in the very department where the want of it is most odious and most rampant. If Mr Carr's experiment meets with the success it deserves, he and Mr D'Oyly Carte between them will have done much to put the rowdiness of the ordinary comic-opera chorus out of countenance and out of fashion.

The stage is the most exclusive profession in the world; and that being so, and necessarily so, there is no reason why we should hesitate to insist on a high standard of manners there. The merest novice in the chorus expects twenty-five shillings a week as a minimum wage; and a man expects thirty. Considering the degree of address and appearance exacted from young women in shops and restaurants who get much worse paid and have to work abominably long hours, I cannot see why so much less social amenity should be expected from a lady of the chorus than from a parlormaid.

On the whole, Mr Carr has reason to congratulate himself. The subject of the opera is an ideal one for his purpose; and his company, his dresses, and his scenery illustrate it in a highly artistic way, the stage spectacle having the quality of a good picture-book. Mr Buchanan has gone to play rather than to work in making an opera-book of the legend; but Mr Buchanan's imagination never fails him: no matter what he writes, or even how he writes, he can always put the story-teller's spell on us. There was not a prosaic moment in the performance; and some of the moments were quite affecting —I do not think that is too strong a description of the sensation produced by the close of the first act with the departure of the children after the Piper. The atmosphere of romantic illusion was proof against even the stage rats.

The principals, too, were all competent and interesting. Miss Lena Ashwell would have made a greater hit by her grace and good looks, and by the sincerity of her acting as Liza, if she had not apparently had the misfortune to have derived her ideas of voice production from some particularly conscientious professor of the academic art of How Not to Do It; but even with this drawback she came off very well.

As to the Piper, Mr Wyatt, decidedly "fluffy" at times as to his words and music, and not by any means emancipated from the ridiculous Mephistophelean tradition in his grotesque attitudes, yet rose successfully to the occasion at the end of the first act, and was once or twice really striking. The tenor, Mr Leonard Russell, was not a bit insufferable —quite the contrary, in fact; and little Gladys Doree, as the lame child Hans, was so intensely rapt in her part that she made an exceptional impression.

But—for I am loth to have to add that all this is only leading up to a great BUT—why did not Mr Buchanan, Wagner-like, compose the music to his own play? Mr F. W. Allwood, the composer who relieved him of that task, is a gentleman with a very great knowledge of Italian opera and English drawing room ballad music, from Mercadante down to Mr Cowen; and he has used his knowledge unsparingly. Unfortunately, his memory is not note perfect. He repeatedly tried to make the Piper play It was a dream; but not even at the end, when he brought the whole orchestra to aid him in two heroic final attempts, did he succeed in getting it right. Only for this unlucky infirmity Mr Allwood would have produced a passable *potpourri*.

As it was, from the opening reminiscence of the exordium to Mendelssohn's Ruy Blas, and the bold resurrection of Regnava nel silenzio, which immediately follows, down to the curiously unsuccessful shot at God Save the Queen, which closes the opera, I heard hardly a theme which did not differ from the authentic version by several notes, and differ for the worse, too. No doubt the truth is that Mr Allwood honestly mistook his memory for his invention; but I do not see how I could have mistaken his invention for my memory; and therefore I am reluctantly compelled to except his score from my otherwise favorable verdict on The Piper of Hamelin.

After the Piper came a burlesque of Sandford and Merton, by Messrs Burnand and Solomon, with Mr Lionel Brough as Barlow. Frankly, I did not like it. That sort of burlesque never entertained me even when it was in the hey-day of its popularity; and what is more, I have never seen an audience shew any convincing signs of differing from me in this respect except when some exceedingly droll performer was providing the fun from his own personal resources. However, Sandford and Merton is not, as far as I can judge, worse than other burlesques of its kind; and possibly the peashooters, squirts, squibs, and birchings will amuse the grown-up people among the audience. Need I add that none of the more questionable enchantments of burlesque are permitted: hence, probably, the term operetta instead of burlesque in the playbill.

The book of The Piper, well printed by the Chiswick Press and capitally illustrated by Mr Hugh Thomson, is sold in the theatre for eighteenpence. This is, perhaps, the most startling of all Mr Carr's reforms. I never saw anything that a respectable printer would call a book sold in a theatre before.

10 *January* 1894

I AM, I suppose, in the west country, by which I mean generally any place for which you start from Paddington. To be precise, I am nowhere in particular, though there are ascertained localities within easy reach of me. For instance, if I were to lie down and let myself roll over the dip at the foot of the lawn, I should go like an avalanche into the valley of the Wye. I could walk to Monmouth in half an hour or so. At the end of the avenue there is a paper nailed to a tree with a stencilled announcement that The Penalt Musical Society will give a concert last Friday week (I was at it, as shall presently appear); and it may be, therefore, that I am in the parish of Penalt, if there is such a place. But as I have definitely ascertained that I am not in England either ecclesiastically or for the purposes of the Sunday Closing Act; as, nevertheless, Wales is on the other side of the Wye; and as I am clearly not in Ireland or Scotland, it seems to follow that I am, as I have honestly admitted, nowhere. And I assure you it is a very desirable place—a land of

quietly beautiful hills, enchanting valleys, and an indescribable sober richness of winter coloring. This being so, need
I add that the natives are flying from it as from the plague?
Its lonely lanes, where, after your day's work, you can
wander amid ghosts and shadows under the starry firma-
ment, stopping often to hush your footsteps and listen to a
wonderful still music of night and nature, are eagerly exchanged for sooty streets and gaslamps and mechanical
pianos playing the last comic song but two. The fact is,
wages in the district do not reflect the sufficiency of the scenery: hence ambitious young men forsake their birthplace to
begrime themselves in "the tinworks," symbolic of the great
manufacturing industries of the nation, which have all, figu-
ratively speaking, the production of tin as their final cause.
I cannot walk far without coming upon the ruins of a deserted cottage or farmhouse. The frequency of these, and
the prevalence of loosely piled stone walls instead of hedges,
gives me a sensation of being in Ireland which is only dis-
pelled by the appearance of children with whole garments
and fresh faces acquainted with soap. But even children are
scarce, the population being, as far as I can judge, about one
sixth of a human being per square mile. The only fit pleasures of the place are those of contemplation. Yet one day,
as I was coasting a neighboring valley, the sylvan echoes
were wakened by an abjectly monotonous Too Too too-
too-too-too, Too Too too too-tooting on a poor sort of horn;
and presently a huntsman appeared jogging along, followed
by a pack of hounds full of eager excitement, which they had
to waste, for want of anything else to do, in a restless wag-
ging of their multitudinous tails which quite hid their bodies
from me, exactly as the swordsman in the German tale kept
himself dry in a shower of rain by waving his sword above
his head. Then came some young gentlemen, their bored
human instincts struggling with those which they shared
with the pack. With them were many older men, of whom a
few, if my observation is to be trusted, eke out their incomes
by selling horses to the younger ones. Usually, when the

hunt is up, my sympathies are with the fox, and I have nothing but contemptuous indignation for its pursuers; but on this occasion the foxless cortège, as it clattered slowly along, comforting itself with flasks and sandwiches, was such a hopeless failure that I pitied it, and would have even provided it with a quarry had I possessed a spirited young tiger or other carnivorous animal able to bring out the manly qualities which are the pride of the sportsman. Had these hunters been wise, they would have satiated their destructive instincts by criticizing musical performances in town, and devoted their country holidays to benevolence and poetry.

There is a band in this place. Two little cornets, four baritone saxhorns, and a euphonium, all rather wasted for want of a competent person to score a few airs specially for them; for the four saxhorns all play the same part in unison instead of spreading themselves polyphonically over the desert between the cornets and the tuba. When their strains burst unexpectedly on my ear on Christmas Day, I supposed, until I went cautiously to the window to reconnoitre, that there were only three instruments instead of seven. With a parish organist to set this matter right for them, and a parish bandmaster to teach them a few simple rules of thumb as to the manipulation of their tuning-slides, the seven musicians would have discoursed excellent music. I submit that, pending the creation of a Ministry of Music, the Local Government Board should appoint District Surveyors of Brass Bands to look after these things. There are also carol singers; but of them I have nothing to say except that the first set, consisting of a few children, sang with great spirit a capital tune which I shall certainly steal when I turn my attention seriously to composition. The second set came very late, and had been so hospitably entertained at their previous performances that they had lost that clearness of intention and crispness of execution which no doubt distinguished their earlier efforts.

But the great event of the Penalt season was the concert.

133

It was taken for granted that I, as an eminent London critic, would hold it in ineffable scorn; and it was even suggested that I should have the condescension to stay away. But, as it happened, I enjoyed it more than any native did, and that, too, not at all derisively, but because the concert was not only refreshingly different from the ordinary London miscellaneous article, but much better. The difference began with the adventurousness of the attempt to get there. There were no cabs, no omnibuses, no lamps, no policemen, no pavement, and, as it happened, no moon or stars. Fortunately, I have a delicate sense of touch in my boot-soles, and this enabled me to discriminate between road and common in the intervals of dashing myself against the gates which I knew I had to pass. At last I saw a glow in the darkness, and an elderly countryman sitting in it with an air of being indoors. He turned out to be the bureau, so to speak; and I was presently in the concert-room, which was much more interesting than St James's Hall, where there is nothing to look at except the pictures of mountain and glacier accidentally made—like faces in the fire—by the soot and dust in the ventilating lunettes in the windows. Even these are only visible at afternoon concerts. Here there was much to occupy and elevate the mind pending the appearance of the musicians: for instance, there was St Paul preaching at Athens after Raphael, and the death of General Wolfe after West, with a masonic-looking document which turned out to be the school time-table, an extensive display of flags and paraffin lamps, and an ingenious machine on the window-blind principle for teaching the children to add up sums of money of which the very least represented about eleven centuries of work and wages at current local rates. It presently appeared that the Penalt Musical Society had adopted one of the most advanced suggestions in Wagner's famous Dresden plan for the reformation of the theatre: to wit, the constitution of a Concert and Theatre department under the Minister of Public Worship. In Penalt, accordingly, the music was under the supreme control of the clergyman. He was conductor, he was accompanist, he was *entrepreneur*, he was (in emergencies) leader of the choir, he was chairman, he was master of the ceremonies, and he had written and composed all the comic songs and trios on local topics. He even mingled the politician and sociologist with the composer—again reminding one of Wagner in Dresden; for one of his compositions dealt with the Parish Councils Bill, and another with the recent coal difficulties. Furthermore, he had rehearsed the concert thoroughly; and this is the beginning and the end of true righteousness.

The program shewed how varied are the resources of a country parish compared to the helplessness of a town choked by the density and squalor of its own population. We had glees—Hail, Smiling Morn, The Belfry Tower, etc.—by no means ill sung. We had feats of transcendent execution on the pianoforte, in the course of which the Men of Harlech took arms against a sea of variations, and, by opposing, ended them to the general satisfaction. But it was from the performances of the individual vocalists that I received the strongest sense that here, on the Welsh border, we were among a naturally musical and artistic folk. From the young lady of ten who sang When you and I were young, to the robust farmer-comedians who gave the facetious and topical interludes with frank enjoyment and humor, and without a trace of the vulgarity which is the heavy price we have to pay for professionalism in music, the entertainment was a genuine and spontaneous outcome of the natural talent of the people. The artists cost nothing: the pianoforte-tuner, the printer, and the carpenter who fixed the platform can have cost only a few shillings. Comparing the result with certain "grand concerts" at St James's Hall, which have cost hundreds of pounds, and left me in a condition of the blankest pessimism as to the present and future of music in England, I am bound to pronounce the Penalt concert one of the most successful and encouraging of the year.

If I dared, I should proceed to criticize the singers in detail. But only an experienced critic knows the frightful

135

danger of doing this. Everywhere alike, in the most out-
landish village and the greatest capital, amateur singers are
the same—one incautious word of appreciation and they
are off to study for the operatic stage, abandoning all their
real opportunities in life for a doubtful chance of reaching
that mirage which looks like the Albert Hall and the Opera,
but which is really a huge casual ward of vagabonds and
humbugs, whose punishment for having attempted to make
Art their catspaw in snatching at riches and fame is perpetual
envy and disappointment. Let me, therefore, explicitly fore-
warn all concerned that when I confess to having been
touched and charmed by some of the songs—nay, to having
caught a gleam of that "sacred fire" of which we used to talk
long ago in the performance of He thinks I do not love him,
and of Mr Blockley's old-fashioned setting of Tennyson's
O swallow, swallow, I do not mean that if the singers had
been transferred from the little schoolroom and the mild
cottage-piano to the stage of Covent Garden or the platform
of St James's Hall, with a full orchestra thundering round
them, they could have produced the same effect. Suffice it
that they did produce it in Penalt, and gave me thereby
greater pleasure than I often get from singers with far
greater pretensions. And in one respect their superiority
was absolute as well as relative. All their voices were unspoiled. They sang in low keys and used their chest registers
a good deal; but the moment the music went above the
natural range of that register they unaffectedly quitted it for
the comparatively light and unassertive, but sweet and pure
falsetto. Need I add that they were untaught, though they
probably do not know how heartily they are to be congratulated on that fact. One lady, who sang modern drawing
room ballads by Stephen Adams and Weatherly, rather
alarmed me at first by a very effective use of her lower notes,
as if she were determined to rival Miss Mackenzie. Not that
I objected to her using them effectively, but I feared that
she would presently try to force that rich quality of tone all
over her voice. But no: she also was content to have that

136

quality only where Nature gave it to her; and when the concert was over and we all plunged again into the black void without, where we jostled one another absurdly in our efforts to find the way home, I had quite made up my mind to advise all our fashionable teachers of singing to go to the singers of Penalt, consider their ways, and be wise.

17 January 1894

I T is not often that one comes across a reasonable book about music, much less an entertaining one. Still, I confess to having held out with satisfaction to the end of M. Georges Noufflard's Richard Wagner d'après lui-même (Paris, Fischbacher, 2 vols., at 3.50 fr. apiece). Noufflard is so exceedingly French a Frenchman that he writes a preface to explain that though he admires Wagner, still Alsace and Lorraine must be given back; and when he records an experiment of his hero's in teetotalism, he naïvely adds, "What is still more surprising is that this unnatural régime, instead of making Wagner ill, operated exactly as he had expected." More Parisian than this an author can hardly be; and yet Noufflard always understands the Prussian composer's position, and generally agrees with him, though, being racially out of sympathy with him, he never entirely comprehends him. He is remarkably free from the stock vulgarities of French operatic culture: for instance, he washes his hands of Meyerbeer most fastidiously; and he puts Gluck, the hero of French musical classicism, most accurately in his true place.

And here let me give a piece of advice to readers of books about Wagner. Whenever you come to a statement that Wagner was an operatic reformer, and that in this capacity he was merely following in the footsteps of Gluck, who had anticipated some of his most important proposals, you may put your book in the waste-paper basket, as far as Wagner is concerned, with absolute confidence. Gluck was an opera composer who said to his contemporaries: "Gentlemen, let us compose our operas more rationally. An opera is not a stage concert, as most of you seem to think. Let us give up

137

our habit of sacrificing our common sense to the vanity of
our singers, and let us compose and orchestrate our airs, our
duets, our recitatives, and our sinfonias in such a way that
they shall always be appropriate to the dramatic situation
given to us by the librettist." And having given this excellent advice, he proceeded to shew how it could be followed.
How well he did this we can judge, in spite of our scandalous
ignorance of Gluck, from Orfeo, with which Giulia Ravogli
has made us familiar lately.

When Wagner came on the scene, exactly a hundred
years later, he found that the reform movement begun by
Gluck had been carried to the utmost limits of possibility by
Spontini, who told him flatly that after La Vestale, etc., there
was nothing operatic left to be done. Wagner quite agreed
with him, and never had the smallest intention of beginning
the reform of opera over again at the very moment when it
had just been finished. On the contrary, he took the fully
reformed opera, with all its improvements, and asked the
nineteenth century to look calmly at it and say whether all
this patchwork of stage effects on a purely musical form had
really done anything for it but expose the absurd unreality
of its pretence to be a form of drama, and whether, in fact,
Rossini had not shewn sound common sense in virtually
throwing over that pretence and, like Gluck's Italian contemporaries, treating an opera as a stage concert. The nineteenth century took a long time to make up its mind on the
question, which it was at first perfectly incapable of understanding. Verdi and Gounod kept on trying to get beyond
Spontini on operatic lines, without the least success, except
on the purely musical side; and Gounod never gave up the
attempt, though Verdi did.

Meanwhile, however, Wagner, to shew what he meant,
abandoned operatic composition altogether, and took to
writing dramatic poems, and using all the resources of orchestral harmony and vocal tone to give them the utmost
reality and intensity of expression, thereby producing the
new art form which he called "music-drama," which is no

more "reformed opera" than a cathedral is a reformed stone quarry. The whole secret of the amazing futility of the first attempts at Wagner criticism is the mistaking of this new form for an improved pattern of the old one. Once you conceive Wagner as the patentee of certain novel features in operas and librettos, you can demolish him point by point with impeccable logic, and without the least misgiving that you are publicly making a ludicrous exhibition of yourself.

The process is fatally easy, and consists mainly in shewing that the pretended novelties of reformed opera are no novelties at all. The "leading motives," regarded as operatic melodies recurring in connection with the entry of a certain character, are as old as opera itself; the instrumentation, regarded merely as instrumentation, is no better than Mozart's and much more expensive; whereas of those features that really tax the invention of the operatic composer, the airs, the duos, the quartets, the cabalettas to display the virtuosity of the trained Italian singer, the dances, the marches, the choruses, and so on, there is a deadly dearth, their place being taken by—of all things—an interminable dull recitative.

The plain conclusion follows that Wagner was a barren rascal whose whole reputation rested on a shop-ballad, O star of eve, and a march which he accidentally squeezed out when composing his interminable Tannhäuser. And so you go on, wading with fatuous self-satisfaction deeper and deeper into a morass of elaborately reasoned and highly conscientious error. You need fear nothing of this sort from Noufflard. He knows perfectly well the difference between music-drama and opera; and the result is that he not only does not tumble into blind hero-worship of Wagner, but is able to criticize him—a thing the blunderers never could do. Some of his criticisms: for example, his observation that in Wagner's earlier work the melody is by no means so original as Weber's, are indisputable—indeed he might have said Meyerbeer or anybody else; for Wagner's melody was never original at all in that sense, any more than Giotto's figures are picturesque or Shakespear's lines elegant.

But I entirely—though quite respectfully—dissent from Noufflard's suggestion that in composing Tristan Wagner turned his back on the theoretic basis of Siegfried, and returned to "absolute music." It is true, as Noufflard points out, that in Tristan, and even in Der Ring itself, Wagner sometimes got so rapt from the objective drama that he got away from the words too, and in Tristan came to writing music without coherent words at all. But wordless music is not absolute music. Absolute music is the purely decorative sound pattern: tone poetry is the musical expression of poetic feeling. When Tristan gives musical expression to an excess of feeling for which he can find no coherent words, he is no more uttering absolute music than the shepherd who carries on the drama at one of its most deeply felt passages by playing on his pipe.

Wagner regarded all Beethoven's important instrumental works as tone poems; and he himself, though he wrote so much for the orchestra alone in the course of his music-dramas, never wrote, or could write, a note of absolute music. The fact is, there is a great deal of feeling, highly poetic and highly dramatic, which cannot be expressed by mere words —because words are the counters of thinking, not of feeling —but which can be supremely expressed by music. The poet tries to make words serve his purpose by arranging them musically, but is hampered by the certainty of becoming absurd if he does not make his musically arranged words mean something to the intellect as well as to the feeling.

For example, the unfortunate Shakespear could not make Juliet say:

O Romeo, Romeo, Romeo, Romeo, Romeo;

and so on for twenty lines. He had to make her, in an extremity of unnaturalness, begin to argue the case in a sort of amatory legal fashion, thus:

O Romeo, Romeo, wherefore art thou Romeo?
Deny thy father and refuse thy name,
Or, if thou wilt not, etc., etc., etc.

It is verbally decorative; but it is not love. And again:

> Parting is such sweet sorrow
> That I shall say good-night till it be morrow;

which is a most ingenious conceit, but one which a woman would no more utter at such a moment than she would prove the rope ladder to be the shortest way out because any two sides of a triangle are together greater than the third.

Now these difficulties do not exist for the tone poet. He can make Isolde say nothing but "Tristan, Tristan, Tristan, Tristan, Tristan," and Tristan nothing but "Isolde, Isolde, Isolde, Isolde, Isolde," to their hearts' content without creating the smallest demand for more definite explanations; and as for the number of times a tenor and soprano can repeat "Addio, addio, addio," there is no limit to it. There is a great deal of this reduction of speech to mere ejaculation in Wagner; and it is a reduction directly pointed to in those very pages of Opera and Drama which seem to make the words all-important by putting the poem in the first place as the seed of the whole music-drama, and yet make a clean sweep of nine-tenths of the dictionary by insisting that it is only the language of feeling that craves for musical expression, or even is susceptible of it.

Nay, you may not only reduce the words to pure ejaculation, you may substitute mere roulade vocalization, or even balderdash, for them, provided the music sustains the feeling which is the real subject of the drama, as has been proved by many pages of genuinely dramatic music, both in opera and elsewhere, which either have no words at all, or else belie them. It is only when a thought interpenetrated with intense feeling has to be expressed, as in the Ode to Joy in the Ninth Symphony, that coherent words must come with the music. You have such words in Tristan; you have also ejaculations void of thought, though full of feeling; and you have plenty of instrumental music with no words at all. But you have no "absolute" music, and no "opera."

Nothing in the world convinces you more of the fact that

141

a dramatic poem cannot possibly take the form of an opera libretto than listening to Tristan and comparing it with, say, Gounod's Romeo and Juliet. I submit, then, to Noufflard (whose two volumes I none the less cordially recommend to all amateurs who can appreciate a thinker) that the contradictions into which Wagner has fallen in this matter are merely such verbal ones as are inevitable from the imperfection of language as an instrument for conveying ideas; and that the progress from Der fliegende Holländer to Parsifal takes a perfectly straight line ahead in theory as well as in artistic execution.

The above observations on the perfect consistency of Wagner's theories with the dramatic validity of music without words must not be taken as an endorsement of the Wagner selections given at the London Symphony Concert last Thursday. Not that it was a bad concert: on the contrary, it brought Mr Henschel's enterprise back again to the first-rate standard which it attained last spring, and from which it fell off a little on the resumption of business towards the end of last year. The performance of Schubert's unfinished symphony was admirable, not so much for its technical execution—though that left nothing to be reasonably desired —as for the significant interpretation of several passages which are generally passed over as part of the mere routine of the symphonic form. If all our conductors could "read music" in this fashion we should not hear so much of the tedium of classical music, which certainly is the very dullest infliction in the world when it is served out mechanically from the band parts under the baton of a gentleman to whom conducting a symphony presents itself as a feat exactly analogous to driving eighty trained and perfectly willing horses round a circus ring. But my enjoyment of the symphony did not soften me towards the "arrangements" from Wagner. They may be very well for promenade concerts and provincial tours; but in London there is no reason why we should accept such makeshifts. The procession of the gods into Valhalla with the gods left out does not satisfy me. You may give me the Rhine daughters or not, as you please; but you are not entitled to tantalize me with a ridiculous squeaking oboe imitation of them; and if you are not prepared to build the rainbow-bridge for me with the full complement of harps, then leave the gulf unspanned, and do not make the scene ridiculous by a little thread of a bridge that would not support a sparrow, much less a procession of thunderers. The fact is, these arrangements, except as regards certain string effects, are paltry and misleading. They are allowable when nothing better is attainable; but in a capital city, where plenty of singers, wind-players, and harpists are available, as well as halls big enough to cover their cost, the Nibelungen music ought to be performed as Wagner scored it, and not as "arranged" to suit everybody's purse by Messrs Zumpe, Humperdinck & Co. By this time it ought to be possible to repeat the 1877 experiment of an Albert Hall recital of The Ring with a fair chance of success.

The part of the concert which most excited the audience was the appearance of M. César Thomson, a violinist bearing a certain resemblance to the Chandos portrait of Shakespear, with perhaps—I think I may say so without offence to an artist who evidently cultivates the Paganini tradition of unearthliness—a dash of the Wandering Jew. His tone is remarkably sensitive, and not less so on the fourth string than on the chanterelle; whilst his skill extends to the most morbid impossibilities of trick fiddling. His metrical sense is by no means acute: it is difficult to keep the orchestra with him, as Mr Henschel found in Goldmark's concerto, which the band stumbled through in a state which I can only describe as one of utter botheration.

As to his rank as an artist, I altogether decline to give an opinion on the strength of Paganini's contemptible variations on Non più mesta, to which I listened with the haughtiest indignation, though they of course produced the usual hysterical effect on those connoisseurs of the marvellous to whom great violinists are only side-shows in a world of fat ladies and children with two heads. As to the concerto by

Goldmark, most unwisely substituted at the last moment for that of Brahms, it contained no music good enough to test the higher qualities of the player. It will be remembered chiefly for a gratuitous explosion of scholarship in the shape of an irresistibly ludicrous fugato on the theme of Wagner's Kaisermarsch, and a cadenza so difficult that its execution gave the artist the air of a conjurer, and so disagreeable that it gave me a pain the scientific name of which I cannot at this moment recall. M. César Thomson, however, will be listened to with considerable interest as soon as he has taken the measure of London sufficiently to choose his program properly. He may take my word for it that a first-rate violinist no more dreams of playing Paganini's variations on Rossini at St James's Hall than Paderewski does of dropping Beethoven and Chopin out of his repertory, and replacing them by Thalberg and Gottschalk.

24 January 1894

THE other evening, feeling rather in want of a headache, I bethought me that I had not been to a musichall for a long time. One of the horrors of a critic's life is his almost nightly suffering from lack of ventilation. Now when to the ordinary products of respiration are added the smoke of hundreds of cigarettes and of the hundreds of holes which the discarded ends of them are burning in the rather stale carpets, the effect on a professionally sensitive person who does not smoke is indescribably noxious.

The privilege of smoking and burning the carpets is supposed to make the music-hall more comfortable than the theatre. Also, no doubt, the rousing explosions of cornet, trombone, and side-drum every twenty seconds or so, help to reassure the audience as to the suspension of all usages based on a recognition of the fact that some superfine people are almost as particular about the sounds they hear and the air they breathe as about the opinion of their next-door neighbors as to their respectability.

I foresee the day when our habit of sitting for two and a

half hours at a stretch in St James's Hall or in a theatre, breathing air that is utterly unfit for human consumption, and that becomes steadily worse and worse as the evening wears on, will seem as sluttish—there is really no other adequate expression—as we now consider those habits of the spacious times of great Elizabeth which startle us in Much Ado About Nothing, when Claudio remarks of Benedick, "And when [before he fell in love] was he wont to wash his face?"

Well, I went to a music-hall, where I got a comfortable seat at a reasonable price as compared with theatre accommodation, and where I also got my headache, a thoroughly satisfactory one, which lasted all the next day, and was worth the money by itself alone. For once I resisted the attraction of Cavallazzi and Vincenti at the Empire, and went to the Alhambra instead, curious as to whether that institution still maintained its ancient glories as a temple of the ballet.

I found it much the same as ever. The veteran Jacobi was still there, monarchical as *chef d'orchestre*, bold, ingenious, and amazingly copious as composer of dance music. The danseuses were still trying to give some freshness to the half-dozen *pas* of which every possible combination and permutation has been worn to death any time these hundred years, still calling each hopeless attempt a "variation," and still finishing up with the teetotum spin which is to the dancer what the high note at the end of a dull song is to a second-rate singer. I wonder is there anything on earth as stupid as what I may call, in the Wagnerian terminology, "absolute dancing"! Sisyphus trying to get uphill with the stone that always rolls down again must have a fairly enjoyable life compared with a ballet-master.

Surely it is clear by this time that if the ballet is to live, it must live through dramatic dancing and pantomime. In vain did La Salmoiraghi smile at me and walk about on the points of her toes: she did it very well; but I have seen it done as well as it can be done over and over again until I am heartily tired of it. La Salmoiraghi is a handsome and self-

145

possessed person, rather suggestive of Mrs Merdle; but she is not dramatic; and her head and neck are not those of the perfect dancer: she hardly moves them. Miss Seale, a less accomplished gymnast, dances with much more feeling. Mr Fred Storey, a clever comedian dancer, with *le diable au corps*, divided with Miss Seale the only grain of imagination in the ballet, the subject of which, as far as it had a subject, was Don Quixote—Doré's, not Cervantes'.

On the whole, it might easily have been made much more amusing. Unfortunately, when you get thoroughly "popular" audiences, you may always expect to have to endure a mass of academic pedantry which no really cultivated audience would tolerate for a moment. Your ordinary Englishman is scandalized by anything that interests or amuses him: his criterion of a first-rate entertainment, after he is satisfied as to the splendor of its appearance, is that he shall not understand it and that it shall bore him. His recompense for the tedium of the artistic or *in*side of it is the intense unreality of its outside. For it must not be supposed that the poets and artists are the romantic people, and their readers and audiences the matter-of-fact people. On the contrary, it is the poets and artists who spend their lives in trying to make the unreal real; whereas the ordinary man's life-struggle is to escape from reality, to avoid all avoidable facts and deceive himself as to the real nature of those which he cannot avoid.

No fact is ever attended to by the average citizen until the neglect of it has killed enough of his neighbors to thoroughly frighten him. He does not believe that happiness exists except in dreams; and when by chance he dreams of his real life, he feels defrauded, as if he had been cheated into night-work by his employer or his clients. Hence the more unnatural, impossible, unreasonable, and morally fraudulent a theatrical entertainment is, the better he likes it. He abhors the play with a purpose, because it says to him, "Here, sir, is a fact which you ought to attend to." This, however, produces the happy result that the great dramatic poets, who are all incorrigible moralists and preachers, are

146

forced to produce plays of extraordinary interest in order to induce our audiences of shirkers and dreamers to swallow the pill.

Another result, with which I am more immediately concerned, is that the ballet, being the acme of unreality in stage plays, is by no means unpopular on that account—quite the reverse, in fact. Unfortunately, it is so remote from life that it is absolutely unmoral, and therefore incapable of sentiment or hypocrisy. I therefore suggest that by getting rid of the dreary academic dancing, the "variations," and the stereotyped *divertissement* at the end, and making the ballet sufficiently dramatic throughout to add the fascination of moral unreality to that of physical impossibility, it might attain a new lease of life.

The vocal part of the performance interested me specially because of the frequency nowadays of police cases in which young ladies charge professors with obtaining fees from them under pretence of teaching them the art of music-hall singing, without the smallest qualification for that task. And yet these young ladies have only lost a pound or two and a few weeks' time. I wonder how many ambitious young people have paid eminent professors hundreds of pounds, and taken lessons for many years, only to find themselves hopelessly bankrupt in voice, chance of success, purse, and sometimes health at the end of the process. There you have the justice of this foolish world. The New Cut professor gets three months' hard labor for a venial exaggeration of his own powers; whilst his rival at the West End, who richly deserves to be transported to Saghalien, gets half a dozen new pupils, all guaranteed to be manufactured into Pattis in the course of five years or so. The most distinguished singer at the Alhambra was Miss Katie Lawrence, who, in addition to the staple music-hall qualifications of a fine ear for pitch and the power of making a well-marked refrain go with a perfect swing, has the unusual accomplishment of a pretty *mezza voce*, which derives additional charm from its contrast with the heartily strident tone which she produces, in the received music-hall manner, by vigorously extending her chest register all over the middle of her voice. After Miss Lawrence had sung Keep your nose out of my bonnet, with that thoroughness of style which always marks the successful artist, Jacobi, by the sheer majesty of his personality, rebuked an uneasy audience into silence whilst the band played the overture of Fra Diavolo.

The musical side of Mr Daly's revival of Twelfth Night is a curious example of the theatrical tradition that any song written by Shakespear is appropriate to any play written by him, except, perhaps, the play in which it occurs. The first thing that happens in the Daly version is the entry of all the lodging-house keepers (as I presume) on the sea-coast of Illyria to sing Ariel's song from The Tempest, Come unto these yellow sands. After this absurdity I was rather disappointed that the sea captain did not strike up Full fathom five thy brother lies, in the course of his conversation with Viola.

Since no protest has been made, may I lift up my voice against the notion that the moment music is in question all common sense may be suspended, and managers may take liberties which would not be allowed to pass if they affected the purely literary part of the play. Come unto these yellow sands is no doubt very pretty; but so is the speech made by Ferdinand when he escapes, like Viola, from shipwreck. Yet if Mr Daly had interpolated that speech in the first act of Twelfth Night, the leading dramatic critics would have denounced the proceeding as a literary outrage, whereas the exactly parallel case of the interpolation of the song is regarded as a happy thought, wholly unobjectionable. Later on in the play Shakespear has given the clown two songs: one, Come away, Death, to sing to the melancholy Orsino, and the other, O mistress mine, quite different in character, to sing to his boon companions.

Here is another chance of shewing the innate superiority of the modern American manager to Shakespear; and Mr Daly jumps at it accordingly. Come away, Death, is discarded altogether; and in its place we have O mistress mine, whilst, for a climax of perverse disorder, the wrong ballad is sung, not to its delightful old tune, unrivalled in humorous tenderness, but to one which is so far appropriate to Come away, Death, that it has no humor at all. On the other hand, the introduction of the serenade from Cymbeline at the end of the third act, with Who is Sylvia? altered to Who's Olivia? seems to me to be quite permissible, as it is neither an interpolation nor an alteration, but a pure interlude, and a very seductive one, thanks to Schubert and to the conductor, Mr Henry Widmer, who has handled the music in such a fashion as to get the last drop of honey out of it.

I see that Mr Schulz-Curtius has had all his doubts removed concerning the success of a Wagner concert conducted by Mottl, which will accordingly come off on April 17 at Queen's Hall. As I have never stopped at Carlsruhe I do not know much about Mottl; but quite the most perfect performance I ever heard in my life in point of that precision and refinement of execution which can only be secured by a conductor who is master of his band and of his score, was one of Tristan at Bayreuth under his baton. His visit will be the more interesting as in temperament he is not at all like Richter, who is the only first-rate German conductor of whom we know anything in this country.

31 *January* 1894

IT was too bad of the Bach Choir to give me the slip on such an occasion as the performance of a Mass by Professor Villiers Stanford. Some years ago I enjoyed the favor of the Bach Choir, and could rely on the customary intimations of their concerts without troubling myself to look out for the announcements. One evening, unfortunately, I was invited to Prince's Hall to hear what the Choir could do in pure part-singing, an art exceedingly difficult, but so beautiful within its own rather narrow limits that it has never become extinct in England, where it has been kept up by various societies for glee and madrigal singing here and there throughout the country.

For instance, some time ago, happening to be caught in a pelting shower in St Martin's Lane on a gloomy evening, I took refuge in the entry to a narrow court, where I was presently joined by three men of prosaic appearance, apparently respectable artisans. To my surprise, instead of beginning to talk horses they began to talk music—pure vocal music, and to recall old feats of their own in that department, illustrating their conversation by singing passages in which certain pet singers of theirs had come out wonderfully. This led to a discussion as to whether they could remember some work which had been an old favorite of theirs. Finally one of them pulled out a pitchpipe; the three sang a chord; and away they went, *sotto voce*, but very prettily, into a three-part song, raising their voices a little when they found that the passers-by were too preoccupied by the deluge to notice them. They were wholly untroubled by any consciousness of the distinguished critic lurking in the shadow a few feet off, greatly pleased with the performance, but withal sufficiently master of his business not to be surprised at this survival.

We all know from our books that England was anciently famous for this sort of music; but to know also what the singing of it sounds like when it is well done is a qualification which a London critic may very well lack if his experience is limited to the fashionable round of concerts and operas. But I, alas! knew well enough; and when the Bach Choristers confidently exhibited their accomplishments as gleemen to me, I at once perceived that they were not within fifty rehearsals of any sort of real proficiency—in short, that they were making an execrable noise under the impression that they were singing a Bach motet.

In discharge of my duty, I explained this and analysed the noise, in which I found only a mere trace of vocal tone. The Choir was unable to face such critical chemistry: it fled as the Faubourg St Antoine did from Napoleon's whiff of grapeshot; and since that day I have only heard of its con-

certs by chance. This time, as I have said, chance was un-
propitious; and, to my sincere regret, I missed Professor
Stanford's Mass. I am not fond of modern settings of the
Mass as a rule; but this particular one, as an example of the
artistic catholicity of an Irish Protestant (and if you have
never been in Ireland you do not know what Protestantism
is), especially interests me.

Nothing is more tempting to a keen critic than an opportunity of comparing that religious music into the spirit
of which the composer has entered through his dramatic
faculty alone, with that which is the immediate expression of
his own religious faith. And of such an opportunity I have
been deprived because it fell to my lot to give the Bach Choir
its first taste of really stimulating criticism. Must I, at this
age, come down to studying advertisement columns for concerts like any common mortal?

On Monday last week I looked in at the Popular Concert, where I found myself in so insusceptible a mood that
half an hour passed before I could fix my attention on anything. During that half-hour I think a Schumann quartet
was played—at least I ascribed a passage or two that broke
through my apathy to that composer. Miss Liza Lehmann
sang also; but it seemed to me that her tone was dry and thin,
her style mannered, and her intonation imperfect even from
the German standpoint. This seemed strange; for five years
ago Miss Lehmann was a charming singer. I prefer to believe that she is so still, and that my ill-humor was to blame
for my unfavorable impression. But for the moment I could
not help thinking that we had somehow managed to starve
a very promising artistic talent in our drawing-rooms just at
the point in its development when it most needed nourish-
ment. I saw in Miss Lehmann a ladylike singer with agreeable manners and an amiable personality; but my ears were
no longer charmed, my heart no longer touched.

The only part of the concert I enjoyed was Miss Eibenschütz' playing of a couple of new sets of pianoforte pieces
by Brahms. In them we had Brahms at his best, overflowing

with purely musical impulses and letting them run into their own shapes and not into any academic mould. The music gushes and babbles delightfully; there is no attempt to engineer channels for it; and nobody would suppose for a moment that so charming and wittily brief a composer could be, in that domain where acute and original intellectual power must be brought to bear on musical inspiration, the most stupendous bore in all the realms of sound.

There was something of a crowd at this concert. The attraction, as it turned out, was one of the annual routine performances of Beethoven's septet, with the string quartet reinforced by Mr Reynolds' double bass, and Messrs Egerton, Wotton, and Paersch playing the clarinet, bassoon, and horn parts. It was soon evident, however, that this early work of Beethoven's has lost all power over Lady Hallé. Her effort to play it carefully only led to her playing it slowly. She took the first movement at about two-thirds of the lowest speed needed to sustain life; and the others followed her from note to note, and thought of other things. Poor old septuor! Whether the later movements went any better I cannot say. At the last chord of the allegro I hastily avaunted.

7 February 1894

IN order to save myself from having to cry Music, Music, when there is no music—for there is nothing beyond the barest routine going on—I diligently attend the Popular Concerts and saturate myself with Brahms. I have been accused of indifference to, and even of aversion from, that composer; but there never was a greater mistake: I can sit with infinite satisfaction for three-quarters of an hour listening to his quintets or sestets—four instruments cannot produce effects rich enough for him—in which he wanders with his eyes shut from barcarolle to pastoral, and from pastoral to elegy, these definite forms appearing for a moment on the surface of the rich harmony like figures in the fire or in the passing clouds. But such works are not the successors of the quintets of Mozart or the quartets of Beethoven. They are the direct and greatly enriched descendants of what the eighteenth-century masters used to call serenades—things to delight the senses, not to be thought about.

When a German Brahmsite critic proclaims them the latest products of the great school in chamber music, I feel exactly as if a gorgeous Oriental carpet were being nailed up on the wall at South Kensington as a continuation of the Raphael cartoons for the Sistine tapestry. It seems to me that anyone who can see the difference between Monticelli and Mantegna, or between Mr Swinburne and Shakespear, should also be able to perceive the absurdity of classing one of these big serenades of Brahms' with Mozart's quartets. Brahms, feeling his way from one sensuous moment to another, turning from every obstacle and embracing every amenity, produces a whole that has no more form than a mountain brook has, though every successive nook and corner as you wander along its brink may be as charming as possible.

Mozart never follows his inspiration in this manner: he leads it, makes its course for it, removes obstacles, holds it in from gadding erratically after this or that passing fancy, thinks for it, and finally produces with it an admirable whole, the full appreciation of which keeps every faculty on the alert from beginning to end. And though Haydn was a much commoner man than Mozart, and Beethoven a much less clearheaded one, both of them were, on the whole, also masters of their genius, and were able to think and sing at the same time, and so to produce chamber music which no one would dream of describing as merely sensuous. Brahms is built quite otherwise.

Nature inexorably offers him the alternative of Music without Mind, or Mind without Music; and even this hard alternative is not fairly presented, since the mind is of very ordinary quality, whereas the music is as good as mindless music can be. Sometimes Brahms submits to Nature, and, declaring for Music without Mind, produces the charming serenades which Lady Hallé and Piatti, with Messrs Ries,

Gibson, Hobday, and Whitehead, have been playing at recent Monday Popular Concerts, to the unbounded delight of the audiences, including myself. Sometimes he rebels, and proceeds to shew his mental mastery, in which case we have Requiems and general yawning.

It was at one of these recent Brahmsian Populars that Mr Oswald sang some vocal pieces, and Lady Hallé a new Highland Ballad, by the distinguished principal of the Royal Academy of Music. We received them with deep veneration, and called the composer to the platform with three times three. What they meant I do not know: all I can say is that they consisted of elegant musical sentences put together with a practised hand. The Highland Ballad was hardly an instrumental "ballade" of the Chopin type: it was apparently conceived as a piece of Highland ballad music in the ordinary sense. Had I or any other lay person been taken that way, I should have given my melody with words to a human singer. The P. R. A. M., unable to find words worthy of his strains, frankly accepted the consequences of his own ineffability, and made a violin solo of his ballad.

This procedure must be right: otherwise Dr Mackenzie would not adopt it; but as I do not follow its rationale I will not expose my ignorance by an attempt at criticism. Last Saturday Lady Hallé bade us farewell for the season with some Irish airs by Professor Stanford which made excellent fiddling, and gave us at their best points a sense of the thatched roof, the clay floor, the potcheen, and the entire absence of the professorial spirit proper to genuine Irish violinism. The pianist at these two concerts was Mr Leonard Borwick. When he played Schumann for us his slow *tempi* were much too slow; and though he was warmly applauded by the ladies, who all play Schumann worse themselves, I was not particularly interested: Mr Borwick seemed to me to have been dreaming about the pieces instead of thinking about them. Over a sonata by Schubert he—well, I suppose I must not say that he moodled, or maundered, or anything of that sort. But I may at least beg Mr Borwick to recollect

what happened to Stavenhagen's reputation a few years ago
when he gave up strenuous playing and took to elegant
trifling.

There has been a general clearing out from the hall of
Barnard's Inn, the Art Workers' Guild betaking themselves
to Clifford's Inn, and their whilom tenant, Mr Arnold Dolmetsch, falling back with his viols and virginals on Dowland,
his own house at Dulwich. Here he opened his spring campaign on Tuesday last week with a concert of English sixteenth-century music, including a couple of pieces by Henry
VIII which did more to rehabilitate that monarch in my
estimation than all the arguments of Mr Froude. Sheryngam's dialogue, Ah, Gentill Jhesu, set for four voices, four
viols, and organ, belongs to fifteenth-century art: it has all
the naïveté, the conscientious workmanship, the deep expression, and the devout beauty of that period. The dialogue
is between the Gentill Jhesu and a sinner.

From the Renascence right down to the last provincial
Festival, the distinction made between two such persons
would have exactly reflected the distinction between a university graduate with a handsome independent income, and
a poor tradesman or other comparatively unpresentable
person. The essentially medieval character of Sheryngam's
work comes out in its entire freedom from this very vulgar
convention. His art is as void of the gentility and intellectual
ambition of the Renascence as Van Eyck's pictures are.
Later on in the concert we got into the atmosphere of the
sixteenth and seventeenth centuries.

The pieces by Byrd and Morley, played upon the virginals by Mr Fuller Maitland, differed, after all, only in
fashion from airs by Rossini with variations by Thalberg.
Some of the variations which made the greatest demands on
Mr Maitland's dexterity and swiftness of hand did not contain from beginning to end as much feeling as a single progression of Schumann's. Others were pretty and lively; and
the airs were tender enough. But when the corner is turned
and the middle ages left behind, that charm that is akin to

155

the charm of childhood or old age is left behind too; and thenceforth only the man of genius has any power. Once my bare historical curiosity has been satisfied, I do not value the commonplaces of *circa* 1600 a bit more than the commonplaces of *circa* 1900.

I hope, therefore, that Mr Dolmetsch will dig up plenty of genuine medieval music for us. The post-Renascence part of his scheme (which will deal mainly with great individuals like Locke, Purcell, Handel, and Bach) is unexceptionable. There will be eight concerts altogether, including some devoted to Italian and French music. The quality of the performances, which has always been surprisingly good, considering the strangeness of the instruments, continues to improve. The vocal music is still the main difficulty. The singers, with their heads full of modern "effects," shew but a feeble sense of the accuracy of intonation and tenderness of expression required by the pure vocal harmonies of the old school. Without a piano to knock their songs into them they seem at a loss; and the only vocalist whom I felt inclined to congratulate was a counter-tenor, the peculiarity of whose voice had saved him from the lot of the drawing-room songster.

Mr Dolmetsch himself seems to have increased his command of the lute, a villainously difficult instrument. None of the concerted pieces were so well executed as the two "fantazies" for treble and tenor viols which he played with Miss Helène Dolmetsch; but the three other violists, Messrs Boxall and Milne and Miss Milne, acquitted themselves creditably.

I was able to hear only a couple of acts of Mr Harold Moore's Magic Fountain, produced on Thursday last at St George's Hall. It is practically a ballad opera with the connecting links of dialogue treated as fully accompanied recitative, and certain choral episodes and concerted pieces. The book is a boyish affair—an enchanted fountain, a maiden, a sorcerer, an absent lover, and so forth: one can conceive Scott writing it at eight years old. The seriousness with which Mr Moore has tackled it is boyish too; but it is just this element of nonsensically imaginative youth in the work that pleases. The music, as perhaps need hardly be said under these circumstances, is not novel, nor does it shew any power of characterization or—in connection with the romantic sylvan scenery—much feeling for Nature; but it flows freely, and is melodious and vigorous. I am informed that the score stands exactly as it was originally written before the author began to study composition. If that is so, then I strongly recommend Mr Moore not to study composition, but to go on scoring. As far as I could judge with the harp part played on a pianoforte, and most of the wind parts put in by an organ, Mr Moore, when he first set to work, found out all he wanted for himself. A professor of composition will no doubt put a good many things into his head that he does not want; but I fail to see how that is likely to improve him as a composer. I am sure literary composition is infinitely more difficult than musical composition; yet I never thought of going to a professor to learn it.

14 *February* 1894

AN important point in the translation into English of Wagner's prose works is marked this week by the appearance of the second volume (Kegan Paul, Trübner & Co., 12s. 6d.), in which Opera and Drama is at last placed complete in the hands of the English public. The qualifications which this task required from Mr Ashton Ellis may be mildly estimated at about five or six hundred times those which go to the making of our fashionable books of original art criticism—the Renaissance in this or the other place, Leonardo da Vinci as he really wasnt, and so on. If anyone doubts this, he can verify it by turning to the Musical World for 1855-56, where he will find a serial output of almost inconceivable balderdash, purporting to be a translation of this same Opera and Drama, no doubt published expressly to make Wagner ridiculous, but none the less made in the sincere belief that Wagner *was* ridiculous, and that it

was only necessary to turn what he said into English to prove
that fact.

Unfortunately for the poor old Musical World, which
lived to be nursed by a Wagnerian on its deathbed, in order
to turn what an author says into English it is necessary to
understand what he says. In Wagner's case, that understanding can only be attained through a strong sympathy with the
man, producing an eager susceptibility to his extraordinary
power of making converts for the religion of Art as he held
it. Sympathy alone, however, is not enough: a man may be a
very devout Wagnerian and a disorderly or feeble thinker, in
which case he will be about as able to reproduce the Wagnerian web of thought in another language as a gouty-fingered
old gentleman would be to earn his living as piecer in a
cotton-mill.

Unless you can think with Wagner as well as feel with
Wagner—unless, that is, you can cope with a philosophic
intellect of first-rate force and dexterity, and fill up for yourself those large ellipses which are always unconsciously left
by geniuses who think with all the impetuosity which a vivid
imagination gives—translating him is not your affair. The
difficulty of the task culminates in the third part of Opera
and Drama, partly because, as Mr Ashton Ellis shews, the
author did not give it his usual careful revision, and partly,
as I venture to suggest on my own account, because it was
written before Wagner had firmly gripped that distinction
between the reasoning faculty and the will which is all-
important in his analysis of the work of the artist.

To illustrate: if I am in love with a lady living at Hollo-
way, that feeling sets me thinking whether I shall take a bus
or a Great Northern train to see her. It is clear that my desire
to see her is pure feeling, and therefore a subject for musical
expression, whereas the calculation of the relative expediency
of buses and trains utterly defies artistic expression of any
sort, though Meyerbeer might perhaps have been foolish
enough to attempt it. The distinction here crudely indicated
is that which is in Wagner's mind during the first two parts

of Opera and Drama, where he speaks of the understanding and the feeling; but later on he begins to identify the two under the name of "thought," which, within the last few pages of the third part, he suddenly defines as recollected feeling, adding that "a thought is the bond between an absent and a present emotion, each struggling for enouncement." He works out this new theme very suggestively; but it turns the symphony into a fantasia, so to speak.

This is why Mr Ellis's modest doubt as to whether he has succeeded in finding the final and accurate expression of all Wagner's terms seems to me to arise from the fact that Wagner did not on this occasion find the final expression of all of them himself.

My ignorance of the German language is so stupendous that I can claim no weight for my opinion that Mr Ellis's version is a masterpiece of translation; but I think I could point out a sentence or two in which it is clearer than the original. For Mr Ellis, having mastered Wagner's meaning, has been able to check and emphasize the expression of it. His volumes are, of course, not exactly light reading(though they are remarkably amusing and suggestive); but there can hardly be any place in England where a present of a set to the local public library would not considerably fertilize at least a choice few of the inhabitants.

No doubt some time must elapse before the sale of so fine a piece of work will have produced enough to pay Mr Ellis as much as the wages of a dock laborer for the time he has devoted to it; but as all such enterprises must at present be disinterested—more shame for us, by the bye—he will probably esteem himself happy if he escapes being actually out of pocket by his printer's bills.

Wagner's music, nevertheless, is paying its way merrily. Mr Henschel's Wagner Memorial London Symphony Concert on Thursday last was crammed; and the enthusiasts in the gallery took to cheering towards the end as if they were at a political meeting. This was a notable success, considering that the sole attraction was the band; for no soloist, vocal or instrumental, took any part in the proceedings. The remarkable improvement apparent at the last concert was carried much further on this occasion. There had evidently been very careful preparation; and an altogether exceptional pitch of force and refinement was the result. Even in the Parsifal prelude, in that extraordinary rustling of wings during the sacramental motive, the violins, if they fell short of the full effect, were at least not ridiculous, as they usually are at our concert performances of this prelude.

And in the Good Friday music—that happy inspiration from the Lohengrin period set forth with the wonderful workmanship of the Parsifal period—one could hardly believe that the wood wind was the same that had been so often rough and false during the first half of the winter season. Of the Valkyrie Ride we had an original and very effective reading. Everyone knows how Richter charges headlong through the whole piece from beginning to end, aiming solely at a *succès de fou hullaballou*, with the result that the tone, strained to the utmost from the first, cannot be reinforced at the climax, which gets marked by a mere increase of noise, and that the middle wind parts lose their individuality, the wood and horns jumbling together into an odd, dry sound which strikes the ear like a compound of bugle and bass clarionet. Mr Henschel avoided this perfectly. He began with plenty of force and emphasis, but with complete self-command, enabling the band to get the last inch of effect out without excitement and without muddle; and the advantage was soon apparent, not only in the greater play of orchestral color, but in the splendid power and brilliancy of the *fortissimo* when it came.

In thus certifying that Mr Henschel was fully equal to an important occasion, I feel impelled to confess that I cannot say as much for myself. The fact is, I am not always fortunate enough to arrive at these specially solemn concerts in the frame of mind proper to the occasion. The funeral march in the Eroica symphony, for instance, is extremely impressive to a man susceptible to the funereal emotions. Unluckily,

my early training in this respect was not what it should have
been. To begin with, I was born with an unreasonably large
stock of relations, who have increased and multiplied ever
since. My aunts and uncles were legion, and my cousins as
the sands of the sea without number. Consequently, even a
low death-rate meant, in the course of mere natural decay, a
tolerably steady supply of funerals for a by no means affectionate but exceedingly clannish family to go to. Add to this
that the town we lived in, being divided in religious opinion,
buried its dead in two great cemeteries, each of which was
held by the opposite faction to be the antechamber of perdition, and by its own patrons to be the gate of paradise. These
two cemeteries lay a mile or two outside the town; and this
circumstance, insignificant as it appears, had a marked effect
on the funerals, because a considerable portion of the journey
to the tomb, especially when the deceased had lived in the
suburbs, was made along country roads. Now the sorest be-
reavement does not cause men to forget wholly that time is
money. Hence, though we used to proceed slowly and sadly
enough through the streets or terraces at the early stages of
our progress, when we got into the open a change came over
the spirit in which the coachmen drove. Encouraging words
were addressed to the horses; whips were flicked; a jerk all
along the line warned us to slip our arms through the broad
elbow-straps of the mourning-coaches, which were balanced
on longitudinal poles by enormous and totally inelastic
springs; and then the funeral began in earnest. Many a clinking run have I had through that bit of country at the heels of
some deceased uncle who had himself many a time enjoyed
the same sport. But in the immediate neighborhood of the
cemetery the houses recommenced; and at that point our
grief returned upon us with overwhelming force: we were
able barely to crawl along to the great iron gates where a de-
moniacal black pony was waiting with a sort of primitive
gun-carriage and a pall to convey our burden up the avenue
to the mortuary chapel, looking as if he might be expected at
every step to snort fire, spread a pair of gigantic bat's wings,

and vanish, coffin and all, in thunder and brimstone. Such were the scenes which have disqualified me for life from feeling the march in the Eroica symphony as others do. It is that fatal episode where the oboe carries the march into the major key and the whole composition brightens and steps out, so to speak, that ruins me. The moment it begins, I instinctively look beside me for an elbow-strap; and the voices of the orchestra are lost in those of three men, all holding on tight as we jolt and swing madly to and fro, the youngest, a cousin, telling me a romantic tale of an encounter with the Lord Lieutenant's beautiful consort in the hunting-field (an entirely imaginary incident); the eldest, an uncle, giving my father an interminable account of an old verge watch which cost five shillings and kept perfect time for forty years subsequently; and my father speculating as to how far the deceased was cut short by his wife's temper, how far by alcohol, and how far by what might be called natural causes. When the sudden and somewhat unprepared relapse of the movement into the minor key takes place, than I imagine that we have come to the houses again. Finally I wake up completely, and realize that for the last page or two of the score I have not been listening critically to a note of the performance. I do not defend my conduct, present or past: I merely describe it so that my infirmities may be duly taken into account in weighing my critical verdicts. Boyhood takes its fun where it finds it, without looking beneath the surface; and, since society chose to dispose of its dead with a grotesque pageant out of which farcical incidents sprang naturally and inevitably at every turn, it is not to be wondered at that funerals made me laugh when I was a boy nearly as much as they disgust me now that I am older, and have had glimpses from behind the scenes of the horrors of what a sentimental public likes to hear described as "God's acre." I will even go further and confess that this was not the only ritual as to which my faculty of reverence was permanently disabled at an early age by the scandalous ugliness and insincerity with which I always saw it performed. And for this reason I do not in my inmost soul care for that large part of Parsifal which consists spectacularly of pure ritual, and musically of the feeling which ritual inspires in the genuine ritualist. With Siegfried lying under his tree listening to the sounds of the forest I can utterly sympathize; but Parsifal gazing motionless on the ceremony of the Grail with nothing but an open door between him and the free air makes me feel that he is served right when Gurnemanz calls him a goose and pitches him out. And here let me urge upon pious parents, in the interests of thousands of unfortunate children of whom I once was one, that if you take a child and imprison it in a church under strict injunctions not to talk or fidget, at an age when the sole consciousness that the place can produce is the consciousness of imprisonment and consequently of longing for freedom, you are laying the foundation, not of a lifetime of exemplary churchgoing, but of an ineradicable antipathy to all temples built with hands, and to all rituals whatsoever. That certainly was the effect on me; and one of the secondary consequences was that at this London Symphony Concert, being in a very active and objective state of mind, I became so preoccupied with the ritualistic aspect of the Parsifal music and of the slow movement of the Eroica that I could get into no sort of true communion with the composers, and so cannot say whether Mr Henschel did them justice at these points or not.

21 *February* 1894

I HAVE been unspeakably taken back by a letter from a gentleman who complains of the programs of the last London Symphony Concert as "a curious caricature of what Mr Henschel might be supposed to have imagined the poor Britisher with struggling musical tastes might enjoy." "First," goes on my correspondent, "he must be allowed to hear the Parsifal prelude and another extract [the Good Friday music] very much out of place in St James's Hall; and thereupon, to efface the unavowable and un-British etherealization of temper produced, in spite of surroundings, *he*

*must be relieved by Ride a Cock Horse to Banbury Cross with
variations.*" The italicized sentence quite prostrated me.
What on earth does he mean by Ride a Cock Horse with
variations? I asked myself. The answer was soon only too
obvious. The words of the nursery rhyme automatically
brought back the only tune I ever heard them sung to, which
happened to be that in Mr John Farmer's singing quadrilles.
To my dismay I had no sooner thought of the first four notes
than I perceived that they were identical with the third bar
of the theme of the opening allegro of the Eroica. It has
come to this, then, that men are growing up around us to
whom this allegro, the heroism of which never in my life
seemed to me any less obvious than the shining of the sun in
the heavens, is merely Ride a Cock Horse with variations.
I am so disconcerted that for the life of me I cannot tell
whether I was always of the gentleman's opinion without
knowing it, or whether, like Bunyan's pilgrim, I have been
wounded in my faith, my hope, and my understanding by a
fiend. I must take time to think it over. He may be right:
anyhow, the temptation to be relieved of another old conviction is great.

I have my own moments of impatience over Beethoven;
and an excellent way to produce them is to send me to a
Popular Concert without any dinner, and treat me to a
Rasoumowsky quartet led by Joachim on the first night of
his season here, when, bothered by the change of diapason
from Germany to England, and finding that his violin is
dragging at the pitch somehow, he begins to worry the movement with a notion that perhaps it will come right if it is only
driven hard enough. A tendency to drive is an old fault of
Joachim as a quartet leader, though of late years he has so
far got over it that when he is quite calm and reconciled to
the high pitch, his fine tone and sleeplessly thoughtful style
(if we could only get it combined with Sarasate's sleeplessly
sensitive and steady hand, what a violinist we should have!)
are better worth hearing than ever. But when anything flur-
ries him, you find the critics next day full of that dismally

deep respect which bewrays the man who has not liked something he thinks he ought to like.

As for me, I said with my usual irreverence, "Joachim is flat; and the quartet is not going to be good: I will go and recapture the missing dinner: next week probably he will play splendidly." The next chamber-music concert I was at, however, was not a Monday Popular, but one given by Mr Gompertz, who unearthed a very good quartet in A minor, by Professor Villiers Stanford, which for some reason had not been performed in public before in London. It is a genuine piece of absolute music, alive with feeling from beginning to end, and free from those Stanfordian aberrations into pure cleverness which remind one so of Brahms' aberrations into pure stupidity.

It is true that the composer has done one or two things for no other reason that I can discover except that Beethoven did something like them; but a professor is bound, I suppose, to shew himself a man of taste; and at all events the passages in question have borrowed some of the fire, as well as the form, of the master. Unfortunately, the quartet is very difficult; and I cannot honestly say that Messrs Gompertz, Inwards, Kreuz, and Ould were quite equal to it. The performance lacked delicacy and precision. Mr Gompertz is a courageous player who affects a certain rough warmth and vigor of style which occasionally finds its opportunity; but he is not fastidious, and Professor Stanford is; so the quartet was not made the most of.

The great attraction for me at this concert was Beethoven's posthumous quartet in C sharp minor. Why should I be asked to listen to the intentional intellectualities, profundities, theatrical fits and starts, and wayward caprices of self-conscious genius which make up those features of the middle period Beethovenism of which we all have to speak so very seriously, when I much prefer these beautiful, simple, straightforward, unpretentious, perfectly intelligible posthumous quartets? Are they to be always avoided because the professors once pronounced them obscure and impossible?

Surely the disapproval of these infatuated persons must by this time prejudice all intelligent persons in favor of the works objected to.

The performance, though the opening *adagio* was taken at a tolerably active *andante*, was an enjoyable one—another proof, by the way, that the difficulties of these later works of Beethoven are superstitiously exaggerated. As a matter of fact, they fail much seldomer in performance nowadays than the works of his middle age.

Between the quartets Mr Shakespear obliged us with some songs in his well-known manner. Mr Shakespear's tone always suggests to me that some very sentimental drawing room cornet-player has dissolved the tone of his instrument in sugar and water, and so transmuted it into a human voice. His singing is pretty; but it is not very difficult—is it? And it is certainly not very majestic. He sang, of all songs, that unfortunate setting of By Celia's Arbor in which Mendelssohn harps on the two lines

> Then if upon her bosom bright
> Some drops of dew should fall from thee

in such a way as to obliterate all recollection of the fact that the poet is addressing a "humid wreath" and not Celia's lover.

Mr Dolmetsch devoted his second viol concert to the music of Henry and William Lawes; and very charming music it is too, inferior to that of Purcell and Handel only because Purcell and Handel happened to be much abler men than the Lawes brothers, and not at all on account of any inferiority of the art of music in their time—rather the contrary, perhaps.

The Crystal Palace concerts recommenced last Saturday, the newest thing in the program being a Symphonic Fantasy for orchestra by R. Burmeister, entitled The Chase after Fortune, suggested by a picture of Henneberg's. Henneberg has certainly much to answer for. The symphonic fantasy has as little fantasy about it as the most prosaic person could desire. Ambitious, intelligent, utterly commonplace, without a redeeming moment even of weakness, it is the sort of music that will one day be ordered from Whiteley's at so much a pound by our conductors. The first movement is sixth-rate Rienzi, the rest sixth-rate Raff. The audience took it in high dudgeon, as it prolonged the concert until nearly half-past five. Lady Hallé, in one of her happiest hours, played Beethoven's violin concerto with an intimate knowledge and affection which made the performance a triumph for Beethoven and for herself; and Miss Evangeline Florence, who not so long ago came over here a mere singer, and a rather provincial one at that, sang Schubert's Der Hirt auf dem Felsen to Mr Clinton's obbligato like a cultivated artist, and afterwards gave us the waltz from Mireille, ending in the skies on the upper octave of the keynote with one of those incredible harmonics of hers.

As to the new comic opera at the Vaudeville—Wapping Old Stairs to wit—I condescended to it as hard as I possibly could. I was in the best of humors, ready to be amused by anything. And yet I fear my mirth got hollower and hollower as the evening went on. Miss Jessie Bond, by the most whimsical pursings of her lips and twinklings of her eyelashes and the tip of her nose, "worked loyally," as the dramatic critics say, to secure a success.

But is there no loyalty due to the audience and to art in these matters? Was Kemble disloyal or loyal when he damned Ireland's Vortigern and that play of Godwin's chronicled by Lamb? Suppose Miss Bond and Messrs Temple, Avon Saxon, Sparling, Bouchier, and the rest make Wapping Old Stairs a success, is that to be counted to them for righteousness or the reverse? I will not undertake to settle the point: all I can say is that the composer, Mr Howard Talbot, has a reasonable talent for the composition of shop ballads, in singing which Miss Mary Turner made an immediate and solid hit; and that the author, Mr Stuart Robertson, has arranged his play with consummate art so that any ten minutes of it is exactly like any other ten minutes of it, neither

167

the scene, nor the story, nor the characters suffering any change, or advance, or development from the rising of the curtain to within a page of the end.

The scene-painter, by the way, has moved Wapping across the river to Rotherhithe in order to bring in St Paul's with a background of the northern heights. All that I can say in praise of the opera is that if it is not very clever, it is at least not deliberately base, as many would-be smart comic operas are: its fun, as far as it goes—and there is some fun in it here and there—is entirely light-hearted and decent. The sailors are men, and not rowdy young women; and altogether, though the author might be more comic and the composer more operatic with advantage, their work is a genuine attempt at what it professes to be, and not a quite different sort of exhibition in disguise.

28 February 1894

AN interesting book has just come into my hands—Mr Arthur Hervey's Masters of French Music (published by Messrs Osgood, McIlvaine and Co.). Mr Hervey is just the man for the work: he loves France and French music; he is an enthusiast and a composer; and I know nothing against him except that he is a musical critic, which, as Mr Riderhood remarked of his three months imprisonment, might happen to any man. I will not say that Mr Hervey expresses my own feelings about French music; for no book could be abusive enough for that and at the same time be entirely fit for publication. But then I should write a very bad book on the subject. To my mind, the French would be a very tolerable nation if only they would let art alone. It is the one thing for which they have no sort of capacity; and their perpetual affectation of it is in them what hypocrisy is in the English, an all-pervading falsehood which puts one out of patience with them in spite of their realities and efficiencies.

Mr Hervey has certain engaging qualities of kindliness and modesty which prevent him from forming these violent opinions. He takes a warm interest in the French school, and, if the score of a grand opera has only as much as a pretty waltz in it, will relent over that instead of throwing the score at the composer's head. In sketching the men themselves he is wonderfully lively and sympathetic considering their superficiality and barrenness from that deeper artistic point of view which he takes when expressing his own feelings, whether as writer or composer. For instance, his sixty-five pages about Saint-Saëns give the pleasantest impression of that composer's cleverness, his technical ingenuity, his elegant and fanciful handling of the orchestra, his facility, his wit, his wide knowledge of modern music, his charming execution as pianist and organist, and his triumphs at the Opera and elsewhere as a "master of French music"—observe, not a French master of music: Mr Hervey, instinctively or intentionally, has guarded himself well in turning that phrase. Mr Hervey even declares that Samson et Dalila, with its one heartless, fashionably sensuous love duet, and its whistling Abimelech in the vilest Meyerbeerian manner, ought to be imported to these shores.

Altogether, you would never guess from him that if you take away from Saint-Saëns' music what he has borrowed from Meyerbeer, Gounod, and Bach, or rather from that poetically ornamental vein of Bach which is best sampled in the prelude to the organ fugue in A minor, you will find nothing left but graceful nicknacks—barcarolles, serenades, ballets, and the like, with, of course, the regulation crescendos, aspiring modulations, and instrumental climaxes ending with a crash of the cymbals, which do duty for "symphonic poetry" when Phaeton has to be hurled from his car or some other sublimity taken in hand.

But Mr Hervey, all the same, allows him to sum himself up in these significant words: "I admire the works of Richard Wagner profoundly, in spite of their *bizarrerie*. They are superior and powerful, *which suffices for me*. But I have never belonged, I do not belong, and I never shall belong, to the Wagnerian religion." Here you have the French composer all over. To be "superior and powerful": that is enough for him. Accordingly, he imitates Meyerbeer, who deliberately cultivated *bizarrerie* in order to impress the French with the idea that he was "superior and powerful" (and succeeded); he complains of the *bizarrerie* of Wagner, the most sincere and straightforward of composers, whose hatred of *bizarrerie* amounted to loathing; and he then solemnly disclaims "the Wagnerian religion," as if, in any other country in the world except France, he could be suspected for a moment of even knowing what it means.

Bruneau himself, a far abler composer, who is really a tone-poet in his way, is quoted as saying, "Owing to Wagner's prodigious genius, the musical drama has entered into a new era—an era of true reason, of vigorous good sense, and of perfect logic." Imagine a man admiring Die Walküre for its good sense and its logic! What Bruneau catches is not the poetry and philosophy of Die Walküre, but the *system* of its composition—the system of representative themes, which he finds perfectly intelligible and reasonable, therefore admirable. Not that he stops here: on the contrary, he goes on to discourse very feelingly on the difference between music-drama and opera; but I cannot help suspecting that he thinks the superiority of the Wagnerian drama is the result instead of the cause of the superior logic of the Wagnerian system.

The most notable saying of Massenet's in the book is his avowal that it was at Rome that he felt his first stirrings of admiration for Nature and for Art. The point of this lies in the fact that he ran away from home at fourteen to be a musician, and played the drums at the Théâtre Lyrique for six years at two pounds fifteen a month before he won the *prix de Rome*. Therefore he recognizes in the above avowal the fact that musical propensity and faculty is one thing and artistic feeling another. Should Massenet require any instances to prove this proposition, England can supply him with several eminent professors who have been musicians by irresistible vocation all their lives, without ever having been artists for five minutes.

One of Mr Hervey's stories about Massenet is too characteristically French to be passed over. When he had to give a "reading" of his Werther to the artists and officials of the Imperial Opera House in Vienna, they all looked so imposing as they sat in a magnificent room round the piano, that when he came in, an unfortunate stranger with a reputation to live up to, and was received with appalling solemnity by the director, he naturally wanted to sit down and cry, just like an Englishman. But an Englishman would have died rather than have expressed his feelings: he would have chilled the assembly by an air of stiff unconcern, and played badly until he had recovered his nerve. Massenet, with a frankness entirely honorable to him, promptly sat down and cried away to his heart's content, thereby throwing his audience into the most sympathetic condition. Another anecdote tells us that "the impression made upon Vincent d'Indy by Brahms' Requiem in 1873 was such that he forthwith started for Germany in order to become acquainted with the master." I had a precisely similar impulse when I first heard that unspeakable work; but I restrained myself, whereas Vincent appears to have actually accomplished his fell purpose. "The result," says Mr Hervey naïvely, "does not seem to have been so satisfactory as it might have been, the German composer receiving the young enthusiast with a certain amount of reserve."

Finally, I cannot take leave of Mr Hervey without asking him to reconsider his remarks about "rules" of composition on pages 231-233. After shewing conclusively, in defence of Bruneau's Le Rêve, that there are no valid "rules" whatsoever, he adds, "Undoubtedly there must be rules of some kind," and proceeds to quote some delusively open-minded remarks from the preface to Mr Ebenezer Prout's work on harmony. Now, in so far as Mr Prout's preface means that his own rules are all nonsense, I agree with him. But I submit to Mr Hervey that he must either give up Mr Prout's treatise and its rules unreservedly, or else give up, not only Bruneau, but Mozart, whose conduct in making "a passing note" jump down a whole fifth in his E flat symphony is treated by Mr Prout as a regrettable impropriety which the student must on no account permit himself to imitate.

The fact is, there are no rules, and there never were any rules, and there never will be any rules of musical composition except rules of thumb; and thumbs vary in length, like ears. Doubtless it is bold of me to differ from such great musicians as Albrechtsberger, Marpurg, Kiel, Richter, Ouseley, and Macfarren as against such notoriously licentious musical anarchists as Bach, Handel, Haydn, Mozart, Beethoven, and Wagner; but the fact is, I prefer the music of these insubordinate persons; and I strongly suspect that Mr Prout does too, in spite of his scruples about "passing notes."

Joachim, quite up to English pitch, and in his finest vein, made the Monday Popular Concert last week a memorably enjoyable one. The older I grow, the more I appreciate Joachim's excellences as an artist. His skill as a violinist I knew all about long ago—and, indeed, as far as the mere fiddling goes, he seems to be able to teach young ladies to do that as well as himself. The singer was Miss Gwladys Wood, a talented young lady, in whose appearance there is latent tragedy, which is suggested still more forcibly by the coldness of her voice. She brought the tragedy into action so cleverly and intensely in a song from Handel's Susannah that the Monday Popular audience, which likes to be musically coddled by its favorites, was not half pleased.

These Monday Popular people sometimes put me out of temper. One of their special pets, Miss Ilona Eibenschütz, who played very well when she first came over here, fresh from Madame Schumann's hands, gave us, on this occasion, a trashy suite by Moszkowski, in which the hypnotic persons present at once found a charming antique flavor, especially in one movement, which was boldly compounded of those well-known archaic fragments, the prelude to the

last act of Il Trovatore and the first subject in Schubert's unfinished symphony. Miss Eibenschütz scrambled through
them just as she scrambles through everything now, as if all
music were nothing but one huge toccata to shew how fast
she can play. The result was a volley of applause which would
have flattered Paderewski, and which was only stopped by a
hackneyed encore piece, which Miss Eibenschütz played as
well as the audience deserved—that is, rather worse than
before.

I can only hope that Miss Eibenschütz is under no illusion as to the value of that applause. Her playing of the great
Beethoven concerto in E flat at the London Symphony Concert on Thursday last did not mend matters. I could discover no other idea in her performance except the intention
of making the most of the technical difficulties by playing as
fast as possible. In the slow movement, where this was out
of the question, and where, during the second half, the sole
function of the pianist is to accompany the orchestra sympa-
thetically, she refused even to listen to it, and went on her
own way so egotistically and capriciously that the piano became simply an annoyance. Nothing would induce me to go
and hear the concerto played in that way again; and yet Miss
Eibenschütz has great talent and skill, and was playing quite
lately well enough to give us all the greatest pleasure. I live
in hope, therefore, that what I am now forced to complain of
is only an aberration which will presently pass away and replace her in the honorable artistic position which her first
performances won for her.

A noteworthy event at this concert was a performance of
a very effective setting of some verses from Goethe's Hartzreise in Winter for contralto solo and male chorus, in which,
though Brahms has almost totally dehumanized Goethe, his
musical power sounded godlike immediately after our pil-
grimage through that hopeless failure, Schumann's symphony in D minor, which is barely tolerable for the sake of
the introduction and one or two other beautiful scraps. Miss
Brema sang the solo in the Hartzreise without twopenn'orth

of feeling, but with a thousand pounds' worth of intelligence and dramatic resolution. She has of late made a remarkable conquest of the art of singing.

When I first heard Miss Brema, I said, "It is magnificent; but she will grind her voice to pieces in five years." But she sang the Hartzreise in such a manner as to compel me to extend the five years to fifty. All signs of wear and tear had vanished; and the sustained note at the end was a model of vocal management. In any reasonably artistic country Miss Brema would be pursuing a remarkable career on the lyric stage instead of wasting her qualities on the concert platform.

7 March 1894

MR SCHULZ-CURTIUS announces that the orchestra at the Mottl Wagner Concert at Queen's Hall on April 17 will tune to French pitch. So much the better. I am a confirmed sceptic as to the reality of those poetic differences which musicians imagine they find between one key and another; for I have never known two persons agree as to the alleged characteristics of the keys. Besides, scientific men have explained the differences, and have thereby confirmed my opinion that they do not exist. Accordingly, I do not believe that when the change from Continental to English pitch virtually transposes Beethoven's C minor Symphony into something nearer to C sharp minor, the character and feeling of the composition are totally altered. But neither do I believe anything so foolish as that the difference in absolute pitch does not matter. The difference between the effect of Pop Goes the Weasel played on an oboe and played on a double bassoon is only a matter of absolute pitch; but nobody will deny the difference in the effect on the listener's spirits. And if you take the Funeral March from Götterdämmerung, and play it half a tone higher, you also play it half a tone merrier. Hence the importance of the change announced by Mr Schulz-Curtius.

Another piece of artistic conscientiousness on his part is his promise to provide the four tenor tubas and the bass trumpet for the Nibelungen music. Doubtless the bass trumpet will be a great joy to us; but oh, if we could only get some decent instrument to play the ordinary trumpet parts on! I declare, in all sincerity, to Messrs Ellis, Morrow, and Jaeger that all their skill leaves the cornet as objectionable as ever. I know very well that the slide trumpet of the textbooks is an impracticable nuisance; but cannot something be done with more modern inventions? Has not a gentleman —a Mr Wyatt, if I recollect aright—invented a practicable slide trumpet by making the slide a double one and so halving the length of the shifts?

And what about those so-called Bach trumpets and Handel trumpets that Kosleck, of Berlin, introduced to us here at the Bach bi-centenary, and that Mr Morrow occasionally plays? Or, if all these are impossible, are there not at least compensating pistons to correct those notes which come so diabolically out of tune with the ordinary three valves? Instrument-makers like Besson, for instance, solemnly invite the critics and Lord Chelmsford and a few amateurs from time to time to hear such improvements. They seem satisfactory, but are never heard of again. It is just like the experiments which used to take place on the Thames Embankment, when an inventor would build a wooden house, soak it in petroleum, sit down on a heap of shavings in the parlor, set fire to the house, and be found after the conflagration perfectly comfortable and unsinged, thanks to his patent extinguisher or fireproof overcoat, applicable to every household. And yet people go on getting burnt as if such patents had never been heard of.

The fact is, we want some genuine artist to take up the work of producing fine instruments, just as Mr William Morris has taken up the work of producing beautiful printed books. The instrument-makers will never do it, because all their efforts are aimed at better intonation, greater facility of execution, and perfect smoothness of tone. Now smoothness of tone is all very well in its way; but the question remains, what sort of tone? The instrument-makers care only for that one variety, dear to Kneller Hall, which is the true characteristic tone of the saxhorn or euphonium, but which robs the trumpet, the trombone, and the horn of their individuality.

I verily believe that the instrument-makers would like nothing better than to make all the brass in the orchestra sound as if it consisted of a happy family of saxhorns, from the bombardon to the cornet. Their ideal orchestra would consist of the string quartet with a cavalry band for the brass, and a set of English concertinas, bass, tenor, alto, and treble, for the wood wind. That is why I want an artist-craftsman to take the matter up, with the object, not of inventing some new instrument like the saxophone or sarrusophone which nobody wants, but of giving us back the old instruments which everybody wants, with their individuality developed to the utmost.

In short, we want a maker of instruments for the classical orchestra; and we shall certainly not get him on strictly commercial lines at present, because the great bulk of the instrument business lies with military bands, and with the innumerable bands on the military model which exist throughout the country, from those of the Salvation Army to the amateur bands of the industrial counties, which compete as eagerly for prizes as rival football teams do, and which spend considerable sums out of those prizes in perfecting their instrumental equipment.

The extent to which the evolution of the mechanism of the orchestra is altering its artistic character was impressed on me at a recent Crystal Palace Concert, where we had a flute concerto played by Mr Albert Fransella, an excellent artist who has only recently joined Mr Manns' band. Like Sivori the violinist, who died only the other day, and who, by the way, greatly astonished my small boyhood—he was the first virtuoso I ever heard—Mr Fransella sacrifices boldness of style to delicacy of tone and perfection of execution.

176

He takes his instrument as it is, and does not enlarge the holes to get a big tone, or otherwise spoil it for all ordinary players, and trust to his power of lip to make it practicable for himself. What we got from him therefore was the normal modern orchestral flute, very well played.

But I should like to have met the ghost of Mozart at that concert in order to ask him whether Mr Fransella's instrument was what he would call a flute. I am convinced that he would have declared it a quite new instrument. He would, no doubt, have been delighted with the accurate intonation and the fascinating peculiarity and beauty of the lower octave; but I think he would have repudiated the higher notes as having absolutely no flute quality at all, the quality aimed at by the manufacturer being apparently that of the harmonica, though really, no doubt, that of the clarionet. These harmonica-like sounds got on my nerves after a while; and I am not at all sure that I should not have enjoyed Mr Fransella's skill and taste more if he had played a fantasia by Kuhlau or some other eighteenth-century master on an old-fashioned flute. And yet I was so far from being in an old-fashioned humor at this concert that I went home halfway through Schubert's charming symphony in C in a fit of exasperation at its childishness.

Mind, I do not object to the existence and use of these practically new instruments; but I wish they had not usurped the old names; and I still call for the artist-craftsman to give us once more a flute that is a flute, and a trumpet that is a trumpet. When he has done that he may adapt the inventions of Gordon, Sax, and the rest to his masterpieces as much as he pleases; for naturally I do not want the old defects back—the primitive mechanism, and the faulty, weak, or missing notes. The intonation of the wind is quite bad enough still, without our turning back to the methods of the old days when it was worse.

Talking of instruments reminds me that the Philharmonic band has only fourteen first and twelve second violins. It ought to have had fifteen of both twenty years ago; and today it ought to employ a hundred men for a fully scored modern work. I did not raise this question while the Society remained in St. James's Hall; for one cannot make demands for fresh expenditure without some reference to the size of the hall and the prices charged.

But now that a move has been made to the comparatively huge Queen's Hall, there is no further reason for tolerating a shorthandedness that makes a really effective performance of the works of Berlioz and Liszt impossible. Some of the scores on which Berlioz wrote the words "at least fifteen" before the two violin parts are half a century old now; so it will be seen that I am not unduly hurrying up the venerable directors. They will, I hope, not permit themselves to be beaten in artistic conscientiousness by Mr Schulz-Curtius. And yet I suppose they will disappoint me, as usual. I have no opinion of the Philharmonic directors from the artistic point of view, and never had. Only I think it hard that Art should not have its share of the profit of their move to a larger hall.

For all that, the opening concert of the season on Wednesday last was a great success, thanks to Tchaikowsky's last symphony, which was very interesting, and far too novel and difficult to leave the band any middle course between playing it well and not playing it at all. Tchaikowsky had a thoroughly Byronic power of being tragic, momentous, romantic about nothing at all. Like Childe Harold, who was more tragic when there was nothing whatever the matter with him than an ordinary Englishman is when he is going to be executed, Tchaikowsky could set the fateful drum rolling and make the trombones utter the sepulchral voice of destiny without any conceivable provocation.

This last symphony of his is a veritable Castle of Otranto, with no real depth of mood anywhere in it, but full of tragic and supernatural episodes which, though unmotived, and produced by a glaringly obvious machinery, are nevertheless impressive and entertaining. There are, besides, abundant passages of romance and revelry, with the usual Tchai-

kowskian allowance of orchestral effects which are so purely
that and nothing else that they have absolutely no sense if
played on a pianoforte. Take, for instance, the basso ostinato
at the end of the first movement, and the rushing scale passages for strings and wind in the march. These are, from the
symphonic point of view, simple humbug. There is no separate slow movement, its place being taken by the second subject of the opening allegro, which appears as an andante,
fully developed as such. The innovation is so successful in
its effect that I shall not be surprised if it be generally
adopted.

By way of scherzo, there is a charming movement in five-
four time, which brought the house down. Most musicians,
if asked to note it by ear off-hand, would have written the
first eight bars of five-four time as twenty bars of two-four,
taking the second note as the beginning of the first bar, and
dividing the theme into strains of five bars instead of the
usual four. No doubt such a scoring would produce a number
of accents which Tchaikowsky did not intend; but our sense
of this five-in-a-bar rhythm is still so undeveloped that as I
listened I found myself repeatedly breaking the movement
into two-four and three-four bars; and, what is more, the
band was doing exactly the same thing. After this five-four
movement comes a very elaborate and brilliant march, with,
it must be confessed, a good deal of nonsense about it. The
finale brings us back to the Castle of Otranto, and ends in a
sufficiently melancholy manner to enable us critics (Tchaikowsky having opportunely died) to give our "swan song"
stereo an airing. That reminds me that the list of members
in the Philharmonic programs of this year contains no
fewer than five black borders, round the names of Cusins,
Elvey, Gounod, Tchaikowsky, and Hans von Bulow. As
everybody has said something of Bulow, let me add my
stone to the cairn by confessing that I contracted an early
prejudice against him because his editing of Bach seemed to
me to be impudent, and his playing of Beethoven vulgar.
Perhaps I was wrong; but I dont believe it: I cannot

imagine how anybody could ever have mistaken his odious familiarity with the later pianoforte sonatas of Beethoven for insight into them. His contrapuntal playing was exceedingly clear and intelligent; but his memory would not now be counted a good one: when he was at a loss he used to improvise Schubertian basses in pieces by Handel with an unscrupulousness that ran through all his performances. Of his conducting I know nothing.

To finish the record of this Philharmonic concert, Mr Borwick played Beethoven's E flat concerto blamelessly but unmemorably; and Miss Ella Russell took advantage of her knowledge of how to use her voice by giving us a concert aria—Mendelssohn's "Infelice" to wit. The audience was large and enthusiastic.

14 March 1894

IN a recent magazine article by a musical critic of whose ability I entertain a high opinion, he described the result of his unaided efforts to acquire the art of pianoforte playing. The description gained a certain historical significance from the fact that as his plight was that in which the whole world once was, he did exactly what the whole world once did. Mr Arnold Dolmetsch, at his last concert, made some comments on the article before playing a suite of pieces for the harpsichord by Matthew Lock. Mr Dolmetsch had been lucky enough to get hold of an old copy with the fingering marked; and he improved the occasion by describing the seventeenth-century keyboard technique, which was virtually the same as that rediscovered by the above-mentioned critic, and which produced what Mr Dolmetsch happily described as the "winglike" action of the player's hand as we see it painted in old pictures of St Cecilia and other celestial musicians.

Hereupon I desire to add a word or two, because, for a reason which I will presently give, I am by no means sure that pianoforte teaching has yet completely disentangled the new system from the old. Without going into all the detail

of the subject, which will be found in a very clear and sufficient article by Franklin Taylor in Grove's Dictionary, I
want to invite attention to the main difference between the
two methods. If you put your hand on the keyboard, there is
no particular difficulty in playing the notes that lie under
your fingers. You simply strike the key with the finger that
happens to be over it, and there you are. But the keyboard is
about four feet long; and the question of method comes in
the moment you have to make your hand travel without interrupting the music, as in running up a scale.

The old plan was to make the hand *walk* along from note
to note on two fingers by passing one over (or sometimes
under) the other. The critic quoted by Mr Dolmetsch, for
instance, made his right hand walk up the keyboard by making his ring finger step over his little finger. If he had been
learning at an old organ keyboard, with the old-fashioned
very low seat, he would have found himself compelled to depend altogether on his long fingers, and so would have passed
his middle finger over his ring finger. That, however, is only
a difference as to the couple of fingers walked on, not as to
the walking method. The modern method is to make your
hand *spring* along like a pole-jumper by turning the thumb
under the two or three next fingers, and so shifting the whole
hand along by half or three-quarters its breadth at a time.

Now if you run up a scale on the pianoforte by these two
methods alternately in the way that comes most naturally to
you, you will find that the old method turns your hand out
so much that when you strike the highest note on the keyboard your finger is nearly at right angles to the key, whereas
on the modern method the action of turning the thumb under
naturally tends to turn the hand in. Now for my reason for
going into all this. My mother had the misfortune to be born
at the height of the reputation of the once famous teacher,
J. B. Logier. From 1839 to his death in 1846 he taught her
how *not* to play the pianoforte with such entire success that
she has never been able to play it since with any freedom or
skill. It is a great testimony to his ability as a teacher that she

has been no more able to get rid of his destructive teaching in pianoforte playing than of his instructive teaching in what was then called "thoroughbass," which also remains with her to this day. The secret of her disablement was his insistence on playing with the hands turned out, the wrists lower than the keys, and the body bolt upright.

Now I do not believe Logier simply acted on the general assumption, common enough then and by no means extinct now, that any way of doing things that is unnatural, laborious, and painful is virtuous, and particularly good for children. Granted that Logier, like all pigheadedly and violently wrong people, was to some extent a fool, still, that was not the exact sort of fool he was. I submit that his three notions were superstitions from the days of the old fingering and the low organ seat. Tradition had placed him in possession of a jumble of generalizations made from the attitudes of players in the past, which defeated the fingering of the present so completely that his pupils played worse than if they had been allowed to pick up the art in their own fashion. It may be said, what does all this matter now that Logier is nearly half a century dead? Well, it matters just this, that superstitions die hard.

What Logier was doing fifty years ago, other people are probably doing today, especially those who, having failed as players, have taken to the resource of all musical failures and turned teachers. I have seen many highly skilled pianists in my time, but never two whose action and attitude were the same. The pianist who can sit like Sophie Menter and Madame Schumann at once, or like Rubinstein and Paderewski, has not yet been born, and never will be. If any student thinks that he can make the music sound as it ought to by sitting on top of the instrument and playing with his boots, by all means let him try it. I have heard organists play much better with their feet than some expensively instructed young ladies with their hands. There are three classes of teachers of the pianoforte in this country: those who help their pupils to become players, those who hinder their pupils from becoming players, and those who do neither one nor the other. I recommend the first to the student, the third to the benevolent rich, and the second to the author of all evil.

Mr Dolmetsch's concert interested me especially because it gave us a chance of hearing the chamber music of Matthew Lock, the last English musician who composed for the viols, and the founder of my school of musical criticism. His denunciation of the academic professors of his day is quite in my best manner. Lock's Macbeth used to be known to everybody: whether it is so now I cannot say; but nothing was more firmly hammered into my head when I was a child than the certainty that Macbeth would spill much more blood, and become worse to make his title good. Later on I learnt that Lock had not composed the Macbeth music, a manuscript score of it in the handwriting of Purcell (aged fourteen) having turned up.

Presently, when someone unearths the copies made of Beethoven's symphonies and posthumous quartets by Wagner in his boyhood, we shall all agree that Wagner was the real composer of these works. As a matter of fact, Lock's temperament was about as like Purcell's as Bach's was like Mozart's, or Michael Angelo's like Raphael's. If Purcell had lived to be seventy he would have been younger at that age than Lock was at twenty. If I had a good orchestra and choir at my disposal, as Mr Henschel has, I would give a concert consisting of Purcell's Yorkshire Feast and the last act of Die Meistersinger. Then the public could judge whether Purcell was really a great composer or not, as some people (including myself) assert that he was.

Mr Dolmetsch has taken up an altogether un-English position in this matter. He says, "Purcell was a great composer: let us perform some of his works." The English musicians say, "Purcell was a great composer: let us go and do Mendelssohn's Elijah over again and make the lord-lieutenant of the county chairman of the committee"—an even more intolerable conclusion than Christopher Sly's, "'Tis a very excellent piece of work: would 'twere over," which I am afraid is exactly what most of us say to ourselves at performances of the Ninth Symphony. Mr Dolmetsch gave us the Golden Sonata, some harpsichord lessons, and several songs, one of which, Winter, created quite a burst of enthusiasm by the beauty of its harmony, which Brahms himself, in his very different way, could not have surpassed for richness, much less for eloquence.

The concert wound up with Let the dreadful engines, the finest humorous bass air I know, excepting only Madamina, and not excepting Osmin's songs from Die Entführung aus dem Serail, or even O ruddier than the cherry. It was sung with much spirit and success by Mr Albert Fairbairn, who only needs a somewhat lighter and freer vocal touch to make him a valuable bass singer. So good a voice as his does not need to be ground out as he is apt to grind it. The first part of the program was perhaps the more important, as the quality of Purcell's genius is so much better known than that of Lock's. Lock came at a time when musicians had neither given up counterpoint nor taken to the endless repetitions, sequences, and rosalias, the crescendos, doubles and redoubles, of the operatic instrumental style, the absurdity of which culminated in that immortal composition, the overture to Zampa.

In the pieces selected by Mr Dolmetsch, Lock steers equally clear of the hackneyed imitative entries of the old school and the overdoing of the rosalias of the new. He had not, it seems to me, the delicate poetic sense or dramatic vivacity of Purcell and Mozart, nor the deep feeling of Bach: indeed, I rather doubt whether he was much more "passion's slave" than the elegant Ferdinand Hiller; but he had a depth of musical sense, and a certain force of intelligence and character which enabled him to compose in a genuinely masterly way. The organ fugue which Mr Dolmetsch played had not the gigantic energy and mass of a Bach fugue; but its inferiority was much more one of dimension only than one would have expected: its difference, as distinguished from its inferiority, lay in its intention, which was less exalted

184

then Bach's, but also more captivating to people in search of musical pastime. Its decorative passages were fresh, ingenious, original, and, to my ear, very pretty.

I should perhaps apologize for having devoted so much space to a concert of English music given by a foreigner, when I have on hand plenty of concerts of foreign music given by Englishmen. But if anyone, however unpatriotic, will face the fact that up to the time of Purcell nobody ever supposed that the English were less musical than other people, and that since then they have been blotted out of the music-map of Europe, he cannot but feel curious as to whether any change occurred in the construction of the English ear at the end of the seventeenth century. But that was not what happened; for there were a few later Englishmen—Pearsall, for instance—who took the old school for their starting-point, and shewed that the musical powers of the nation were still as robust as ever.

What broke up English music was opera. The Englishman is musical, but he is not operatic; and since during the last two centuries music has been so confounded with opera that even instrumental music has been either opera without words or else the expression in tone of a sort of poetry which the English express with great mastery in spoken verse, our composers have been able to do nothing but abjectly imitate foreign models: for instance, Sterndale Bennett and Mendelssohn, Bishop and Mozart, Crotch and Handel. It seemed on the point of ending in our being able to compose nothing but analytic programs of foreign masterpieces, when opera, providentially, began to die of its own absurdity, and music at once shewed signs of reviving. Now I am convinced that in this revival the old music must serve as a starting-point, just as thirteenth-century work has served, and is serving, in modern revivals of the other arts. That is why I attach such importance to these concerts of Mr Dolmetsch, which are, besides, highly enjoyable both to experts in music and to the ordinary Englishman who, with every respect for "classical music," has deep down in his breast a rooted belief (which I

185

rather share) that three-quarters of an hour is too long for any one instrumental composition to last.

In this connection let me hail with three times three the proposal of Mr Fuller Maitland and Mr Barclay Squire to republish in modern notation, but otherwise without addition or omission, that treasure of the Fitzwilliam Museum at Cambridge, Queen Elizabeth's Virginal Book, so called because, as it contains several pieces which were not composed until after Queen Elizabeth's death, it could not possibly have belonged to her. The editors, who are, as far as I know, the two most competent men in England for the work, will issue it as The Fitzwilliam Virginal Book. It contains nearly three hundred pieces, many of them of great beauty, and all, at this time of day, of some interest. The publication, through Messrs Breitkopf & Härtel, will be by thirty-six monthly parts, costing, by subscription, thirty shillings a year, or, separately, three shillings apiece. As the enterprise is one of enthusiasm and not of commerce, and the editors will probably wish they had never been born before it is completed, I recommend it confidently to the support, not only of musicians, but of those who are in the habit of buying three new waltzes every month, and are consequently beginning to feel the want of some music that they have never heard before.

21 *March* 1894

I AM not prepared just now to deliver my full mind as to charity concerts. Like all persons in sound mental health, I hate charity, whether as giver or receiver, asker or asked. Those who occasionally try to warp my critical integrity by pleading that their concerts are for a "deserving object" little know that they are stirring up my fiercest instinctive antipathies. I have no patience with the people who think that social evils can be cured by a little gush of sympathy and a dip of their hand into all the pockets within their reach. But there is one point upon which I am prepared to commit myself. If you are an artist, and have promised to sing at a charity concert for nothing, then keep your engagement in all respects as if it were an ordinary professional one, and be in your place when your turn comes.

I looked in at a charity concert at Queen's Hall last week, and found the band of the Coldstream Guards desperately playing one selection after another to keep the audience amused until the arrival of the artists who were first on the program, which had at last to be taken anyhow, Miss Evangeline Florence, Mr Charles Warner, and Mr Watkin Mills throwing themselves into the breach and keeping things going, much out of their turn, with the help of Mr Orlando Harley and Mr Leo Stern, until the missing philanthropists turned up. And now let me venture to sweeten this admonition to charitably disposed artists with a valuable piece of advice concerning the professional services which they throw away every year under the impression that they are giving them to charitable institutions. In nine cases out of ten, probably, the unfortunate charitable institutions only get what little there is left after a committee has wasted all that it can on its own unpunctualities, blunderings, forgettings, and other characteristics of amateur beggars and busybodies.

But even a good committee—and I speak as an experienced committee-man—cannot help having half the steam taken out of it by the consciousness that if it clears a ten-pound note for the charity nobody can find fault with it, and that if it gets a dozen popular artists to perform for nothing, a very moderate exertion in the way of selling tickets and booming the concert will secure that modest minimum. Now suppose it were met by a flat refusal on the part of the artists to abate one farthing of their full terms for the occasion. What would happen? The committee would have to bestir itself in earnest to make the concert successful enough to bring in the artists' salaries as well as the desiderated ten-pound note.

The concert would therefore be handled in a business-like way; the audience would be a paying audience, and not a horde of deadheads entertaining themselves at the expense of the singers and of the purchasers of a few rows of empty stalls; and as the artists would be present on business terms there would be no disappointments, changes of program, apologies, complimentary applause, and squabbles in the green-room as to who should sing first and get away. Then —and this is the cream of my advice from the charitable point of view—the artists could go home and send their cheques straight on to the treasurer of the charity in question, thereby securing to it the full value of their services without the deduction or waste of a single farthing.

I suggest that this might with great advantage be made the professional rule, both for the stage and the concert-room. The present system is a nuisance to everybody, from the artists who feel that they are wasting their time and yet do not like to refuse, to the persons who are pestered to buy tickets for an entertainment which they know will be a slovenly affair, with a disappointment and an apology at every third item. If your services have any real value, have that value coined; and then, if you really believe Mr Clement Scott when he says:

How can we gladden grim misery's features?
The answer is evident—GIVE! GIVE! GIVE!

(and Mr Clement Scott never, I can assure him, made a greater mistake in his life), why, you can hand over the coin and feel that you have really given something instead of merely indulged yourself in a public appearance, a round of applause, and an advertisement, which, to be frank, is the true substance of most of the effusive and thoroughly loose-minded "charity" with which our artists are so open-handed.

4 April 1894

ON my way down to the country for the Easter holidays I disbursed the respectable sum of twelve shillings to Messrs Kegan Paul & Co. for a copy of The Art of Music, by C. Hubert H. Parry, Master of Arts at Oxford; Doctor of Music at Oxford, Cambridge, and

Dublin; and composer of—among other works—those two
famous oratorios, Judith and Job. Dr Parry occupies a position in the history of English art not unlike that occupied by
Charles I in English politics. Any objection to his public
compositions is immediately met by a reference to the extraordinary amiability of his private character. It is my firm
belief that Hampden himself would have paid any assess-
ment of ship money rather than sit out Judith a second time;
and the attempt to arrest the five members seems to me a
trifle in comparison with Job. But the defence is always the
same—that Dr Parry sums up in his person every excellence that the best type of private gentleman can pretend to.

Now it should be remembered that long before people
began to get tired of Judith they got tired of hearing Aris-
tides called the Just; and if Dr Parry is not to end his days
in St Helena, somebody must act as devil's advocate in his
case. Out of pure friendliness, therefore, let me try to find
fault a little with his book. If I do not do this, nobody else
will; for, if I may blurt out the truth for once, without regard
to the feelings of my colleagues, those musical critics who
have sufficient culture and scholarship to grapple with Dr
Parry's learning have been driven by mere isolation to associate themselves with the more scholarly of our musicians
and artists on terms of personal intimacy which practically
involve mutual admiration and logrolling.

These are not the objects of the intimacy, which is perfectly natural and honest, and in some ways beneficial to the
public as well as to the principal parties; but they are among
its inevitable consequences; and, frankly, I would not give
a rap more for any public utterance of our best critics concerning Professor Stanford, Dr Parry, and the rest of their
musical friends, than I would advise them to give for any
public utterance that I could be persuaded to make concerning those friends of mine with whom I have been closely
and specially allied for years past in political matters.

In reading Dr Parry's book I began at the end (my in-
variable custom with histories of music); and I have not yet

quite reached the beginning. However, that does not matter, since it is not with the remoter history of the art that I am now concerned. In the later chapters I find, along with a great deal of criticism with which I agree, and a mass of information which my position as a critic obliges me to pretend that I knew all along, certain observations which smack, to me, of the commoner sort of analytic concert program. Most of these are due to the disturbance of Dr Parry's judgment by his love for Beethoven, which sets him pointing out as choice merits of that composer such features as "insisting on his key," and "often casting his leading idea in terms of the common chord."

If this be a mark of genius, let us not ignore it in Donizetti's choruses, in our comic songs and army trumpet-calls, and in such pretentious platitudes as the first movement of Rubinstein's Ocean symphony. But as it most certainly is not a mark of genius at all, I suggest that Dr Parry should cut all such special pleading out of his second edition, and replace it by a few words as to the manner in which melody follows the development of harmony. When I was a boy, an overture beginning emphatically with an unprepared discord made me expect something tremendous, provided the discord was not more extreme than a third inversion of the dominant seventh (play the common chord C, E, G, C with your right hand, dear lady, and hit B flat as hard as you can in octaves with your left: that's the effect I mean), which I was familiar with from the overture to Prometheus and Trema, trema in Don Giovanni. Later on, the crashing major ninths in the prelude to the second act of Tannhäuser sounded extraordinary to me; and Schumann imposed on me as an enigmatical genius of unfathomable depth, simply because his chords, being strange, were mysterious.

At present nothing surprises me: you may begin the next act of your opera with the sixth inversion of a full chord of the major thirteenth without making me turn a hair. Now the moment I get sufficiently used to a discord to tolerate it unprepared, and to recognize its key and destination, I am

ready to accept a figuration of that discord and its resolution
as a "popular" melody. When other lips, which everybody
recognizes as popular, begins, practically, with a figuration
of the resolution of the dominant seventh. Now that the
finale of the first act of Lohengrin has educated the common
ear to the extension of that familiar discord by another major
third, any modern Balfe can manufacture an equally acceptable melody by substituting a figuration of the ninth for the
seventh, though I doubt whether Dr Parry will compliment
him on his "insistence on the key."

The fact is, it is the enormous part which figuration and
rum-tum play in modern music—harmonic music, as Dr
Parry calls it—that makes it wear so badly in comparison
with the old contrapuntal music. I had rather hear the most
conventional, fashionable overture that Handel ever wrote
than the once brilliant and novel overture to Zampa, with its
"insistence on the key"; and I here prophesy that the extent
to which Wagner, like all the composers of the harmonic
school, resorted to figuration of chords that are daily becoming more familiar and even platitudinous, will one day make
many pages of his mere *melodrame* sound stale and obvious
when Bach's polyphony will be as fresh as when it first came
from his hand. Why, then, should we hold up this "insistence on the key," which is really nothing but reliance on the
chord, as a merit, and, for example, praise the finale to B et-
hoven's symphony in C minor for the features in which it so
strongly resembles Cheer, boys, cheer?

It seems to me that all this part of the book wants restat-
ing. The very interesting contrast made in it between Beethoven's first pianoforte sonata and the finale to Mozart's G
minor symphony is spoiled by an attempt to represent the
difference as a superiority on Beethoven's part. Similarly,
some very suggestive passages on Bach's refusal to join the
harmonic movement are weakened by an assumption that the
harmonic school was a higher development than the contrapuntal one. Surely the truth is that the so-called "development" was really the birth of the modern "tone poetry" or

"music-drama" with which the old music had long been pregnant. The separation was concealed by the extraordinary genius of Mozart, who could produce a piece of music which at once presented to the theatre-goer the most perfect musical reflection of the vagaries of a scene from a farce, and to the professor a "movement" in strict form; but Mozart, none the less, made a European revolution in music with the statue scene in Don Giovanni, unmentioned by Dr Parry, which represents the most sensational manifestation of the only side of his work which was followed up.

Beethoven could not touch Mozart as an "absolute musician": a comparison of his attempts at contrapuntal writing with such examples as the minuets in Mozart's quintets or the Recordare in the Requiem seems to me to shew a striking falling off in this respect. Finally we come to Wagner, who, like Weber, could not write absolute music at all—not even an overture; for the Tannhäuser overture is no more an overture than our old friend William Tell; and the Faust is simply a horrible reduction to absurdity of the attempt to combine the new art with the old, the beginnings of the said reduction being already plain in the first allegro of no less respectable a classic than Mozart's Hafner symphony. But before Wagner died, "absolute music" was reviving in the hands of men who were musicians alone, and not wits, dramatists, poets, or romancers, seizing on music as the most intense expression of their genius.

Mozart, Beethoven, and Wagner, with all the "program-music" men, practised a delightful and highly compound art which can be understood without any musicianship at all, and which so fascinated the world that it swept genuine absolute music out of existence for nearly a century. But now absolute music has been revived with enormous power by Brahms, and is being followed up in this country by Dr Parry himself, and by Professor Stanford. Unfortunately, neither of them sees this as clearly as I, the critic, see it. Dr Parry knocks the end of an admirable book to pieces by following up the technical development of music, which is, of course, continuous from generation to generation, instead of the development and differentiation of the purposes of the men who composed music. Thus, he treats Mozart as the successor of Bach, and Brahms as the successor of Wagner.

The truth is that Brahms is the son of Bach and only Wagner's second-cousin. Not understanding this, Brahms feels bound to try to be great in the way of Beethoven and Wagner. But for an absolute musician without dramatic genius to write for the theatre is to court instant detection and failure, besides facing a horribly irksome job. Therefore he falls back on a form of art which enables absolute music of the driest mechanical kind to be tacked on to a literary composition and performed under circumstances where boredom is expected, tolerated, and even piously relished. That is to say, he writes requiems or oratorios. Hence Brahms' Requiem, Job, and Eden! Eden is evidently the work alluded to in this volume as "one of the finest of recent oratorios, in which the choruses of angels and of devils sing passages which express the characteristic impulses of angelic and diabolic natures to a nicety." O those mixo-Ionian, hypo-Phrygian angels, and those honest major and minor devils! shall I ever forget them?

The future is bright, however: Dr Parry's latest composition is an "overture to an *unwritten* drama"—precisely the right sort of drama for an absolute musician to write an overture to. In process of time he will see that his particular "art of music," though a very noble art, has nothing to do with tragedies, written or unwritten, or with Jobs, or Judiths, or Hypatias, or anything else of the kind. In the meantime I must acknowledge my deep obligation to him for having written a book from which I have learned much. No critic can afford to leave it unread.

11 *April* 1894

THE audience at the Crystal Palace Saturday Concerts lately had a much better opportunity of judging Professor Villiers Stanford's Becket music than ever Mr Irving enjoyed. Technically, it is a very good piece of work—it has qualities that may almost be described as moral excellences. For instance, the handling of the orchestra is first rate: by which I do not mean, if you please, that there are sensational tremolandos, or voluptuous murmurs for the wind, or delicate embroideries for the flute, or solos for the English horn, or scintillations for the triangle, or, generally speaking, any of that rouging of the cheeks of the music and underlining of its eyes which is so cheap nowadays: I mean that the composer knows how and where to get his tone of the right shade and of the best quality, how to balance it, how to vary it otherwise than by crudely obvious contrasts, and how to get from the full band that clear, smooth, solid effect for which one has to go to Brahms, or even back to Cherubini, for satisfactory examples.

Add to this a complete intellectual mastery of harmony, and you have an equipment which enables the composer to do anything he wants to do within the known limits of musical composition. As to what he wants, I approach that subject with less than my usual confidence. Something is happening to my attitude towards absolute music. Perhaps I am fossilizing, perhaps I am merely beginning to acquire at last some elementary knowledge of my business as a critic: I cannot say. I am not sure that I did not think at one time that absolute music was dead: that Mozart had been faithless to it; that Beethoven had definitely deserted it; and that Wagner had finally knocked it on the head and buried it at the bottom of the Red Sea. And certainly, whenever an attempt was made to galvanize it by attaching it to an oratorio libretto, or festival cantata, or mayhap to the Requiem Mass, its appearance was sufficiently ghastly and ridiculous to make me regard it as a product, not of composition, but of decomposition; so I reviled its professors for not burying it decently, and devoting themselves with frank singleness of purpose to tone poems and music-dramas.

For example, it seemed to me that Professor Stanford would have done better to follow up his Cavalier Romances and write for the stage than to hammer away at absolute music. Unfortunately, he did neither the one nor the other: he tried to combine the two in such hybrid works as Eden and The Revenge, concerning which I remain impenitent, more convinced than ever that they are hopeless mistakes. The only opening for critical error concerning them lay in the doubt as to whether the case was one of an absolute musician hampered by a libretto, or a dramatic musician hampered by the traditions of absolute music.

Naturally I was sure to decide in the latter sense when once I had assumed beforehand that absolute music was dead. This decision of mine proves—what it concerns every reader of these columns to bear constantly in mind—that I can be incredibly prejudiced and stupid on occasion, considering that I am in many ways rather an intelligent man. For could anything have been more obvious than that the disturbing element in all these oratorios and cantatas is the libretto—that it is in his efforts to be a poet and dramatist that the composer is an ineffectual amateur, while in his counterpoint he often shews ten times the skill and knowledge of an opera composer? The man who roused me into common sense on this subject was no other than our friend Brahms.

The truth in his case was too clear to be overlooked. The moment he tried to use music for the purpose of expressing or describing anything in the least degree extraneous to itself he became commonplace and tedious, there being nothing distinguished either in his own or in his view of other men's ideas. On the other hand, when he made music purely for the sake of music, designing sound patterns without any reference to literary subjects or specific emotions, he became one of the wonders of the world: I found myself able

195

to sit listening to him for forty-five minutes at a stretch without being bored. Absolute music was in him abundant, fresh, hopeful, joyous, powerful, and characterized by a certain virile seriousness and loftiness of taste which gave great relief after the Byzantine corruption of the latest developments of operatic music. It was only when he touched a literary subject of any dimensions that he became, by overpowering contrast with his other self, a positive blockhead. Even his songs are remarkably deficient in vividness after those of Gounod or Schubert.

In other men the ascendant movement of absolute music was less apparent; but the *dégringolade* of dramatic music was obvious. Test it by the operas of European popularity —Don Juan a century ago, Carmen today. Or take program music, with Beethoven's Pastoral Symphony to begin with, and Moszkowsky's Joan of Arc and Benoit's Charlotte Corday to finish with. Or compare Mozart's Requiem and Rossini's Stabat Mater with Dvořák's. Surely we have along these lines the most frightful degeneration, which has only been masked from us by the irresistible power with which Wagner drew out attention to himself alone while he was crowning the dramatic movement by his combination of all the arts into the Bayreuth music-drama, just as Bach crowned the contrapuntal movement at the moment when it was worn out and tumbling to pieces in all directions.

Even with Wagner the wearing out of the purely musical material is patent to all unsympathetic critics. If you take Parsifal, and set aside that large part of the score (the best part) which is senseless apart from the poem, and consider the rest from the point of view of absolute music, you find that a good deal of it will not bear comparison for a moment with the musical material of the Leonora overture or the Ninth Symphony.

Music, in fact, is now in revolt against the union of all the arts, since it has meant to her a ruthless exploitation not only by the poet and higher dramatist, but by the sensation-monger and pander. She is now, like our revolting daughters

196

and Doll's House Noras, insisting on being once more considered as an end in herself; and so the union of all the arts falls to pieces before Wagner's cement is dry, and his Art Work of the Future is already the art work of the past.

Of late this view has been pressed home on me in another way. One of the unsolved problems which all critics have been conscious of for a long time has been the collapse of English music in the eighteenth century. So long as our knowledge of the old music was confined to the madrigals and other vocal pieces—that is, to the least absolutely musical specimens—the problem remained inert at the back of our minds.

Some of us, of course, had a paper knowledge of the old instrumental music; but I am so deeply sceptical as to the value of such paper knowledge that whenever a musician tells me that reading a score is to him the same as hearing it performed, I either give him credit for deceiving himself, or else accept the statement exactly as I would accept it from a deaf man. Those who make it usually contradict themselves, whenever they get the chance, by taking the trouble to attend performances of the very scores which are on the shelves of their libraries.

Now, for some time past Mr Arnold Dolmetsch has been bringing the old instrumental music to actual performance under conditions as closely as possible resembling those contemplated by the composers; and under this stimulus the unsolved problem has suddenly become active and begun to struggle after its solution as a discord struggles after its resolution. And the explanation appears to be the very simple one that the English gained their great musical reputation up to the eighteenth century in absolute music. In the eighteenth century the world left off writing absolute music and took to operatic music, for which the English—to the great credit of their national character—had no sort of aptitude. And if they wish to regain their old fame, they must begin where they left off.

While I was still in my teens, the verbal horrors of "opera

197

in English," by the Carl Rosa and other companies, convinced me that if the English language is to be musically treated at all it must be done in the style of Purcell, and not in that of Verdi. This was my first superficial formulation of the solution which completed itself quite lately in my mind at the viol concerts at Mr Dolmetsch's house at Dulwich. Here the music, completely free from all operatic and literary aims, ought, one might have supposed, to have sounded quaintly archaic.

But not a bit of it. It made operatic music sound positively wizened in comparison. Its richness of detail, especially in the beauty and interest of the harmony, made one think of modern "English" music of the Bohemian-Girl school as one thinks of a jerry-built suburban square after walking through a mediæval quadrangle at Oxford. The operatic charms that were once irresistible—the freedom of melody, the determinateness of form and harmonic movement, the intelligibility of treatment gained by the establishment of a single popular scale and its relative minor as the mode for all music—these seemed for the moment almost as contemptible as the cheapness of workmanship and the theatrical vulgarity and superficiality of aim which they had brought with them.

But the most significant feature of the old English music was its identity in kind with the best music of Brahms, and with all that is hopeful and vital in the efforts of Parry, Stanford, and our latest composers. So that I had no sooner reached the conviction that English music must come to life again by resuming its old exclusive aims, than I began to see that this was what it was actually doing. Consequently the whole problem for the critics at present is how to make Professor Stanford and the rest see their own destiny clearly, and save themselves from the fate of Lot's wife, which will most assuredly overtake them if they look back to the librettos, operatic and "sacred" (save the mark!), which are superstitions from the age of England's musical impotence. Let them leave the theatrical exploitation of music to

Kistler, Mascagni, and the rest of the brood of young lions:
they themselves, the absolute musicians, will only succeed
by sticking to absolute music, wherein their strength lies.

Having thus, I hope, made my critical position clear, I
may say of Professor Stanford's Becket music that, together
with those excellences which I have already indicated, it
marks an advance in the only direction along which he now
can advance, and that is the intensification of his grip of his
thematic material. He no longer resorts to clever technical
trifling to conceal his want of interest in his own work: he
now keeps to the point; only the grip is not yet so earnest or
the vision so penetrating as—shall I say Beethoven's, since
he has reminded me of that mighty man by unconsciously
transferring one of the most striking phrases in the finale of
the Eighth Symphony to the Becket overture. The mills of
the gods have not yet ground his cleverness small enough
nor his inner purpose fine enough to make it wise to claim
for him the place among European composers which he is
probably capable of reaching, for he is in some ways a tough,
incorrigible subject; but I confess I am more than commonly curious to hear what his next symphony will be like.

18 *April* 1894

LAST Thursday England came into possession of another oratorio, called Bethlehem, music by Dr Mackenzie, P.R.A.M.; poetry and analytic program by
Mr Joseph Bennett. I was duly present at the performance
at the Albert Hall, with its thousand choristers, its lavish
orchestra, its gigantic organ, and above all its huge audience
applauding the composer to the echo—or rather to the two
or three echoes which the building harbors—with evident
enthusiasm and enjoyment. But I am somehow deficient in
the sense to which Bethlehem appeals; and I am so conscious
of this that I shall make no attempt to criticize the work
seriously.

The music of Bethlehem is noteworthy as a popular development. When Gounod took to writing oratorio, the ob-

vious identity of his devotional music with his love music did
not cause any particular scandal, perhaps because Dr Henry
Maudsley's essays had convinced the public that a great deal
of what passes as religious ecstasy is really only a fantastic
manifestation of quite another instinct, perhaps because the
love music had been so seraphically refined. At any rate,
Gounod met with no remonstrances as he proceeded to build
up his oratorios out of the most exquisitely sensuous elements of his operatic music. The only fault found with them
was that their sweetness made them cloy after half an hour
or so, full-length performances being all but insufferable.

Dr Mackenzie has followed Gounod's example. He is
determined that nobody shall accuse him, because he is a
Scotchman, of asceticism or Calvinism. His score is crammed
with all the luxuries of the musical confectioner. His ultra-
sentimental cantabiles for the violins, his chimes of bells, his
pianissimo shakes on the cymbals, his glittering touches
with the triangle and pretty breathings on the cornet, make
up an abandonedly voluptuous orchestration; and his actual
use of the well-known figure from the Tannhäuser Venus-
berg music, altered as to the notes, but unmistakeable in
its rhythm (Mr Bennett calls it "the Shepherds' Terror"),
comes in quite naturally in the instrumental saturnalia.

But, as Dr Mackenzie is a hard-headed, vigorous man,
proof against an excess of any sort of ecstasy, devotional or
romantic, the effect he produces is entirely his own; and instead of suggesting Gounod, he rather suggests a morally
reformed Offenbach. There is a Christmas carol at the end
of the first part of Bethlehem which is Offenbach all over
(minus, of course, the Bohemianism). It is in six-eight time,
treated in the most popular fashion, with the orchestra mark-
ing the swing of the two divisions of the bar like a huge accordion, and making it like a pious cousin of the pastoral in
the first act of Orphée aux Enfers. Another point of resemblance to Offenbach is in the way in which the imposing
effects are produced.

Offenbach was no master of harmony: he could write an

accompaniment to a tune; but the moment he wanted to produce any harmonic effect he had to modulate, and trust to the gay effect of jumping from one key to another to conceal the fact that when he got into the new key he could do nothing but repeat the rum-tum he had just been exploiting in the old one. When this resource was exhausted, he whipped up the score by making the tunes move more busily and increasing the speed. Finally, there was the big drum to fall back on, and the mere piling up of brute sound.

A great musician, capable of noble part writing, and provided with a patient and serious audience, need not fall back on such cheap expedients. Within the limits of a single key he commands a range of harmonic progressions of sufficient variety of effect and expression to enable him to give a thoughtful inside to his work instead of a popular outside. Now I cannot say that I found Dr Mackenzie's part writing interesting. I even inferred that he did not find it so himself, not alone from the extreme orchestral bedizenment which I have already described, but from the more conclusive fact that whenever he wished to intensify the emotional effect, he immediately began to emphasize the rhythms, to make his melodies stump about more vigorously, and to pile Pelion on Ossa with organ, chorus, and instruments of percussion.

This, with the obviousness and popularity of the rhythms employed, was what suggested to me the apparently incongruous idea that Offenbach, if he had suppressed his humor, and become a respectable British P.R.A.M., might have given us just such a work as Bethlehem. I do not, however, allege this against Dr Mackenzie as a grievance. I only wish to define the artistic rank of his work. If it is once clearly understood that oratorios like Bethlehem stand in the same relation to the works of the great masters as modern blank verse melodramas to the masterpieces of dramatic poetry, then let us by all means applaud it as a well-knit work of its kind.

But I am not convinced that any such understanding has

been established. I rather suspect that the public, when it reads the eulogies which we critics lavish on these works, thinks that our words mean exactly the same thing as when we apply them in a cooler, more perfunctory way, to Bach and Handel. Therefore I am forced to be ungraciously explicit as to the distinction I make between Dr Mackenzie and Handel and between Mr Bennett and Milton.

I should explain that Bethlehem is constructed on the system of representative themes. The second part opens with a chorus entitled Cometh a heavenly legion to guard the New Born King. The representative theme employed here is the first strain of the old tune Fare you well, my own Mary Ann, familiar to playgoers who remember Mrs Barney Williams. Probably Dr Mackenzie never heard that lady sing; but to me, who remember her very well, the way in which the cornet would every now and then cap the rhetoric about shining ranks and lofty crests and glittering spears, with a sly, soft echo of A lobstere in a lobstere-pot, had something derisive in it, as if the player were having a little joke in disparagement of the enthusiasm of the cherubim.

Were there no artistic moral to be drawn from this ridiculous reminiscence of mine, my mention of it would be a mere impertinence. But it brings to light one of the limiting conditions of the use of representative themes. Since their effect depends altogether on the intimacy and vividness of their association with the idea they represent, it is important that they should not have pre-established associations with other ideas. It is, therefore, dangerous to give them the form of a tune, or of a fragment of a tune, especially when they are introduced, as in the case of the Mary Ann theme, without a strongly characteristic harmony.

Further—and this condition goes deeper—they should only be attached to leading ideas. Now suppose there are no leading ideas in a poem—suppose it is not a poem at all, but only the contents of a bag of tricks emptied out on a sheet of paper, without any intellectual design, for the use of a composer in search of a libretto! Under such circumstances the wisest thing for the composer to do is not to set the libretto at all. But if he must meddle with it, then let him treat it in the old-fashioned way, as a mere excuse for writing set pieces of music—choruses, marches, songs, duets, and so on, without making a pretence of intellectual architectonicity by dragging in the system of representative themes, which was called into existence for the purpose of a musician who was not only a poetic dramatist, but a psychologist and philosopher.

The notion that the Wagnerian method consists simply in picking out stray ideas and ticketing them with a tune opens up in the path of the oratorio composer abysses of absurdity before which I must really try to place a board marked "Danger." Let me illustrate. Suppose some composer, inferring from the case of Mr Joseph Bennett that a musical critic is the proper person to write a libretto, asks me to provide him with words for a cantata, and resolves beforehand to employ "the system of representative themes" because that is the fashion now.

Let us further suppose that the following is a section of my libretto, designed to combine the pious with the popular:

Recit.—Let us eat and drink; for tomorrow we die.

Chorus.—We wont go home till morning,
We wont go home till morning,
We wont go home till morning,
Till daylight doth appear.

In the above there is one leading idea and only one— an idea which plays a huge and significant part in every world drama, from the plague described by Thucydides to the London of our day. No composer of Wagnerian capacity would miss the central thought, or confuse it by introducing themes representing the inessential ideas mentioned.

But your composer who should set to work merely to imitate the Wagner fashion would regard this as a very feeble and barren view of the case. He would say, with relish, "Aha, here we have plenty of material! In the phrase, 'Let us eat and drink,' we shall require a food theme and a drink theme, with orchestration to suggest the clatter of knives and forks and the clinking of glasses. In the following phrase we have a death motive, just as in Tristan, as well as the first hint of a morning theme, which can be fully developed on the word 'morning,' in the following chorus, and raised to its utmost musical splendor at the phrase 'daylight doth appear.' " Naturally a man occupied with the elaboration of such brilliant opportunities would entirely overlook the central thought which is the real substance of the passage.

And the audience, occupied solely with that central thought, would entirely overlook the food and drink and death and morning themes unless there were an elaborate analytic program to point out the ingenuities of the work. Mr Bennett has saved Dr Mackenzie from such oversights by providing him with a book in which there are no central thoughts or leading ideas. Nevertheless, the analytic program quotes a dozen or two of representative themes from the score. I can only say that without Mr Bennett's assistance I should not have identified one of them, save only Fare you well, my own Mary Ann.

25 *April* 1894

I MUST entirely applaud Mr Henschel's spirited cutting-in between Herr Felix Mottl and the expectant public with a Wagner program identical, save as to one item (the Flying Dutchman overture), with that announced for Herr Mottl's first appearance in England. I have heard people say that such a challenge was in bad taste; but in this case, as in ninety-nine out of a hundred others in which the same complaint is made, good taste would have meant simply moral cowardice, a quality in which we in England are always anxious to be kept in countenance. Mr Henschel was quite right, in the face of the flourish of trumpets which heralded Mottl's arrival, to decline to admit the pretensions of the stranger to give us lessons in Wagner-conducting; and he could only protest effectively by at once offering a performance by his own band as a sample of what London can do, thus tacitly daring Herr Mottl to beat him.

Nothing could be fairer; nothing could be bolder; nothing could be more entirely creditable to the challenger. If I could add that the invader had been put to shame—that he had done nothing that Mr Henschel had not done as well, or better, then indeed it would be a proud day for London. But to that length I must not go. Mr Henschel, in the heat of his spirit, underrated his adversary. He was not bad; but Mottl bettered him in every bar. Before the Rienzi overture was half through it was evident that London was going to have a most exemplary beating from Carlsruhe. One after another the blemishes and stupidities to which we have become so inured here that we have ceased to record them against our conductors vanished under Mottl's hand.

Let me, before speaking of his highest qualities, give an illustration or two of his resources as a manager of the orchestra. We all know the overture to Tannhäuser by heart by this time. Well, have we not often shrunk from the coarse and unsatisfactory effect of the three trombones at the climax of the pilgrims' march in the first section of the overture? With Richter it is rather worse than with the others, since he insists on the full power of the fortissimo. Mottl effected a magical transformation. The chant was as powerful as Richter could have desired; and yet it was beautiful, broad, easy, with a portamento which an Italian singer might have envied.

How was this brought about? In the simplest way in the world. Instead of keeping strict Procrustean time for the florid work of the violins, thus forcing the trombones to chop their phrases so as to fit the accompaniment, Mottl gave the trombones a free hand, allowing them to give the time to the whole band, and making the violins wait, when necessary, between the bars, so to speak, until the slow-speaking brass instruments had turned their phrases with unembarrassed majesty. The effect was magnificent. In exactly the same way, and with still more splendid effect, he gave us the great passage at the end of Die Walküre, where the trombones reaffirm the last words of Wotan.

Again, take the Flying Dutchman overture. In the second half of this, the contrast between the furious raging of the storm on the one hand, and the consolation of the salvation theme on the other, should be so obvious, one would think, to any ordinarily imaginative conductor, that Wagner thought it sufficient to indicate the necessary changes of tempo by such hints as ritenuto, stringendo, and the like, depending on their apparent inevitability for their full comprehension. Yet we are accustomed to hear our bands dragged tearing through the salvation theme at almost the same speed as through the storm, some attempt being made to strike a balance by taking the one too slow and the other too fast. Mottl varied his speed from allegro to adagio, managing the transitions with perfect address, and producing the full effect which everybody except our conductors knows to be what Wagner intended.

His allegro, too, was a true *allegro con brio*, as marked, and not the customary *allegro pomposo*. His treatment of those batteries of chords which lead up to the first forte in the quick movement reminded me of Wagner himself, whom I once saw stamping to them with his foot, and, I am afraid, swearing at the band between his teeth because they would not hit them out tremendously enough for him. He would certainly have been satisfied with the cannonade which Mottl got from the drums in this passage. It is one of Mottl's salient characteristics as a conductor that he seizes on the accents of the music with immense energy, always using them to obtain force of expression, and never merely to set people dancing, in the manner of an Austrian band.

This distinction came out strikingly in the instrumental version of Tannhäuser's pæan to Venus in the overture, commonly played as if it were something between a march and a galop, under which treatment the two trumpet blasts with which the opening notes are emphasized sound like a
206

rather boyish bit of decoration, as if someone had tipped two out of a row of iron railings with gilding, for no particular purpose except to see the gold glitter. In Mottl's hands these two trumpet notes explained themselves at once as necessary reinforcements of two all-important accents; and the effect was not to make the movement still more march-like, but, on the contrary, to entirely prevent any such suggestion, and to produce the true accent of oratorical passion, the intensive impulses of which are no more like the merely go-ahead lilt of a march or dance than a furnace is like a sky-rocket.

In short, though Mottl is a very forcible conductor, and, in spite of all that has been said about his slowness, a very fast conductor when the right tempo happens to be very fast, he is not in the least an impetuous one: his self-possession is completed instead of destroyed by excitement; and his speed and energy are those of a strong man on level ground, and not those of an ordinary one going downhill. It must not be supposed that this intensive, concentric force, characteristic of the true art passion, is always manifesting itself in the energetic way in him.

For example, his conducting of the Lohengrin prelude was quite a study in physical expression of just the opposite mode of musical feeling. Needless to say, the band fell considerably short of the ethereal perfection of sound at which the composer aimed. Mottl's face and gesture, entreating, imploring, remonstrating, deprecating, pleading, would have softened hearts of stone; and the violins made it as easy for him as they could, which was perhaps not very easy, especially in the first section.

In the Tannhäuser, too, the fine tone and expressive phrasing of the violoncellos at their first entry in the pilgrims' march was something to be for ever grateful for; while the perfect freedom allowed to the clarinet to develop all the sweetness of the Venus strain (which I heard then, for the first time in my life, as it was meant to be heard) produced an effect only surpassed when, at the end of the Tristan prelude, the Liebestod, usually murdered by being taken too fast, came stealing in, with the conductor doing exactly what Wagner declared to be the whole duty of a conductor, "giving the right time to the band." Is it vain to hope that nobody will ever take it too fast again?

⁋ Perhaps the most convincing instance of Mottl's delicacy of touch was the way in which he managed to veil the cheapness and Rossinian tum-tum of the Rienzi overture, which Mr Henschel had stripped naked with a ruthless hand. But it is unnecessary to multiply illustrations. Those which I have given will serve to shew that I am not merely turning an empty phrase in compliment to a Bayreuth reputation when I say that Mottl is a conductor of the very first rank, with, to boot, immense physical energy and personal influence. I was filled with admiration by his efficiency and insight; and I imagine my feelings were shared by all present who were capable of discriminating between one conductor and another. It is greatly to be desired that Mr Schulz Curtius should follow up the great success of his enterprise (the room was crammed, and the seats had all been sold months in advance) by establishing an annual series of concerts under Mottl. A second concert is already announced for May 22; but the program will have to be changed in one particular. As it stands at present, Beethoven is represented by the overture to Egmont only. This—with due respect to the authors of the program—is all nonsense. Mottl must conduct the C minor symphony: that is the sample of Beethoven for which all his qualities mark him out. By all means, however, let us have Egmont as well, and sacrifice one of the Wagner selections.

And this brings me to the question of that recent artistic phenomenon, the Wagner program, which, as we are assured by the directors of the Crystal Palace, is the most attractive program nowadays. It may be so; but it is an artistic misdemeanor all the same. In satisfying our craving for the sound of Wagner's music, the concert-room is, against its own nature, doing the work of quite another social organ—to wit, the theatre.

We have, unfortunately, no Wagner theatre here; and we must either leave Wagner unheard, or else stuff our concert programs with selections arranged for orchestra alone, as in the second part of a Covent Garden promenade concert. For an arrangement of the Liebestod for a band is really not a bit more defensible at a first-rate concert than an arrangement of the Miserere scene from Il Trovatore or a Pinafore potpourri. It is better to hear the Bayreuth music done in this way than not to hear it at all, perhaps; but it need not on that account be allowed to squeeze concert music proper out of our concerts. I confess that towards the end of Mr Henschel's program my attention began to wander; and if I had seen Mottl conducting as often as I have seen Mr Henschel, I doubt whether even his concentrated power could hold me with the Parsifal prelude played as postlude to ninety minutes' music.

Indeed, to make the confession complete, I may as well add that my attention to the last piece at the Mottl concert cost me a distinct effort. Something comparatively cheap and violently self-assertive, like the Walkürenritt (which Mottl very properly left out of his scheme), is needed to end long concerts, if long concerts must be inflicted on us. Indeed it would be far more reasonable to take these chronological-order programs backwards, so that we could give our unwearied attention to the best pieces first, and reserve the Rienzi overture to waken us up and demoralize the band when our edge has been well dulled.

I have one other strong reason for desiring to see Mottl established here as a conductor. His greatest rival, Richter, is so far above the heads of the public that he has no external stimulus to do his best in London. Only a very few people can perceive the difference between his best and his second best; but the difference between his second best and Mottl's best would be felt at once by a considerable body of amateurs. Now I do not suggest that Richter ever consciously does less than his best; but I am materialist enough in these matters to believe that even the best man does more work under pressure than in a vacuum. Mr Henschel, for instance, whose concert was not up to his own standard, much less to Mottl's, will be quite able, now that he is put on his mettle, to surpass himself.

It is so long since I have mentioned the pianoforte in this column that I must add, before concluding, that Sophie Menter and Sapellnikoff are in London. I was unable to attend the Philharmonic when Sapellnikoff played there on Thursday last; but I heard Madame Menter at the Crystal Palace on Saturday. She is still irresistible; but there were signs of wear and tear on her playing of the two transcriptions from Schubert. Probably she has played them too often; at all events, there was more of her old power and audacity in her playing of the concerto (Liszt in E flat). Mr Frederick Dawson has given a recital. He is a pleasant, frank-looking, somewhat irresponsible young gentleman with a technique which enables him to rattle off Beethoven's sonatas quite cheerfully. His best effort, as far as I heard, was Mendelssohn's Variations Serieuses, in which he seemed to be quite in his depth. With Beethoven and Schumann he was just a little too light-hearted.

2 *May* 1894

I HAVE been indulging in five shillings' worth of Ruskin on Music, in a volume just published by Mr George Allen. As it happened, the first sentence I lighted on when I opened the book was "the oratorio, withering the life of religion into dead bones on the Syren sands." Immediately I woke up; for the fact that modern oratorio is mostly a combination of frivolity and sensuality with hypocrisy and the most oppressive dullness is still sufficiently a trade secret to make its discovery by an outsider interesting. A few pages off I found Mr Ruskin describing the singing he heard south of the Alps. Usually the Englishman in Italy, carefully primed beforehand with literary raptures concerning a nation of born musicians speaking the most vocal language in the world, is sufficiently careful of his own credit as a man of taste to discover a Giuglini in every gondolier and St Cecilia's lute in every accordion.

Mr Ruskin innovated so far as to use his own judgment; and here is the result: "Of bestial howling, and entirely frantic vomiting up of damned souls through their still carnal throats, I have heard more than, please God, I will ever endure the hearing of again, in one of His summers." I take the liberty of squeezing Mr Ruskin's hand in mute sympathy with the spirit of this passage. In Italy, where the chance of being picked up off the streets and brought out as *primo tenore* at the Opera occupies the same space in the imagination of the men as the chance of selecting a Derby winner does in England, you cannot get away from the ignoble bawling which Mr Ruskin describes so forcibly—and yet not too forcibly, or forcibly enough; for language will not hold the full pretentiousness and cupidity of the thing, let alone the unpleasantness of the noise it makes.

It is at once the strength and weakness of Mr Ruskin in dealing with music that he is in love with it. There is always a certain comedy in the contrast between people as they appear transfigured in the eyes of those who love them, and as they appear to those who are under no such inspiration—or, for the matter of that, as they appear to themselves. And the tragi-comedy of the love of men and women for one another is reproduced in their love for art.

Mr Ruskin is head and ears in love with Music; and so am I; but I am married to her, so to speak, as a professional critic, whereas he is still a wooer, and has the illusions of imperfect knowledge as well as the illuminations of perfect love. Listen to this, for example:

"True music is the natural expression of a lofty passion for a right cause. In proportion to the kingliness and force of any personality, the expression either of its joy or suffering becomes measured, chastened, calm, and capable of interpretation only by the majesty of ordered, beautiful, and worded sound. Exactly in proportion to the degree in which we become narrow in the cause and conception of our passions, incontinent in the utterance of them, feeble of perseverance in them, sullied or shameful in the indulgence of them, their expression by musical means becomes broken, mean, fatuitous, and at last impossible: the measured waves of heaven will not lend themselves to the expression of ultimate vice: it must be for ever sunk in discordance or silence."

I entirely agree with Mr Ruskin in this; but it will not hold water, for all that. "The measured waves of heaven" are not so particular as he thinks. Music will express any emotion, base or lofty. She is absolutely unmoral: we find her in Verdi's last work heightening to the utmost the expression of Falstaff's carnal gloating over a cup of sack, just as willingly as she heightened the expression of "a lofty passion for a right cause" for Beethoven in the Ninth Symphony. She mocked and prostituted the Orpheus legend for Offenbach just as keenly and effectively as she ennobled it for Gluck. Mr Ruskin himself has given an instance of this —a signally wrong instance, by the way; but let that pass for a moment:

"And yonder musician, who used the greatest power which (in the art he knew) the Father of Spirits ever yet breathed into the clay of this world; who used it, I say, to follow and fit with perfect sound the words of the Zauberflöte and of Don Giovanni—foolishest and most monstrous of conceivable human words and subjects of thought—for the future amusement of his race! No such spectacle of unconscious (and in that unconsciousness all the more fearful) moral degradation of the highest faculty to the lowest purpose can be found in history."

This is a capital instance of Mr Ruskin's besetting sin— virtuous indignation. If these two operas are examples of "foolishness and most monstrous" words fitted and followed with perfect sound—that is, with true music—what becomes of the definition which limits true music to "the natural expression of a lofty passion for a right cause"? Clearly, that will not do.

And now may I beg Mr Ruskin to mend his illustration, if not his argument? The generation which could see nothing in Die Zauberflöte but a silly extravaganza was one which Mr Ruskin certainly belonged to in point of time; and he has for once sunk to the average level of its thought in this shallow criticism of the work which Mozart deliberately devoted to the expression of his moral sympathies. Everything that is true and vital in his worship of music would be shattered if it were a fact—happily it is not—that the music of Sarastro came from a silly and trivial mood. If I were to assure Mr Ruskin that Bellini's Madonna with St Ursula, in Venice, was originally knocked off as a sign for a tavern by the painter, Mr Ruskin would simply refuse to entertain the story, no matter what the evidence might be, knowing that the thing was eternally impossible. Since he sees no such impossibility in the case of Die Zauberflöte, I must conclude that he does not know the masterpieces of music as he knows those of painting.

As to Don Giovanni, otherwise The Dissolute One Punished, the only immoral feature of it is its supernatural retributive morality. Gentlemen who break through the ordinary categories of good and evil, and come out at the other side singing Finch' han dal vino and La ci darem, do not, as a matter of fact, get called on by statues, and taken straight down through the floor to eternal torments; and to pretend that they do is to shirk the social problem they present. Nor is it yet by any means an established fact that the world owes more to its Don Ottavios than to its Don Juans.

It is, of course, impossible to make a serious stand on a libretto which is such an odd mixture of the old Punch tradition with the highly emancipated modern philosophy of Molière; but whether you apply Mr Ruskin's hasty criticism to Punch and Judy or to Le Festin de Pierre, you will, I think, see that it is fundamentally nothing but an explosion of pious horror of the best Denmark Hill brand. The hard fact is that Don Giovanni is eminent in virtue of its uncommon share of wisdom, beauty, and humor; and if any theory

of morals leads to the conclusion that it is foolish and monstrous, so much the worse for the theory.

I must, further, remonstrate with Mr Ruskin about his
advice to the girls of England. First, like a veritable serpent
in the garden, he tempts the young English lady, already
predisposed to self-righteousness, with the following wicked
words: "From the beginning consider all your accomplishments as means of assistance to others." This is Denmark
Hill with a vengeance. But the artist in Mr Ruskin is always
getting the better of Denmark Hill; and on the very next
page he says, "Think only of accuracy; never of effect or
expression."

Now, will anyone kindly tell me how a young lady is to
consider all her accomplishments "as means of assistance to
others"—that is, to think of nothing but effect and expression, and consequently to cultivate self-consciousness and
its attendant personal susceptibility up to the highest point
—and at the same time not to think of effect or expression at
all, but only of accuracy. Speaking as a rival sage—as one
who, in musical matters at least, considers himself fitted to
play Codlin to Mr Ruskin's Short—I earnestly advise the
young ladies of England, whether enrolled in the Guild of
St George or not, to cultivate music solely for the love and
need of it, and to do it in all humility of spirit, never forgetting that they are most likely inflicting all-but-unbear-
able annoyance on every musician within earshot, instead of
rendering "assistance to others."

The greatest assistance the average young lady musician
can render to others is to stop. Mind, I speak of life as it is.
Some day, perhaps, when it is like a page out of Wilhelm
Meister or Sesame and Lilies, when the piano is dead and
our maidens go up into the mountains to practise their first
exercise on the harp, Mr Ruskin's exhortations as to the
sinfulness of doing anything merely because you like it may
gain some sort of plausibility. At present they will not wash.

"It is, I believe," says Mr Ruskin, "as certain that in the
last twenty years we have learnt to better understand good

music, and to love it more, as that in the same time our
knowledge and love of pictures have not increased. The
reason is easily found. Our music has been chosen for us by
masters; and our pictures have been chosen by ourselves."

Alas! how easy it is to find a reason for the thing that is
not! Not that there is not here, as usual, a hundred times
more insight in Mr Ruskin's mistake than in most other
men's accuracies. It is quite true that the favorite works at
our good concerts are of a much higher class than the favorite
works at the Royal Academy, and that the difference is due
to the fact that Beethoven and Wagner are still in a position
to dictate to the public what is good for them. But the public
is not really conscious of that part of Beethoven's work which
raises it above the level of popular painting. It finds a great
deal of Beethoven incomprehensible, and therefore dull,
putting up with it only because the alternative is either no
music at all or something a good deal duller. But will it put
up with it when vulgar musicians have completely mastered
the trade of producing symphonies and operas containing
all the cheap, popular, obvious, carnal luxuries of the Beet-
hovenian music, without its troublesome nobilities, depths,
and spiritual grandeurs?

I doubt it. Wagner accused Meyerbeer of following the
great masters as a starling follows the plough, picking up
the titbits which their force unearthed, and serving them up
to Paris unmixed with nobler matter. That process, which
has been going on in music for less than a century, has been
going on in painting for three or four hundred years, so that
our contemporary popular painters have rid themselves far
more completely of what was greatest in the great masters
of Florence, Rome, and Venice, than our contemporary
composers of what was greatest in Mozart, Beethoven, and
Wagner; but the process is going on all the same under
the influence of popular demand; and we shall soon have
the field held by vulgar music as much as by vulgar painting,
as is right and proper in a country with a vulgar population.

I need hardly add that Mr Ruskin himself, true to his

method of never collating his utterances, but taking his inspiration as it comes, so that on every possible subject he says
the right thing and the wrong thing with equal eloquence
within the same ten minutes, does not really believe any such
nonsense as that people can be kept on high ground by having their music chosen for them by masters. For instance:

"You cannot paint or sing yourselves into being good
men. You must be good men before you can either paint or
sing; and then the color and the sound will complete all in
you that is best."

Neither can people appreciate good music, whether
chosen for them by masters or not, except to the extent to
which they are "good" themselves. You can chain a terrier
to Richter's desk, and force it to listen to all the symphonies
of Beethoven, without changing its opinion one jot as to the
relative delights of rathunting and classical music; and the
same thing is true in its degree of mankind. The real point
is, that most of us, far from being chained to the desk, never
get the chance of finding out whether we can appreciate
great music or not.

Mr Ruskin is probably right in anticipating that a change
in the tone of public feeling would be produced "if, having
been accustomed only to hear black Christy's, blind fiddlers,
and hoarse beggars scrape and howl about their streets, the
people were permitted daily audience of faithful and gentle
orchestral rendering of the work of the highest classical
masters."

Here I must leave an infinitely suggestive and provoca-
tive book, the publication of which no musical critic can very
well ignore. To finish, I will give, without comment, one
more quotation as a sample of what Mr Ruskin's musical
criticism would, perhaps, have been like if he had taken to
my branch of the trade instead of to his own:

"Grisi and Malibran sang at least one-third slower than
any modern cantatrice; and Patti, the last time I heard her,
massacred Zerlina's part in La ci darem, as if the audience
and she had but the one object of getting Mozart's air done

216

with as soon as possible. . . . Afterwards I was brought to the point of trying to learn to sing, in which, though never even getting so far as to read with ease, I nevertheless, between my fine rhythmic ear and true-lover's sentiment, got to understand some principles of musical art, which I shall perhaps be able to enforce, with benefit on the musical public mind, even today."

9 *May* 1894

I HAVE again had the privilege of hearing Paderewski play that Polish Fantasia of his, this time by special request of the Philharmonic directors, who were probably afraid that he might otherwise have played Beethoven or some other tedious classical composer. I have now heard that Fantasia three times; and though Paderewski seems to be entirely of Macbeth's opinion as to crying "Hold, enough!" I confess I do not want to hear it again, at least not for another week or so. The fact is, he can play much better music than he has yet composed; and it offends all my notions of artistic economy to see Paderewski the first-rate player thrown away on Paderewski the second-rate composer.

That Fantasia does not contain a bar of pianoforte music of the highest class: it is brilliant, violent, ingenious, here and there romantic; but what do I care for all that at my age? Now that I have worn out the somewhat obvious charms of the themes, I care for little more than the careful and intelligent workmanship. As for those flashy rapid traits, played on a piano which has been spoiled to make them practicable, they are lost on me: Liszt, and even Tausig, in spite of his vulgar vandalism, were more amusing in this department. People who challenge musical criticism in a double capacity put me in a difficulty.

Take Rubinstein for instance. He was a player of stupendous manual dexterity, with immense power, passion, and spontaneity. Had his intellect been as keen as his will was energetic he would have been unsurpassable: as it was, he

217

stood, after the retirement of Liszt, the foremost player of his time. But he insisted on composing profusely, strenuously, earnestly, loading up Europe with big instrumental compositions which it was most painful, in view of one's regard for him as a pianist, to have to set down as huge trumperies, intolerably diffuse considering their commonness, and containing no qualities that were not far more suitably employed on his songs, duets, pianoforte pieces, and other domestic ware.

Rubinstein's place has now been taken by Paderewski, intellectually his superior, and made of steel where he was made of iron, consequently rather less ready to glow and melt. And now Paderewski, too, is beginning to compose, with the same earnestness and the same ambition. The result is very different: the Russian pitted against the Pole comes out as childishly in intellectual and critical power as an ancient Roman or modern Bulgarian against a Greek; but the old difficulty none the less reproduces itself: Paderewski stands higher as a player than he does as a composer; and consequently his playing of his own works is a waste of his finest powers.

Were I he, I should not condescend to play that Polish Fantasia at a Philharmonic concert: I should say to the directors, "No, gentlemen: at your classical concerts I play Beethoven, or Bach, or Chopin, or some other great composer, instead of that deserving but not as yet exactly first-rate young aspirant Paderewski, on whose behalf I must, however, thank you for your kind encouragement." We so rarely hear Paderewski with an orchestra behind him that the choice between a Beethoven concerto and one of his own works is forced upon us rather sharply; and I should belittle him as a player if I hesitated to say that I now want to hear him play Beethoven in G for the first time, or Beethoven in E flat for the second time, much more than I want to hear him play that Fantasia for the fourth time.

Now that the Crystal Palace Saturday Concert season is over, the recitals at Queen's Hall will perhaps come in for a larger share of attention. I have been 'present at two, and found them enjoyable enough. Mr Cowen has a first-rate band; and he conducts with more freedom than he used to. I cannot say that his curious freak of taking the Walkürenritt in the slow tempo proper to the Lohengrin prelude, and the Lohengrin prelude in the lively tempo proper to the Walkürenritt, revealed any new beauties in these works: rather the contrary, in fact; but still it was interesting—for once. The recital of an act of Lohengrin, without the usual stage cuts, is artistically valuable in this unhappy town, where everything is mutilated to fit the dinner hour.

And it is a mistake to suppose that you can "cut" Lohengrin as you can cut an Italian opera. The first (and last) time I ever caught a lizard by the tail, it disconcerted me extremely by breaking itself into three pieces, and making off with the piece in which its head happened to be. This power is one of the privileges of low organization: if a man were to elude a police constable in that manner he would die: and possibly the policeman would die too, of the shock. Now there is almost as great a difference in complexity of organization between an Italian opera and a Wagerian music-drama as between a reptile and a man. The degree of mutilation which is only inconvenient to the opera is fatal to the music-drama.

Those who heard at Queen's Hall the transition from the first to the second scene of the third act of Lohengrin given without the usual opera-house butchery must have been astonished at the effect of all that gathering of legions and clangor of trumpets which makes the opening of the final scene so exciting and impressive. Last Saturday we had the third act of Tannhäuser, less of a novelty, and perhaps for that reason more of a favorite on the concert platform. Mr Edward Lloyd fills the tenor parts at these entertainments, occasionally playing a little to the gallery by a style of declamation not precisely classic, though sufficiently sincere and effective; and Miss Ella Russell, a very capable artist, of whom we have rather failed hitherto to make any adequate use, is the leading soprano.

There are the materials for excellent performances at Queen's Hall; and all Mr Cowen need do to realize them is, not to conduct like Mottl, since he is not built that way, but simply to faithfully carry out Wagner's instructions; insist on accurate reading of the notes and nuances; and get from his band at least five gradations of tone, pianissimo, piano, mezzoforte, forte, and fortissimo, over and above those mechanically produced by the increase or decrease of the number of instruments employed, instead of slopping along with a lazy piano and mezzoforte only. I do not mean to imply that Mr Cowen is consciously careless: far from it, the activity of his conscience is visible to all; but there are a good many indications in the score which he either overlooks or fails to value adequately.

Mention of Mottl reminds me that my feeling that he should break ground as a Beethoven conductor here by the C minor symphony is evidently shared by Mr Schulz-Curtius and himself; for the program for the 22nd now includes that work, along with six pieces by Wagner and two by Berlioz. As we never hear Berlioz handled successfully in London, except on one of the scarce visits of the Manchester Band, it will be interesting to hear what Mottl, whose appreciation of Berlioz carried him to the length of producing Les Troyens at Carlsruhe, will be able to do with him.

It is impossible not to admire the vigorous individuality and irrepressible musical talent of Signor Scuderi, who gave a concert the other day at Steinway Hall; and I am indebted to him for letting me hear the obbligato to the serenade in Don Giovanni played on the instrument for which it was written, that is, the mandoline, though I do not believe in the least that Mozart meant it to be "double-tongued," if I may borrow that expression to describe the effect of turning each semiquaver into a rapidly repeated demisemiquaver. But much as I admire the way in which Signor Scuderi can adapt himself to any instrument, I protest against his readiness to adapt any instrument to any piece of music. The very quality which makes the mandoline the ideal instrument to accompany Deh vieni alla finestra, puts it quite out of the question for Wolfram's apostrophe to the evening star in Tannhäuser; yet Signor Scuderi plucked out the harp part to that song on his mandoline, whilst Mr Oscar Noyes sang the foolish Italian arrangement of it for concert use in two verses. I can only describe the instrumental effect as blasphemous. Mr Noyes, who is by no means an unpromising singer, might get more effect out of the serenade by singing it exactly as Mozart wrote it, instead of muddling away the effect of the low D at the end by a rather clumsy gruppetto.

The Crystal Palace Saturday Concerts are now over for the season. I have still to complain of the excessive length of the concerts. I admit that my desire to shorten my work operates in the contrary direction to the desire of the public to get as much value as possible for its money; but if anyone will compare a modern Philharmonic program with an ancient one, or a playbill of the palmy days with Mr Irving's of last night, he will see that the march of evolution involves shortening. It is not that people are less tolerant of music than they were: on the contrary, it is because they listen with an intensity formerly undreamt of.

We do not all realize how modern an institution the silent audience is. Even in the dreariest moments of a bad concert nowadays we do not talk, or go in and out noisily, or beat time with our boots, unless, indeed, we are country-cousins, unfamiliar with concert-room usages, in which case our neighbors generally make us aware very soon that we are misbehaving. Critics have had to eliminate from their stereo such phrases as "the vast audience was hushed," etc., because audiences always are hushed. Even "the Bayreuth hush" has acquired its eminence solely through its being quite the noisiest thing of the kind, owing to the way in which the older English ladies, confused by the darkness, and not realizing the solemnity of the moment, will ask questions of their daughters and provoke angry "Sh-sh-es" from incontinent foreigners and fanatic Wagner worshippers.

But things were not always on this footing. An audience in a concert-room or play-house formerly kept up a continual buzz of conversation, nobody having any notion that he should not talk if he wanted to, and, what is more surprising nowadays, nobody listening to the performance with any such strain on their attention as is necessary to make the buzz of conversation unendurable. The relics of this state of things are to be seen in the Crystal Palace concert-room in the shape of notices requesting people not to talk, and informing them, as something that they are not likely to know, that any noise made by them will interfere with the enjoyment of their neighbors. These hints on good behavior have long been out of date as far as the Saturday audiences are concerned; and my contention is that this change involves the suppression of the long program half listened to by the short program thoroughly listened to.

The fatigue of thorough listening is so great that when the concentration is carried to the utmost, as at Bayreuth, where the fact that nothing is visible except the stage produces great intensity of observation, you come out from a two hours' shift, such as the last act of Die Meistersinger, in a state of exhaustion not to be described. I suggest, therefore, that an hour and three-quarters should be fixed as the extreme outside limit for a concert of high-class music, and that the addition of any item whatsoever to a program containing the Ninth Symphony should be punished by imprisonment without option. When this work was done a few Saturdays ago at the Crystal Palace the concert was almost spoiled by the unnecessary addition of three or four songs which, with the honorable exception of one by Miss Fillunger, were so abominably sung that I cannot believe that the singers themselves would dispute the point with me, especially the gentleman who had forgotten Adelaida and had to fall back on improvization once or twice. But this leads me to a consideration of the music we have had at the

Palace; and I must postpone that matter for the present for want of space.

16 *May* 1894

ANOTHER great artist has come. I suppose I ought to have been quite familiar with her performances already when I went to her reception of the English Press (musical critics *not* included) at the Savoy Hotel last week; but as a matter of fact I had never heard her before. The fact is I am a very bad Parisian. I have never been to the Chat Noir: I have looked at its advertisements on the Boulevards time after time without the least conviction that my sense of being in the fastest forefront of the life of my age would culminate there. To me, going to Paris means going back fifty years in civilization, spending an uncomfortable night, and getting away next morning as soon as possible. I know, of course, that there must be places and circles in Paris which are not hopelessly out of date; but I have never found them out; and if I did, what figure could I make in them with my one weapon, language, broken in my hand?

Hence it is that I had never seen Mdlle Yvette Guilbert when Monsieur Johnson, of the Figaro, introduced her to a carefully selected audience of the wrong people (mostly) at the Savoy Hotel as aforesaid. Monsieur Johnson, as a veteran, will not feel hurt at any comment which only goes to prove that "the power of beauty he remembers yet"; therefore I need have no delicacy in saying that the remarks which he addressed to the audience by way of introducing Mdlle Guilbert were entirely fatuous when his emotion permitted them to be heard. When the young lady appeared, it needed only one glance to see that here was no mere music-hall star, but one of the half-dozen ablest persons in the room. It is worth remarking here, that in any society whatever of men and women there is always a woman among the six cleverest; and this is why I, who have a somewhat extensive experience of work on the committees of mixed societies, have been trained to recognize the fact that the Efficient Person in this

223

world is occasionally female, though she must not on that account be confounded with the ordinary woman—or the ordinary man, for that matter—whom one does not privately regard as a full-grown responsible individual at all.

You do not waste "homage" on the female Efficient Person; you regard her, favorably or unfavorably, much as you regard the male of the Efficient species, except that you have a certain special fear of her, based on her freedom from that sickliness of conscience, so much deprecated by Ibsen, which makes the male the prey of unreal scruples; and you have at times to defend yourself against her, or, when she is an ally, to assume her fitness for active service of the roughest kinds, in a way which horrifies the chivalrous gentlemen of your acquaintance who will not suffer the winds of heaven to breathe on a woman's face too harshly lest they should disable her in her mission of sewing on buttons.

In short, your chivalry and gallantry are left useless on your hands, unless for small-talk with the feminine rank and file, who must be answered according to their folly, just like the male rank and file. But then you get on much better with the female master-spirits, who will not stand chivalry, or gallantry, or any other form of manly patronage. Therefore let others, who have not been educated as I have been, pay Mdlle Guilbert gallant compliments: as for me, no sooner had the lady mounted the platform with that unmistakeable familiarity with the situation and command of it which shews itself chiefly by the absence of all the petty affectations of the favorite who has merely caught the fancy of the public without knowing how or why, than I was on the alert to see what an evidently very efficient person was going to do.

And I was not at all deceived in my expectancy. It amuses her to tell interviewers that she cannot sing, and has no gestures; but I need not say that there would be very little fun for her in that if she were not one of the best singers and pantomimists in Europe. She divided her program into three parts: Ironic songs, Dramatic songs, and—but perhaps I had better use the French heading here, and say Chansons Legères. For though Mdlle Guilbert sings the hymns of a very ancient faith, profusely endowed and sincerely upheld among us, we deny it a name and an establishment. Its Chansons Ironiques are delivered by her with a fine intensity of mordant expression that would not be possible without profound conviction beneath it; and if there is anything that I am certain of after hearing her sing Les Vierges, it is the perfect integrity of her self-respect in an attitude towards life which is distinctly not that of the British matron.

To kindle art to the whitest heat there must always be some fanaticism behind it; and the songs in which Mdlle Guilbert expresses her immense irony are the veil of a propaganda which is not the propaganda of asceticism. It is not my business here to defend that propaganda against the numerous and highly respectable British class which conceives life as presenting no alternative to asceticism but licentiousness: I merely describe the situation to save people of this way of thinking from going to hear Mdlle Yvette, and proposing to treat her as their forefathers treated Joan of Arc.

Perhaps, however, they would only laugh the innocent laugh of the British lady who, not understanding French, and unwilling to let that fact appear, laughs with the rest at the points which prevented Mdlle Guilbert from inviting the episcopal bench as well as the Press to her reception. In spite of her superb diction, I did not understand half her lines myself. Part of what I did understand would have surprised me exceedingly if it had occurred in a drawing-room ballad by Mr Cowen or Sir Arthur Sullivan; but I am bound to add that I was not in the least shocked or disgusted, though my unlimited recognition of an artist's right to take any side of life whatsoever as subject-matter for artistic treatment makes me most indignantly resentful of any attempt to abuse my tolerance by coarse jesting.

The fact is, Mdlle Guilbert's performance was for the most part much more serious at its base than an average Italian opera scena. I am not now alluding to the avowedly dramatic songs like Le Conscrit and Morphinée, which any ordinary actress could deliver in an equally effective, if somewhat less distinguished, manner. I am thinking of Les Vierges, Sur la Scène, and the almost frightful La Pierreuse. A *pierreuse*, it appears, is a garrotter's decoy. In the song she describes how she prowls about the fortifications of Paris at night, and entraps some belated bourgeois into conversation. Then she summons her principal with a weird street cry; he pounces on his prey; and the subsequent operations are described in a perfect war dance of a refrain.

Not so very horrible, perhaps; but the last verse describes not a robbery, but the guillotining of the robber; and so hideously exquisite is the singing of this verse that you see the woman in the crowd at La Roquette; you hear the half-choked repetition of the familiar signal with which she salutes the wretch as he is hurried out; you positively see his head flying off; above all, you feel with a shudder how the creature's impulses of terror and grief are overcome by the bestial excitement of seeing the great State show of killing a man in the most sensational way.

Just as people would not flog children if they could realize the true effect of the ceremony on the child's pet playmates, to whom it is supposed to be a wholesome warning, so the French Government would certainly abolish public executions *sans phrase* (and perhaps private ones too) if only they would go and hear Mdlle Guilbert sing La Pierreuse.

Technically, Mdlle Guilbert is a highly accomplished artist. She makes all her effects in the simplest way, and with perfect judgment. Like the ancient Greeks, not to mention the modern music-hall artists, she relies on the middle and low registers of her voice, they being the best suited for perfectly well-controlled declamation; but her cantabile is charming, thanks to a fine ear and a delicate rhythmic faculty. Her command of every form of expression is very remarkable, her tones ranging from the purest and sweetest pathos to the cockniest Parisian cynicism.

There is not a trace of the rowdy restlessness and forced

"go" of the English music-hall singer about her; and I suggest to those members of the London County Council who aim at the elevation of the music-hall, that they could not do better than offer Mdlle Guilbert handsome terms to follow up her reception of *la Presse Anglaise* by a series of receptions of Miss Marie Lloyd, Miss Katie Lawrence, and other eminent English prima donnas, in order that they might be encouraged to believe that there is room in music-hall singing for art of classic self-possession and delicacy without any loss of gaiety, and that the author of a music-hall song may not be the worse for being a wit, or even a poet.

Some time ago Mr Bonawitz invited me to an invisible concert. I did not go, because I felt that I had been entirely misunderstood. I do not at all object to seeing the performers at a concert: it is hearing them that upsets me. If Mr Bonawitz will try an inaudible concert, he may rely on my eager support: meanwhile, I actually did, one day last week, succeed for the first time in my life in going to a concert without hearing a note of music. It was given by Mrs Clarinda Webster, and was called a Mendelssohn concert. When I arrived, some gentleman who had evidently covered himself with glory was retiring, violin in hand, amid thunders of applause. I had settled myself down comfortably to enjoy the next item, when Mrs Webster, observing that a Mendelssohn concert would be incomplete without a sketch of the life of Mendelssohn (which seemed no more than reasonable), proceeded to read a biography of the master. This was all very well for the ignorant multitude; but it was very poor fun for me, who know all about Mendelssohn. However, I reflected that as he died young, the biography could not last very long; and I held on until Mrs Webster began to read a letter from the composer descriptive of his reception at Buckingham Palace. I regret to say that my loyalty broke down under this strain. I stole out as quietly as I could, hoping Mrs Webster would not look up from her manuscript and catch me in the act. And so, though I have no doubt the concert was a capital one, I heard none of it. It was rather an unlucky day in this way; for in the evening I repaired to the same place (Queen's Hall, the concert-room at the top of the building) to hear Mr Charles Fry recite Eugene Aram to an accompaniment composed by Dr Mackenzie. I arrived just in time to have the door closed in my face, under the very proper rule which forbids people to come in during the performance of a piece. And here I discovered the value of Mr Bonawitz's invention of the invisible concert; for the spectacle of Mr Fry, apparently making faces at me through the glass-door (which cut off all sound) in derision of my baffled plight outside, was more than I could bear; and I again retreated musicless.

Mr Max Laistner's choir distinguished itself at St James's Hall last week by an excellent performance of Max Bruch's setting of Schiller's Lay of the Bell. Mr Laistner is a capital choirmaster; and it is a pity that his concerts are not more frequent, in view of the dearth at the West End of good choral concerts with choirs of reasonable size and manageableness. But why on earth did Mr Laistner play Schumann's pianoforte concerto in public? Surely he must know that his hands, musicianly as they are, have not the trained strength of the pianoforte athlete's. I did not hear half the notes. Besides, it made the concert absurdly long. Bruch's work, passionate and grandiose at best, and lively and interesting at worst, is so very superior to the sort of thing we turn out here, that I cannot, for very shame, insist on its limitations in an English paper. It might well be heard oftener.

I see that Mr Daniel de Lange has again brought his choir over from Amsterdam. He did so ten years ago, when I vainly tried to draw public attention to the extraordinary merit of his performances of the old choral music of the great Netherlandish school. I came upon one of his concerts at the Inventions Exhibition at South Kensington, quite accidentally; and I shall never forget the effect produced on me, or the stupendous insensibility of most of the other droppers-in to the fact that they were listening to one of the very finest and rarest performances they had ever heard in their lives.

I have not heard the choir since, and so do not know whether it maintains its former excellence; but it gives me great pleasure to acknowledge my old debt to Mr de Lange by urging all lovers of the pure choral counterpoint of the fifteenth and sixteenth centuries (than which, in its way, there is no more beautiful music in the world) not to lose this opportunity as that of 1885 was lost.

23 May 1894

I HAVE been to the Opera six times; and I still live. What is more, I am positively interested and hopeful. Hitherto I have had only one aim as regards Italian opera: not, as some have supposed, to kill it; for it was dead already, but to lay its ghost. It was a troublesome phantom enough. When one felt sure that it had been effectually squeezed out at last by French opera, or Hebraic opera, or what may be called operatic music-drama—Lohengrin, for instance—it would turn up again trying to sing Spirito gentil in the manner of Mario, raving through the mad scene in Lucia amid childish orchestral tootlings, devastating Il Trovatore with a totally obsolete style of representation, or in some way gustily rattling its unburied bones and wasting the manager's money and my patience.

The difficulty was to convince those who had been brought up to believe in it (as I was myself) that it was all over with it: they *would* go on believing that it only needed four first-rate Italian singers to bring the good old times back again and make the rum-tum rhythms, the big guitar orchestration, the florid cabalettas, the cavatinas in regular four-bar lines, the choruses in thirds and sixths, and all the rest of it swell out to their former grandeur and sweep Wagner off the boards. I have no doubt they believe it as devoutly as ever, and that if Mr Mapleson were to start again tomorrow, he would announce Lucia and Il Barbiere and Semiramide with unshaken confidence in their freshness and adequacy, perhaps adding, as a concession to the

229

public demand for novelty, a promise of Ponchielli's La Gioconda.

But now an unlooked-for thing has happened. Italian opera has been born again. The extirpation of the Rossinian dynasty, which neither Mozart nor Wagner could effect, since what they offered in its place was too far above the heads of both the public and the artists, is now being accomplished with ease by Mascagni, Leoncavallo, Puccini, and Verdi. Nobody has ever greeted a performance of Tristan und Isolde by such a remark as "We shall never be able to go back to L'Elisire d'Amore after this," or declare that Lucrezia was impossible after Brynhild. The things were too far apart to affect one another: as well might it be supposed that Ibsen's plays could be accepted as a substitute for popular melodrama, or Shakespear wean people from the circus. It is only by an advance in melodrama itself or in circuses themselves that the melodrama or circus of today can become unpresentable to the audiences of ten years hence.

The same thing is true of Italian opera. The improvement of higher forms of art, or the introduction of new forms at a different level, cannot affect it at all; and that is why Tristan has no more killed L'Elisire than Brahms' symphonies have killed Jullien's British Army Quadrilles. But the moment you hear Pagliacci, you feel that it is all up with L'Elisire. It is true that Leoncavallo has shewn as yet nothing comparable to the melodic inspiration of Donizetti; but the advance in serious workmanship, in elaboration of detail, in variety of interest, and in capital expenditure on the orchestra and the stage, is enormous. There is more work in the composition of Cavalleria than in La Favorita, Lucrezia, and Lucia put together, though I cannot think—perhaps this is only my own old-fashionedness—that any part of it will live as long or move the world as much as the best half-dozen numbers in those three obsolete masterpieces.

And when you come to Puccini, the composer of the

latest Manon Lescaut, then indeed the ground is so transformed that you could almost think yourself in a new
country. In Cavalleria and Pagliacci I can find nothing but
Donizettian opera rationalized, condensed, filled in, and
thoroughly brought up to date; but in Manon Lescaut the
domain of Italian opera is enlarged by an annexation of German territory. The first act, which is as gay and effective and
romantic as the opening of any version of Manon need be,
is also unmistakeably symphonic in its treatment. There is
genuine symphonic modification, development and occasionally combination of the thematic material, all in a dramatic way, but also in a musically homogeneous way, so that
the act is really a single movement with episodes instead of
being a succession of separate numbers, linked together, to
conform to the modern fashion, by substituting interrupted
cadences for full closes and parading a Leitmotif occasionally.

Further, the experiments in harmony and syncopation,
reminding one often of the intellectual curiosities which
abound in Schumann's less popular pianoforte works, shew
a strong technical interest which is, in Italian music, a most
refreshing symptom of mental vigor, even when it is not
strictly to the real artistic point. The less studied harmonies
are of the most modern and stimulating kind. When one
thinks of the old school, in which a dominant seventh, or at
most a minor ninth, was the extreme of permissible discord,
only to be tolerated in the harsher inversions when there was
a murder or a ghost on hand, one gets a rousing sense of getting along from hearing young Italy beginning its most
light-hearted melodies to the chord of the thirteenth on the
tonic.

Puccini is particularly fond of this chord; and it may be
taken as a general technical criticism of the young Italian
school that its free use of tonic discords, and its reckless pro-
digality of orchestral resources, give its music a robustness
and variety that reduce the limited tonic and dominant harmonic technique of Donizetti and Bellini, by contrast, to
mere Christy minstrelsy. No doubt this very poverty of the

231

older masters made them so utterly dependent on the invention of tunes that they invented them better than the new men, who, with a good drama to work on, can turn out vigorous, imposing, and even enthralling operas without a bar that is their own in the sense in which Casta Diva is Bellini's own; but Puccini, at least, shews no signs of atrophy of the melodic faculty: he breaks out into catching melodies quite in the vein of Verdi: for example, Tra voi, belle, in the first act of Manon, has all the charm of the tunes beloved by the old operatic guard.

On that and other accounts, Puccini looks to me more like the heir of Verdi than any of his rivals. He has arranged his own libretto from Prevost d'Exiles' novel; and though the miserable end of poor Manon has compelled him to fall back on a rather conventional operatic death scene in which the prima donna at Covent Garden failed to make anyone believe, his third act, with the roll-call of the female convicts and the embarkation, is admirably contrived and carried out: he has served himself in this as well as Scribe ever served Meyerbeer, or Boito Verdi.

If now it is considered that this opening week at Covent Garden began with Manon, and ended with Falstaff; Cavalleria and Pagliacci coming in between, with nothing older than Faust and Carmen to fill up except the immortal Orfeo, it will be understood how I find myself with the startling new idea that Italian opera has a future as well as a past, and that perhaps Sir Augustus Harris, in keeping a house open for it, has not been acting altogether as an enemy of the human race, as I used sometimes to declare in my agony when, in a moment of relenting towards that dreary past, he would let loose some stout matron to disport herself once more as Favorita, or spend untold gold in indulging Jean de Reszke with a revival of that concentrated bore and outrage, Le Prophète, when I wanted to see the prince of tenors and procrastinators as Siegfried or Tristan.

Falstaff drew an enormous house on Saturday, and was received with an enthusiasm which was quite unforced up to

the end of the clothes-basket scene. After that the opera suf-
fered for a while from the play outlasting the freshness of the
subject, a fate that invariably overtakes The Merry Wives
of Windsor, except when the actor who plays Falstaff has
an extraordinary power of inventing humorous and varied
character-traits.

The first scene of the third act was undeniably a little
dull. The merry wives cackled wearisomely; Pessina's comic
stock was exhausted, so that he could do nothing but repeat
the business of the earlier scenes; and Mrs Quickly, who
had been charming for the first ten minutes in the novel character of the youthful and charming Signorina Ravogli, gave
the final blow to the dramatic interest of the scene by not
being her detestable old self.

Fortunately, the excitement revived in the forest scene
at the end, which is full of life and charm. It ends with a sort
of musical practical joke in the shape of a fugue which is
everything that a fugue ought not to be, and which, failing
more rehearsal than it is worth, has to be execrably sung in
order to get the parts picked up. It was listened to with deep
reverence, as if Verdi, in his old age, had clasped hands with
Sebastian Bach. Always excepting the first scene of the third
act, the opera went like wildfire.

Boito's libretto is excellent as far as it is a condensation
of Shakespear, except that he has not appreciated the great
stage effectiveness of Falstaff's description to Ford of his
misadventure in the basket, with its climaxes, dear to old
Shakespearean actors, of "Think of that, Master Brook."
His alterations, notably the screen business in the basket
scene, make some fun; but they also make the scene in Ford's
house quite outrageously impossible. As far as acting is concerned, the weight of the whole opera lies in the scene between
Ford and Falstaff at the Garter Inn; and here Pessina played
with considerable humor and vigor, though without any particular subtlety.

Pini-Corsi's acting was better than operatic acting generally is; but it hardly satisfied those of us who have seen any-

thing like an adequate impersonation of Ford on the English stage. The women were rather unintelligently and monotonously merry; and on the whole the success was, past all question, a success of the musical setting, which is immensely vivacious and interesting. The medieval scenery is attractive, especially the garden and the room in Ford's house. The interior of the inn is not sunny enough: modern painting, with its repudiation of the studio light, and its insistence on work in the open air, has made the traditional stage interior look old-fashioned in this respect.

The company at Covent Garden is a very strong one. The representations of Cavalleria and Pagliacci derive an altogether exceptional dramatic force from the acting of De Lucia and Ancona in parts which are in constant danger of being handed over to a second-rate tenor and baritone. Beduschi, who plays Des Grieux in Manon with success, is another tenor of the Gayarré school, without the goat-bleat and tremolo of its extreme disciples. He is a capable actor, small in figure, with a face which will probably be described as dark and ugly by a good many people, nevertheless by no means an unprepossessing face. Cossira, a tenor of heavier build than Beduschi, made some effect by his passion and sincerity in the love scene in the second act of Carmen. Albers, a baritone, made his first appearances as Valentine in Faust and the Toreador in Carmen. His treatment of Bizet's daintily written scene between José and Escamillo before the fight in the third act gave me an extremely unfavorable impression of the delicacy of his musical sense; but the rougher part of his work was presentably done. Bonnard, a French tenorino, made a satisfactory Philémon in Philémon et Baucis, in which, however, the honors went to Plançon for a splendid appearance as Jupiter.

Philémon brought back Mdlle Simonnet, whose voice is somewhat thicker and richer, especially in the middle, than when she charmed us first in Bruneau's Le Rêve. I am not sure that the same remark does not apply, in a slight degree, to Mdlle Simonnet's figure, though she was certainly as trim and youthful as could be desired as Michaela in Carmen. She also played Marguerite in Faust, of which I saw only the last act and a half. Her Michaela was not good: she slipped through the music in a pointless way, apparently finding the part trivial and uninteresting, and certainly making it so. Her Marguerite—what I saw of it—was clever and pretty, but prosaic. It was only as Baucis that she fully justified the admiration excited by her first performances in this country, though none of her three appearances passed without a burst of applause for some happily sung passage. The leading parts in the two new operas were taken by Olga Olghina, a clever Russian lady with chiselled features and a somewhat courtly fastidiousness of manner, just a little too ladylike for Manon and a little too mundane for Anne Page, but able to make a distinct mark in both by her acting in the embarkation scene of the one opera and her singing in the forest scene of the other. Mdlle Pauline Joran played Siebel and Lola in Cavalleria, the latter cleverly. Of Bauermeister the invaluable, the inevitable, I need not speak; and of Signorine Zilli and Kitzu I shall perhaps speak later on, when my impressions of them are more definite. Of the two great dramatic artists of the company, Giulia Ravogli struck me as suffering from underwork; and as to the incomparable Calvé, at least a week must elapse before I can trust myself to speak of her Carmen and her Santuzza, or, indeed, of herself, with a decent pretence of critical coolness.

The Amsterdam Choir, after a brief spell at St Martin's Hall, is singing this week at Queen's Hall. The expectations I expressed last week have been far surpassed. The choir now consists of twenty-two singers, each of them a singer in a thousand. In England we should set the whole thousand bawling together, and then brag all over Europe about our supremacy in choral music.

Mr Daniel de Lange eliminates the worst nine hundred and ninety-nine from each thousand, and produces with the remainder a choir the fortissimo of which would drown the biggest of our feebly monstrous choral societies, and the pianissimo of which almost embraces perfect silence. I wish I had space to do justice to the extraordinary excellence of their execution and the surpassing interest and beauty of the music, sacred and secular, of Josquin, Orlando, Sweelinck, and the rest of the heroes of the old Netherlandish school.

30 May 1894

WE live in an age of progress. Patti has been singing a song by Wagner. Never shall I forget the sensation among the critics at the Albert Hall when, on turning over the pages of their programs, they saw among the names there that of The Master, cropping up like a modest crocus among those of Mozart, Rossini, and other contemporaries of Madame Patti's grandmother. There is now no denying the fact that Madame Patti—Adelina Patti —*the* Patti—the lady who used to appear and reappear as Rosina in Il Barbiere at Covent Garden until the old régime died of it, actually did, on the afternoon of Saturday, May 19, 1894, sing the study on Tristan und Isolde, No. 5 of the Five Poems composed by Richard Wagner, late of Bayreuth, in 1862. What is more, she sang it extremely well, and, when the inevitable encore came, repeated it instead of singing Home, Sweet Home or Within a Mile.

And yet there was something exasperating in the thought that this demonstration by a fine singer that Wagner's music is as singable as Mozart's came just twenty years after it was most needed. Nobody now supposes that in Wagner's works the women must shriek and the men howl, and that no human voice can stand the wear and tear for more than a year or two. But that was once a very common opinion, most devoutly acted on by many operatic artists, with, of course, fully corroborative results as far as the prophesied wear and tear was concerned. What was Madame Patti doing in those dark days, when she might have rescued Tannhäuser from the horrors of its first performance at Covent Garden in the decline and fall of the seventies? Alas! in those days she sang Bel raggio in the key of A, and did not sing Wagner at all.

It was left to Jean de Reszke, by his Walther in Die Meistersinger, to give the final proof that Wagner requires and repays the most delicate lyrical treatment; and now Madame Patti, with the ground made safe for her, comes forward and, having first propitiated the first quarter of the expiring century by singing Bel raggio in the key of G, at last ventures on this simple little Träume, and is perhaps surprised to find that the thrill is deeper and the applause more sincere than that which follows Rossini's shallow bravura. For my part, I regard Patti's brilliancy as a singer of florid decorative music as one of her greatest misfortunes. In the first place, she has never done it superlatively well: it has always been a little jerky and tricky in comparison with the finest execution of such a perfect singer of roulade as Marimon, for instance, not to mention others.

I never fully appreciated Patti until one night at Covent Garden when I heard her sing, not Una Voce or anything of that sort, but God save the Queen. The wonderful even soundness of the middle of her voice, its beauty and delicacy of surface, and her exquisite touch and diction, all qualify her to be great in expressive melody, and to occupy a position in the republic of art high above the pretty flummery of newspaper puffs, flowers, recalls, encores, and so forth which makes it so difficult for people who take art seriously to do justice to the talent and the artistic pains with which she condescends to bid for such recognition.

I am so far from regretting that Time has stolen some of the five or six notes above the high B flat which she once possessed, and has made the rest hardly safe for everyday use, that I shall heartily congratulate her when the day comes when Bel raggio and Ah, non giunge, in any key whatsoever, must be dropped, and replaced in her repertory by more such songs as Träume; for it is my firm belief that Patti is capable of becoming a great singer, though the world has been at such pains and expense to spoil her for the last thirty-five years. At her concert on the 19th, her voice was better than at last year's concerts; and altogether she

237

was brighter, more efficient, more successful—if there can be said to be degrees in Patti's success—than when I last heard her.

The difference between the old order in opera and the new suggests to my imagination such a vast period of time, that it seems odd to me that I should have witnessed Patti's latest triumph on the morrow of Calvé's appearance at Covent Garden as Carmen. It is only fair that I should warn the public against attaching too much importance to anything I may say about Madame Calvé. As I have often explained, it is one of the conditions of that high susceptibility which is my chief qualification as a critic, that good or bad art becomes a personal matter between me and the artist.

I *hate* performers who debase great works of art: I long for their annihilation: if my criticisms were flaming thunderbolts, no prudent Life or Fire Insurance Company would entertain a proposal from any singer within my range, or from the lessee of any opera-house or concert-room within my circuit. But I am necessarily no less extreme in my admiration of artists who realize the full value of great works for me, or who transfigure ordinary ones. Calvé is such an artist; and she is also a woman whose strange personal appearance recalls Titian's wonderful Virgin of the Assumption at Venice, and who has, in addition to that beauty of aspect, a beauty of action—especially of that sort of action which is the thought or conception of the artist made visible—such as one might expect from Titian's Virgin if the picture were made alive. This description will perhaps sufficiently shew the need for a little discount off such eulogies as I may presently be moved to in speaking of her performances in detail.

But I have no eulogies for her Carmen, which shocked me beyond measure. I pointed out on a previous occasion, when dealing with a very remarkable impersonation of that character by Giulia Ravogli, that the success of Bizet's opera is altogether due to the attraction, such as it is, of seeing a pretty and respectable middle-class young lady, expensively dressed, harmlessly pretending to be a wicked person, and that anything like a successful attempt to play the part realistically by a powerful actress must not only at once betray the thinness and unreality of Prosper Merimée's romance, but must leave anything but a pleasant taste on the palate of the audience. This was proved by the fact that Giulia Ravogli's Carmen, the most powerful that had then been seen in England, was received with a good deal of grumbling, and was shelved to make way for that pretty little imposition, the Carmen of Miss De Lussan, who was, as everybody could see, a perfect young lady innocently playing at being naughty.

And yet Giulia Ravogli flattered Carmen by exhibiting her as a woman of courage and strength of character. Calvé makes no such concession. Her Carmen is a superstitious, pleasure-loving good-for-nothing, caught by the outside of anything glittering, with no power but the power of seduction, which she exercises without sense or decency. There is no suggestion of any fine quality about her, not a spark of honesty, courage, or even of the sort of honor supposed to prevail among thieves. All this is conveyed by Calvé with a positively frightful artistic power of divesting her beauty and grace of the nobility—I had almost written the sanctity —which seems inseparable from them in other parts. Nobody else dare venture on the indescribable allurements which she practises on the officers in the first act, or such touches as the attempt to get a comprehensive view of her figure in Lillas Pastia's rather small looking-glass, or her jealously critical inspection of Micaela from the same point of view in the third act.

Her death-scene, too, is horribly real. The young-lady Carmen is never so effectively alive as when she falls, stage dead, beneath José's cruel knife. But to see Calvé's Carmen changing from a live creature, with properly coordinated movements, into a reeling, staggering, flopping, disorganized thing, and finally tumble down a mere heap of carrion, is to get much the same sensation as might be given by the reality of a brutal murder. It is perhaps just as well that a great artist should, once in a way, give our opera goers a glimpse of the truth about the things they play with so light-heartedly. In spite of the applause and the curtain calls, it was quite evident that the audience was by no means as comfortable after the performance as Miss de Lussan would have left them.

But nothing would induce me to go again. To me it was a desecration of a great talent. I felt furious with Calvé, as if I had been shewn some terrible caricature by Hogarth of the Titian. That, however, may have been a personal sentiment. What I am perfectly sure was a legitimate critical sentiment was my objection to Carmen carrying her abandonment to the point of being incapable of paying the smallest attention to the score. I have never seen, at Bayreuth or anywhere else, an operatic actress fit her action more perfectly and punctually to its indication in the orchestra than Giulia Ravogli did as Carmen. And I have never seen, even at Covent Garden, the same artistic duty so completely disregarded as it was by Calvé. She acted out of time the whole evening; and I do not see why artists should act out of time any more than sing out of time.

I go back with relief from Carmen to Cavalleria, in which her Santuzza was irresistibly moving and beautiful, and fully capable of sustaining the inevitable comparison with Duse's impersonation of the same part.

But Duse makes the play more credible, not because an opera is less credible than a spoken play—for though that can be proved logically, the facts are just the other way, the superior intensity of musical expression making the opera far more real than the play—but because Duse makes the woman not only intensely pitiable, but hopelessly unattractive, so that Turiddu's preference for Lola seems natural, whereas in the opera his desertion of Calvé is not to be tolerated as the act of a sane man: one cannot take any interest in such an ass.

The desolating Arctic wind which parched the liver of

London last week swept blightingly through the ranks of Mottl's band at his second concert, and laid the program waste. Himself in something less than his highest spirits, he nevertheless made a brave effort to rally his prostrated forces. But he got nothing like the response they made to him at the previous concert. The effect of this general indisposition was unfortunately emphasized by the change from Wagner to Berlioz and Beethoven. Beethoven did not know how to get his effects with the orchestra as Wagner did: some of the most powerful traits in his musical designs are disappointing in orchestral execution. Berlioz, of whom this cannot be said, is a Frenchman; and though Mottl's freedom from anything like German heaviness makes him as good a Berlioz conductor as it is in the nature of any German who lives and works in his own country to be, yet he simply sent me asleep with the extracts from Roméo et Juliette; for his fine reflective handling took all the passion and pathos out of Romeo's brainless reveries, and his splendid self-possession equally took all the brimstone out of the dance music, which makes but a poor show in the vein of Die Meistersinger. With all these deductions, and the slackness of the band, the hateful wind, and the somewhat injudicious order and excessive length of the program into the bargain, Mottl made a strong impression on those who had not been present at his first appearance as a conductor in England; and I have nothing to retract or modify in the opinion I then expressed of his ability.

6 June 1894

AFTER the freshness of the opera season, come in inevitable course the stalenesses of it. I sat out Les Huguenots the other evening; and I cannot quite pass it over without asking whether something cannot be done to recover the original flavor of what is, after all, an interesting and effective piece of stage work. Would it not be possible for the chorus and Bevignani to be born again with certain modifications, and for someone to compile Tales from Meyerbeer in the style of Lamb's Tales from Shakespear, and make a present of a copy to the stage manager? I am a person of strong economic instincts, cultivated by circumstances as well as by study; and when I calculate the appalling sum it must cost to send the curtain up at Covent Garden, it infuriates me to see the minimum instead of the maximum of value given to the manager and the public for all that gigantic expenditure.

Nobody who does not know the score can have any idea of the mutilated state of the work as performed at Covent Garden, or how completely obsolete is the phase of public taste which influenced the mutilators in their choice of cuts. A couple of years ago Maurel restored a page in the first act for the sake of a bravura passage which he wanted to sing. This year Plançon has done the same in the third act in order to get one more turn at his chorale. Nothing is gained by this, except to make the original cut rather more ridiculous than it was before; and, to counterbalance it, there is a new cut in the first act, from the beginning of the scene where Nevers and the rest begin to vie with one another in flattering Raoul, up to the exclamation "Tous," which is the cue for the last movement of the finale.

The third act is too silly for description. The duel in which, after the most heroic preliminaries, the parties no sooner cross swords than they bolt, every man of them, without any apparent reason except their conviction that he who fights and runs away may live to fight another day, is only an example of the insensate way in which the work was cut fifty years ago; but even in the earlier parts of the act, which stand much as they were written, all pretence of knowing or caring what the scene is about has been dropped by everyone except the principals. When the Catholics remonstrate with Marcel for not taking off his hat during the Ave Maria, they keep their own hats tightly on; and though, for once in a way, the Huguenot soldiers who back Marcel did not last Thursday take their helmets off or kneel down, I can only regard that as a lazy neglect on their parts of what they doubtless still believe to be their duty.

The whole stage business of the act is like blindman's buff from beginning to end, the crowd caring for nothing but to get out of the way of the principals; and the choral singing matches it exactly. Just as a railway porter who has been told to call out the name of his station soon allows the words he pronounces to muddle themselves away into a cry which conveys no import and renders no service to any human traveller, so, at Covent Garden, the choristers have come in the course of long years to gabble over something that was once the Rataplan Chorus or the Vesper Hymn, but which is now nothing but a public indulgence of an intolerably slovenly habit. I cannot understand why Sir Augustus Harris allows himself to be so badly served in these matters as he is.

I am quite well aware of the impossibility of rehearsing every opera adequately; and though it is my business as a critic to put all that aside and proceed on the plain assumption that things that cannot be done reasonably well should not be done at all, I am nevertheless anxious to make every possible allowance for the difficulties of the situation. But I will only do so on condition that the difficulties are struggled with to the utmost. The moment they are made an excuse for letting things slide, then all tolerance is out of the question. If the supreme authority is goodnatured enough to accept from his stage manager and conductor an assurance that the third act of Les Huguenots cannot be done any better than that under the circumstances, then I am not; and if Sir Augustus, as impresario, will not make himself unpleasant, I, as critic, will. Rehearsal or no rehearsal, I expect at Covent Garden to see the stage full of people who are punctual, alert, in earnest, under the eye of a conductor who is not to be trifled with.

If we cannot have, at what professes to be the leading opera house in Europe, a great conductor, before whom everyone will be ashamed not to do his or her best, let us at least have a martinet before whom they will be afraid to risk

a mistake. There are few persons whom I have less desire to
see alive again than Costa; but there are moments when
Bevignani makes me miss him. I do not wish to do Bevignani an injustice: I admire the obligingness and adroitness
with which he accompanies the principal singers through all
their extremely *ad libitum* readings, and the determination
and briskness with which he thwacks the choruses along so
as to get the opera over early and leave plenty of time for
very long waits between the acts, so that the critics may have
ample opportunities for saying to one another in the foyer
what they never say to the public in print.

The more *blasé* I grow the more the performance of an
opera becomes to me a piece of routine which has to be got
through somehow every night in the season with as little
friction as possible, the more do I feel inclined to stand by
Bevignani. But sometimes the thought will come unbidden
that I have heard Richter conduct Die Meistersinger, Mottl
Tristan, and Faccio Otello; and that not only was the music
much more effective, but the whole character of the performance, from the attitudes and tone of the chorus down to
the frequency with which they were willing to shave, changed
under the eye of these strong men. In short, to be quite
frank, though I appreciate the way in which the Covent
Garden conductors pull things through under difficulties,
none of them is such a Napoleon of the orchestra as is
needed to establish himself as ruler by divine right in the
prevailing anarchy of a London opera-house.

Pending the re-cutting and consequent re-rehearsal of
Les Huguenots, I need only record what is necessary of the
performance last week. The Valentina was a Mdlle Adini, a
tall, powerfully built lady with a serviceable high C, and
plenty of feeling of a not uncommon kind, but without invention as an actress, even in the matter of stage business.
Cossira has not the range for Raoul—who has? Instead of
transposing the duel septuor, and driving the basses into
their boots as De Reszke does, he sang it in the original key
and replaced the C sharp by a B natural. I cannot say that it

244

did as well; but it was the frankest and wisest thing to do under the circumstances. He sang the duet with the queen very well. Plançon carried off the honors of the performance for his Marcel, which, as he happens to have that first important requisite for the part, a true bass voice, was a relief after the attempts of Edouard de Reszke to squeeze it into the compass of a somewhat limited basso cantante.

Mdlle Olitska, who played Urbain, should have omitted the song in the second act, since she was unable to execute the volley of little runs down half the scale, which are a leading feature in it. She is a clever and ambitious artist; but her method, artificially throaty and naturally rather nasal, runs counter to my prejudices as to what is desirable in vocal tone. Mdlle Adini did not make any serious pretence of giving us the double chromatic scale in the duet with Raoul; but nobody seems to mind these little licences nowadays; and indeed I cannot say that I think an artist should be disqualified from attempting a part like Valentina merely by the difficulties of a trait of this sort. The Nevers of Albers was a great improvement on his bullfighter in Carmen.

On Saturday last we had Faust, with Melba as Margaret. De Lucia accosted her in the second act in Italian; she snubbed him in French; Bauermeister kept her in countenance by conversing with her in French in the garden; and Mephistopheles, at home in all countries, tempted Faust in Italian and Marta in French. And, to give the devil his due, his French was the best in the collection: Margaret's, in particular, being occasionally rather like mine. De Lucia's dramatic instinct helped him well through a part in which he seemed likely to be overweighted. Several times in the garden scene he found the right musical treatment with exceptional success.

Ancona's Valentine is the best we have had for a long time. His Dio Possente, sung in the original key with great expression and with a magnificent high G, was one of the features of the representation. But he should go over the part with the book some morning; for he has forgotten the exact notation of one or two passages. I am not, of course, alluding to his intentional taking of the first line of the *reprise* in Dio Possente right up the scale to the high E flat. Melba, with her unspoiled, beautiful voice, and, above all, her perfect intonation—you never realize how wide a gap there is between the ordinary singer who simply avoids the fault of singing obviously out of tune and the singer who sings really and truly in tune, except when Melba is singing—received boundless welcome, and, with the usual mysterious luck of American and colonial prima donnas, received flowers across the footlights in those large baskets which English ladies and gentlemen invariably carry with them in the theatre, and which they present to singers in moments of uncontrollable admiration. Melba has commanded Sir Augustus to put on that favorite Donizettian *chef-d'œuvre* Lucia di Lammermoor, for the better display of her roulades; and Sir Augustus has gallantly consented. Having heard the work rather frequently in the course of my early career, I do not look forward to the occasion with much curiosity.

The second Patti concert at the Albert Hall ended with a recital of a "lyric drama, in one act, entitled Gabriella, specially composed for, and dedicated to, Madame Adelina Patti, by Emilio Pizzi." I came rather late: in fact, if the honest truth must be told, I did not get to the Albert Hall until a quarter of an hour before the close of the concert, by which time all the characters were in their death agonies, struggling with a tempestuous orchestration, and uttering ejaculations like "Madre infelice," "alla morte," "Ohime! perduto," and so on. There was nothing whatever to take exception to in what I heard of the music. Of the tenor, Mr Robert Kaufmann, I must say a word. This gentleman made his first appearance here lately at a concert which was declared by some high musical authorities to be England's absolutely finest musical achievement, and by others, including myself, to be one of the severest afflictions of the century. I did not hear Mr Kaufmann again until he sang the other day at Mdlle Kleeberg's pianoforte recital at St James's Hall, when he proved himself a singer of exceptionally fine artistic sensibility and intelligence, doing a great deal with a by no means extraordinary voice. On this occasion Miss Kleeberg who, if not so perfectly neat and even-handed as she used to be, has gained in freedom of expression, began solemnly by playing Beethoven, that being the proper thing to do in St James's Hall. I bore it like a man, and even enjoyed one variation in the sonata Op. 110, which gave Mdlle Kleeberg an opportunity in the style of playing in which she excels. I have also heard M. Sevadjian, in appearance at least a pianist to the last few inches of his hair. His reading of Beethoven's Funeral March sonata was entirely original; but it did not carry conviction to me as the reading intended by the composer. M. Sevadjian, too, though an accurate player, has a peculiar way of scrutinizing the keyboard as if he did not quite know where he would find the note he wanted, which gives him an odd resemblance to a person trying to write a word on a typewriter for the first time. These peculiarities of manner perhaps handicapped him a little unfairly with the audience. My apologies to the givers of many other concerts and recitals, notice of which must stand over for the present.

13 June 1894

DR VILLIERS STANFORD has been favoring us with his views on Some Aspects of Musical Criticism in England in the shape of a magazine article. I am very strongly tempted to quote it here at full length; for it is the best article I ever saw on the subject, unexceptionally judicious and accurate, and much better written than most musical criticisms are. I shall at least quote his exposition of his main point, as I cannot paraphrase it to any advantage:

"A new opera, which has been, perhaps, the work of years, and the outcome of the daily thought and labor of composer and librettist, is produced on a Monday night; and by 2 A.M. on Tuesday morning a critic, who has just made his first acquaintance with the composition, is expected to have completed a full and just chronicle of its merits and

247

faults, its workmanship and its effect, fit to be put into print, and intended to instruct the public before breakfast as to what attitude they should be prepared to take when they find themselves in the audience. I say, as one who is, from much experience in the musician's craft, perhaps exceptionally quick in seizing the points of a new work at first hearing, that to expect the best possible criticism, or indeed criticism of any lasting value at all under such circumstances is grotesque; and the insistence upon such hot haste production is a hardship to the writer, an injury to the producer, and a mischief to the public."

True as this is, and deeply as I am touched by the tribute here implied, and elsewhere explicitly rendered, to the superiority of those weekly articles of which my own may be taken as examples, I am not sure that the opinion elaborated in a week is always so much more valuable than the impression made in a moment. The only musical compositions which will bear thinking of for more than half an hour are those which require an intimate acquaintance of at least ten years for their critical mastery. As to the weekly article being any more "just" than the daily one, I do not see how that can be sustained for a moment. Let us try to vivify our ideas on the subject by getting away from the abstraction "criticism" to the reality from which it is abstracted: that is, the living, breathing, erring, human, nameable and addressable individual who writes criticism.

To avoid getting into trouble I shall not cite any musical critics. The dramatic and parliamentary ones will serve my turn as well. Two of the best dramatic critics in London, Mr Clement Scott and Mr Walkley, write both weekly essays and two-o'clock-in-the-morning notices of new plays. Both write the immediate notice as impressionists. Mr Scott writes his deferred notice also as an impressionist, rubbing in his first impression, and as often as not spoiling it. Mr Walkley is an acute analyst; and in his case the gain in intellectual elaboration in the deferred notice is immense. But has anyone ever observed any gain in either case in the matter of justice? I certainly never have.

Take another case in point. I have for years urged upon editors the necessity of sending a fine critic into the House of Commons to write notices of the sittings of the House exactly as they send a critic to the Opera. The result of giving such a critic a brief for Lord Rosebery against Lord Salisbury is as absurd as it would be to give me a brief for Calvé as against Melba, or my colleague W. A. a brief for Mr Irving as against Mr Tree. Of late years the custom of prefacing the verbatim reports of the sittings of the House by a descriptive report has been developing parliamentary criticism on my lines.

For example, Mr Massingham, a typical parliamentary critic of the new kind, will, in criticizing a debate, praise the performances of Mr Balfour and Mr John Burns, and slate Sir William Harcourt and Mr Chamberlain, or vice versa, as if there were no such thing as party politics in the world. This sounds impartial; but does anybody find Mr Massingham "just"; or is it likely that he would be any the juster if his extraordinary small-hour performances were replaced by weekly ones? The fact is, justice is not the critic's business; and there is no more dishonest and insufferable affectation in criticism than that impersonal, abstract, judicially authoritative air which, since it is so easy to assume, and so well adapted to rapid phrase stringing, is directly encouraged by the haste which Dr Stanford deprecates.

In Dr Stanford's article, which is a masterpiece in the way of tact, no individual critic now alive and working on the English press is talked either of or at. Instead, we have "the critic," "the musical correspondent," and so on. Now "the critic" is a very fine character. One can quite believe that if only the noble creature is given time to consider his utterances, he will hold the scales balanced to a hair's breadth. But just substitute for "the critic" the initials G. B. S. Instantly the realities of the case leap to light; and you see without any argument that the lapse of a few days between the performance and the notice, far from obliterating the writer's partialities and prejudices, his personal likes and dislikes, his bias, his temperament, his local traditions, his nationality —in a word, himself, only enables him to express them the more insidiously when he wishes to conceal their influence.

No man sensitive enough to be worth his salt as a critic could for years wield a pen which, from the nature of his occupation, is scratching somebody's nerves at every stroke, without becoming conscious of how monstrously indefensible the superhuman attitude of impartiality is for him. If the countless injustices which I have done in these columns had been perpetrated in that attitude I should deserve hanging. I therefore add to Dr Stanford's plea for the more considerate utterance of the weekly feuilleton, a further plea for sincerity of expression, not only of the critic's opinion, but of the mood in which that opinion was formed.

We cannot get away from the critic's tempers, his impatiences, his sorenesses, his friendships, his spite, his enthusiasms (amatory and other), nay, his very politics and religion if they are touched by what he criticizes. They are all there hard at work; and it should be his point of honor—as it is certainly his interest if he wishes to avoid being dull—not to attempt to conceal them or to offer their product as the dispassionate dictum of infallible omniscience. If the public were to receive such a self exhibition by coldly saying, "We dont want to know the sort of person you are: we want to know whether such a work or artist or performance is good or bad," then the critic could unanswerably retort, "How on earth can you tell how much my opinion on that point is worth unless you know the sort of person I am?" As a matter of fact the public never does meet a good critic with any such rebuff. The critic who cannot interest the public in his real self has mistaken his trade: that is all.

Dr Stanford touches a painful point when he speaks of "the danger that editors who happen themselves to be ignorant of music, should engage the services of writers almost equally ignorant merely because they possess the gift of literary style." Here, for almost the only moment in his article,

Dr Stanford speaks without inside knowledge of journalism. Editors, by some law of Nature which still baffles science, are *always* ignorant of music, and consequently always abjectly superstitious on the subject. Instead of looking the more keenly to the critic's other qualifications because they cannot judge of his musical ones, they regard him with an awe which makes them incapable of exercising any judgment at all about him.

Find me an editor who can tell at a glance whether a review, a leading article, a London letter, or a news paragraph is the work of a skilled hand or not, and who has even some power of recognizing what is money's worth and what is not in the way of a criticism of the Royal Academy or the last new play; and I, by simply writing that "the second subject, a graceful and flowing theme contrasting happily with the rugged vigor of its predecessor, appears unexpectedly in the key of the dominant," will reduce that able editor to a condition so abject that he will let me inundate his columns with pompous platitude, with the dullest plagiarisms from analytic programs, with shameless puffery, with bad grammar, bad logic, wrong dates, wrong names, with every conceivable blunder and misdemeanor that a journalist can commit, provided I do it in the capacity of his musical critic.

Not that my stuff will not bore and worry him as much as it will bore and worry other people; but what with his reluctance to risk a dispute with me on a subject he does not understand, and his habit of considering music as a department of lunacy, practised and read about by people who are not normally sane and healthy human beings, he will find it easiest to "suppose it is all right" and to console himself with the reflection that it does not matter anyhow. Dr Stanford says, "If editors appoint an incompetent person, public opinion is pretty sure, sooner or later, to find out and expose the ignoramus." This expectation is so entirely and desperately unwarranted by experience, that I may take it that Dr Stanford only offers it rather than leave the difficulty without at least a pretense of a solution.

But why not form a Vigilance Committee of musicians for the exposure of incompetent critics? The other day, as we all remember, five eminent musicians published a protest against a certain musical critic. Being new to their work, they did not do it well; and the critic got the best of it; but I sincerely hope the five will not be discouraged. After a few trials, a Vigilance Committee would learn to attack cautiously and effectively, and to avoid the professional weakness of exaggerating the importance of those blunders as to historic facts and musical technicalities which sometimes give a ludicrous air to really shrewd and essentially sound criticism.

Musical criticisms, like sermons, are of low average quality simply because they are never discussed or contradicted; and I should rejoice were such a committee to be formed, especially if Dr Stanford were to be chairman, and would undertake the drafting of such public protests as it might be deemed advisable to issue.

The Philharmonic orchestra has been distinguishing itself at the last two concerts in the hands of Grieg and Saint-Saëns. Grieg is so successful in getting fine work out of the band that if the directors were wise they would make him a handsome offer to take it in hand permanently.

Saint-Saëns also persuaded it to give him a very smooth and fine-drawn performance of his symphony for orchestra with pianoforte and organ, a model of elegant instrumentation, in which the effect of the adoption of what I may call the Lohengrin orchestra, with three wood wind instruments of each kind instead of two, is to my ear conclusive as to the advisability of its general employment in symphony. It is a pity that this particular work of Saint-Saëns degenerates so frightfully at the end. All that barren coda stuff, with its mechanical piling of instruments, its whipping of rhythms, and its ridiculous scraps of fugato, should be ruthlessly excised: it has no real theme, and only spoils the rest. Grieg's suite of entr'actes and incidental music is, for a composer of his pretension, trumpery stuff enough, except for a fanciful and delicate movement for muted violins pianissimo, with

252

starts and shudders on the drum, representing somebody's uneasy dreams. Whether Grieg was clever enough to get all the rehearsal to himself I do not know; but a rather abject performance of Beethoven's eighth symphony suggested that he had not left much time to Dr Mackenzie, who, by the way, was exceptionally successful with Wagner's Faust overture at the next concert.

Mr Ben Davies self-sacrificingly added his name to the long list of tenors who have failed in Beethoven's Adelaida, which is virtually a sonatina for tenor voice, and should be treated accordingly. This was rather a drop after the clever singing of Mdlle Landi on the previous occasion.

Mr Bispham's Schumann concert last week was so prodigiously successful that I had to retreat unwillingly into the fresh air before it was quite over. Mr Bispham's artistic judgment served him well in his choice of Mrs Henschel and Miss Marguerite Hall as colleagues no less than in his own fine singing, which is getting almost too gentle in its touch for large popular audiences, and will probably be all the better for the greater sharpness of definition and vigor of stroke which Drury Lane will demand from him in the forthcoming German Opera season there.

Mr Henry Bird, in the very important position of Schumann accompanist, divided the honors with the singers, his only failure being in the scene from Faust, which requires a broad orchestral handling altogether different from that of the songs. However, I rejoice to find Mr Bispham turning his attention to this undeservedly neglected piece of Schumann's work; and I take the opportunity to repeat my old suggestion that he should be invited by the Philharmonic or Crystal Palace directors, or by Richter or Mottl, to take part in a performance of the whole of the middle section of the work, from the sunrise scene to the death of Faust.

20 *June* 1894

WHOEVER has not seen Miss Eames as Charlotte has not realized the full force of Thackeray's picture of the young lady who, when she saw the remains of her lover

> Borne before her on a shutter,
> Like a well-conducted person,
> Went on cutting bread-and-butter.

I never saw such a well-conducted person as Miss Eames. She casts her propriety like a Sunday frock over the whole stage, and gives Mr Steadman's choir-boys, as she cuts the bread-and-butter for them, a soapy nosed, plastery haired, respectable-aged-mothered appearance which they totally lack in Carmen under the influence of Calvé. Like Goldsmith's hero in She Stoops to Conquer, I am ill at ease in the company of ladylike women; and during the first act of Werther at Covent Garden I grew shyer and more awkward in my stall, until, upon Charlotte informing Werther that she was another's, I felt ready to sink into the earth with confusion. In the third act, when Werther, breaking down under the strain of a whole year's unintermitted well-behavedness, desperately resolved to have a kiss, and to that end offered the young lady violence, the whole audience shared the chills with which he was visibly struggling. Never, since Miss Mary Anderson shed a cold radiance on the rebuked stage, have virtue and comeliness seemed more awful than they do at Covent Garden on Werther nights. How I envy Miss Eames her self-possession, her quiet consciousness of being founded on a rock, her good looks (oh, those calmly regular eyebrows!), and, above all, that splendid middle to her voice, enabling her to fill the huge theatre without an effort!

Werther is a more congenial subject for Massenet than even Manon was. When he gets away from the artificial and rhetorical into the regions of candid sentiment and the childlike sincerities of love and grief he is charming. Des Grieux, a hero whom we forgive even for cheating at cards, suited him well: Werther suits him still better. The surroundings suit him too. The constant hum and murmur of the country evening, and the pleasant noisiness of the children when they are not rehearsing their carol or munching the bread-and-butter, make the first act quite delightful to a jaded critic sitting in a well-situated and comfortable stall.

In the rococo of the following scenes the modishness is made interesting by a certain frank naturalness which never deserts Massenet as long as he is treating subjects that give it a chance—that is, as long as he steers clear of the traditions of Parisian grand opera. On his own ground he has an engaging force and charm of expression; and though he is not exactly a creator in harmony or orchestration, yet in both he has a lively individual style. At all events, he has succeeded in keeping up the interest of a libretto consisting of four acts of a lovelorn tenor who has only two active moments, one when he tries to ravish a kiss from the fair as aforesaid, and the other when he shoots himself behind the scenes.

Naturally, the success of the work in performance depends a great deal on the artist who plays Werther; and Massenet is certainly fortunate in Jean de Reszke, whose performances as Werther and Romeo last week were masterly. His grip of these two parts is now extraordinarily firm and intimate: he is in the heart of them from the first note to the last. Not a tone nor gesture has a touch of anything common or cheap in it: the parts are elaborately studied and the execution sensitively beautiful throughout, the result, aided by his natural grace and distinction, being in both operas an impersonation not only unflaggingly interesting, but exquisitely attractive. His voice leaves nothing to be desired: at the beginning of the evening there is the slightest possible fur on the first two or three notes; but it wears off at once, and leaves him in the most confident possession of all his forces.

In Werther there are several formidable declamatory

passages, accompanied by the full power of the orchestra. He attacks these with triumphant force, and next moment is singing quietly with his voice as unstrained, as responsive, as rich in quality as if it had been wrapped in cotton wool for a week, instead of clashing against Massenet's most strenuous orchestration with a vehemence that would put most tenors practically *hors de combat* for several minutes. He seems to me to be at the height of his physical powers, and at the same time to have perfected his artistic integrity, if I may so express myself, my meaning being that he is now magnificently in earnest about his work and undivided in his attention to it.

The effect of this on his colleagues is excellent: Melba especially surpasses herself when playing with him. I must admit reluctantly that these performances of Werther and Romeo seem sure of a place in the front rank of my operatic recollections. I say reluctantly, because, after all, Romeo is *vieux jeu* and Werther is hardly to be counted a great part; therefore it still rankles in me that we have to send for Herr Alvary to play Tristan and Siegfried.

Edouard de Reszke made his re-entry for the season as Frère Laurent. In that matter of artistic integrity he lags behind his brother. The old Adam is strong within him, and tempts him to bawl occasionally. When he yields, he invariably adds an apologetic attempt at a piano passage, which gets out of tune from the after-effects of the bawling, and leaves him abashed. When he sings with a dignified reticence, content with the normal strength of his abnormally powerful voice, he is hugely satisfying from the musical, if not from the severely intellectual, point of view. Bonnard was not precisely the man for Tybalt, a part which requires before all things a swordsman.

If Jean de Reszke had gone for him as he used to go for the condescending Montariol, he would infallibly have stained the Covent Garden boards with his gore. On the whole, the duels were made failures by the extreme caution needed to prevent their becoming mortally realistic suc-

256

cesses. Miss Lucile Hill, who ought to have played Romeo's page very well, missed her chance, apparently for want of a few hours' scale practice. Her voice was in very indifferent order; her French diction was hardly presentable after De Reszke's; and the effect of certain passages—for instance, the skip of an octave in Que fais-tu—was quite unworthy of her former performances. She got through the part on the strength of her appearance and reputation, instead of doing justice to it. I invite her to retrieve this shortcoming: she can do it easily enough if she likes. Of Albers as Mercutio I cannot speak, as I was prevented by a concert from hearing the first act.

In Rigoletto the final duet was restored. As far as I know, it has never been done on the stage since its excision immediately after the opera was first produced. Its orchestration is celestially pretty, so much so, that as I have not a full score within my reach, I will not undertake to swear that it has not been touched up by Mancinelli, or someone with all the latest discoveries at his fingers' ends.

Ancona's Rigoletto was a disappointment. Considering that he has shewn considerable dramatic feeling, and that he has exactly the voice for which the part was written— that is, a rich baritone of such range as to enable him not only to sing with ease up to G, but to keep singing for pages together above the bass stave, as if that were the middle of his voice—great things were expected of him; and I am almost compelled to admire the ingenuity with which he avoided doing them.

In all the less important moments he was tremendous, or looked as if he was going to be; but when the crises arrived, and one expected those terrible explosions of ferocity or paroxysms of abasement which are the great opportunities of the part, he somehow slipped round them with an entirely gentlemanlike aversion to anything like making a scene.

He sang the music with consummate ease, always excepting his consistent failure from beginning to end to seize and strike the right dramatic accent; but after Maurel, who

257

only gets through the music by an occasionally almost painful exercise of vocal ingenuity, he made no mark; and the honors of the performance went to Giulia Ravogli for a very clever piece of playing as Maddalena; to De Lucia, who, over-parted as he was, got through with the Duke's music adroitly and pluckily; and, of course, to Melba, whose acting, if conventional, was earnest and careful, and whose long shake at her exit after Caro nome was as beautiful as ever.

Monterone was impersonated by that versatile artist De Vaschetti, who has played, since the season commenced, more parts than most of the leading artists have ventured upon in all their lives. Innkeeper, nobleman, courtier, ghost, bandit, soldier, statesman, chemist, buffoon: nothing comes amiss to De Vaschetti, whose brazen voice rings throughout all operas, and whose old weakness for singing the most unexpected and startling wrong notes—he once, as the statue in Don Giovanni, planted one of these unearthly intervals on me with such deadly effect that, before I could think, I had bounded out of my stall with a shriek, to the great terror of my neighbors—has now yielded to experience and, presumably, study. He has gained a firm hold on the affection of the subscribers, and will, I doubt not, flourish usefully at the Royal Italian Opera for the next thirty or forty years, outliving as many reputations as that veteran tenor Rinaldini.

I am glad that Mr Leonard Borwick's recital on Tuesday last week gave me an opportunity of renewing the regard for him as a pianist which has of late been almost destroyed by the frequency with which I have come upon him when he has been dealing with Beethoven. He cannot play Beethoven: his attempts to sentimentalize and prettify that virile master's work are quite beyond my patience. But his playing of Chopin's sonata in B flat minor is really worth hearing, and was deservedly received with enthusiasm. In Mendelssohn's fine prelude and foolish fugue in E minor, Saint-Saëns' Alceste caprice, and some pieces by Schumann, he gave the concourse of young ladies who filled St James's Hall further excellent value for their money. The Don Juan fantasia he had better, perhaps, have let alone.

At Mr Isidor Cohn's recital a trio by Dvořák in E minor, called Dumky for some reason, was played for the first time by Mr Cohn, Mr Whitehouse, and Lady Hallé. What I heard of it—I missed the first movement—was mere rhapsody, with more or less pretence of sonata form about it, pretty enough, but not getting much higher than that. Miss Lydia Müller sang some German songs very competently.

27 June 1894

ON Wednesday last week, at about half-past ten at night or thereabout, the inhabitants of Covent Garden and the neighborhood were startled by a most tremendous cannonade. It was the beginning of La Navarraise; and it did heavy execution among the ladies and gentlemen who cultivate their nerves on tea and alcohol. As one who has relieved the serious work of musical criticism by the amusement of dramatic authorship, I can testify to the great difficulty of getting artillery and musketry fire of really good tone for stage purposes; and I can compliment Sir Augustus Harris unreservedly on the thundering amplitude of sound and vigorous attack of his almost smokeless explosives.

They gave the piece a magnificent send-off: Calvé had no need to shake a ladder behind the scenes, according to the old receipt, in order "to strike twelve at once"; for before the curtain had been up thirty seconds, during which little more than half a ton of gunpowder can have been consumed, she was a living volcano, wild with anxiety, to be presently mad with joy, ecstatic with love, desperate with disappointment, and so on in ever culminating transitions through mortification, despair, fury, terror, and finally— the mainspring breaking at the worst of the strain—silly maniacal laughter. The opera, which lasts less than an hour, went like lightning; and when the curtain came down there

was something like a riot both on the stage and off. All sorts
of ridiculous incidents crowded upon one another. Plançon,
fetching bouquets for Calvé, turned to present them to her
with stately courtesy, and found himself bowing elaborately
to the curtain, which had just descended behind him and cut
him off from the main body of the stage army. When it went
up—and stayed up, there being no prospect of the applause
stopping—it became evident that Massenet was bashfully
concealed in the wing. Calvé rushed off to fetch him, but
returned empty-handed, breathless, and conveying to the
audience by speaking gestures that the composer had wres-
tled with her victoriously. Then the stalls, forgetting the de-
corum proper to indispensable evening dress, positively
yelled for Massenet. Calvé made another attempt, and again
returned defeated. The tumult thereupon redoubled; and
she, resolving in her desperation to have somebody out,
made a fresh plunge, and came up with Flon of Brussels, the
conductor. But the house would not be satisfied with Flon;
and finally Sir Augustus himself had to appear. As he
stepped forward to the footlights a deep hush fell on the assembled multitude. He looked for a moment at some person
behind the scenes; and immediately I was reminded of Captain Cuttle's last appeal to Bunsby when that unfortunate
mariner was allowing himself to be married to Mrs Mac-
stinger for mere want of resolution enough to run away.
Everyone remembers the formula, "Jack Bunsby, will you
once?" "Jack Bunsby, will you twice?" and so on. If Sir
Augustus had actually uttered the words "Jules Massenet,
will you once?" the situation could not have been more
patent. But, like the fated Bunsby, Jules Massenet wouldnt
once; and Sir Augustus, looking the audience in the face
with that steadfastness to which the mere truth can never
nerve a mortal man, explained that M. Massenet had left
the theatre to smoke a cigaret, and that the gratifying news
of the success of his work should be communicated to him,
by telegraph or otherwise, as soon as possible. I immediately
withdrew, feeling that I could no longer lend the moral sanc-

tion of my presence to the proceedings; and for all I know, the audience may be there calling for Jules still.

As to the work itself, there is hardly anything to be said in face of the frankness with which Massenet has modelled it on Cavalleria. He has not composed an opera: he has made up a prescription; and his justification is that it has been perfectly efficacious. The drama is simple and powerful, the events actually represented being credible and touching, and the assumptions, explanations, and pretexts on which they are brought about so simple and convenient that nobody minds their being impossible. Alvarez, in the tenor part, seconded Calvé with almost brutal force and vividness, dividing the honors with her in the final scene: that is to say, making a remarkable success as an actor.

But no triumph of the genius of an individual artist has half the significance in operatic history of the fact that in La Navarraise we had the management at last in full artistic activity. La Navarraise has not been shovelled on to the stage: it has been really *produced*. It was no mere matter of extravagance in gunpowder: the whole staging of the piece was excellent. The scenery was not ordered from the painter and exhibited anyhow: it was lighted, placed, and considered in the exits and entrances of the troops in such a manner as to secure the utmost illusion and make the audience imagine much more than it was possible to make them actually see. The change from night to morning during the intermezzo, with the mountain summit brightening in the sun while the town below was still in darkness, and the stealing down of the light, were capitally represented.

The couple of bells sounding the F sharp and G an octave below the bass stave (which means that they were huge and expensive pieces of bell-founding) must have been cast expressly for the occasion. In short, when Sir Augustus came on the stage at the end, he was, as manager, in his place as an artist who had taken a leading and highly successful part in the performance.

But in criticism there is no such thing as gratitude. I

have got, in La Navarraise, what I have been clamoring for all these years; and now I want more. The newly born operas are splendid; but when are the old operas going to be born over again? I have spoken of shovelling operas on to the stage, and trusting to the genius of the principal artists to pull them through; and I know quite well that, with such a repertory as the London one, shovelling is forced on the management by the mere limits of time, space, and skilled labor. But even shovelling can be carefully or carelessly done; and what I have said in praise of the way in which La Navarraise has been handled would carry no weight if I did not couple it with a most vehement protest against the way in which Die Walküre was shovelled on at Drury Lane on Tuesday last week, when the German opera season opened.

Take the second act, for example, which is supposed to take place in a mountain gorge. Now I am not going to be unreasonable. I do not ask for a new scene. I do not object to the mountains being provided with flights of stairs and galleries exactly like the hall of an old manor house; for however seldom these freaks of natural architecture may be met with by the chamois, they are undoubtedly convenient for opera singers who have to bound up four thousand feet or so and cross from one range to another whilst the orchestra is playing a dozen bars. Neither do I complain of the venerable smuggler's cave which provides a useful entrance on the ground floor of the valley. To bring these things into some remote harmony with nature would involve a revolution; and you cannot, let it be fairly admitted, make revolutions at Drury Lane and produce La Navarraise at Covent Garden on successive evenings.

But there are some things that you can do, or at least blow up the responsible official for not doing; and one of them is lighting the stage properly. When a rock in the foreground, supposed to be illuminated by the sun overhead, throws a strong black shadow *upwards* on a rock behind which is higher than itself; and when this system of black shadows is carried out through the whole scene, destroying all effect of distance, and making the stage look like a mere store-room for dingy canvases, then you can go round and speak burning words to the person whose business it was to have seen that there were sufficient lights placed on the floor between each set of rocks to overcome the shadow from the footlights and to make the back of the stage look five miles away from the front.

The fact is, the music of Die Walküre so enthrals the imagination of both Sir Augustus and most of the audience that they are unconscious of things that would instantly leap to their apprehension in Faust or Carmen. I am under no such spell, the music being as familiar to me as God save the Queen, and the work as capable of boring me as any old-fashioned opera when it is not finely executed.

There is another reform in the staging of these Nibelung dramas upon which I must appeal to the leading artists. Why is it that Brynhild always looks ridiculous and ugly, no matter how attractive the artist impersonating her may be? And why, on the night in question, did Fräulein Klafsky, in bounding up the mountain staircase, trip, tumble, and have a narrow escape of adding to the year's list of Alpine casualties? Simply because she would go mountaineering, according to German etiquette, in a trailing white skirt. Imagine a helmeted, breastplated, spear-armed war-maiden dashing through battles and scaling crags in a skirt in which no sensible woman would walk down Regent Street! I do not suggest gaiters and a tailor-made skirt, nor yet bicycling knickerbockers, though either would be better than the present Valkyrie fashion; but I do urge the claims of a tunic.

Surely the antique Diana is more beautiful and more decent than the late Hablot Browne's picture of Mrs Leo Hunter as Minerva in a gown, which is exactly the model followed by the Valkyries. The modern lyric drama owes to the German nation three leading features. First, the works of Wagner. Second, tenors who never sing in tune. Third, prima donnas who dress badly. I plead earnestly with Sir Augustus for a strenuous resistance to the two last, combined with a hearty welcome to the first. It must never be forgotten that on De Reszke nights, when Covent Garden is at its best, there are moments when Bayreuth is left positively nowhere in point of vocal beauty and dramatic grace; and in bringing the other moments—which are certainly rather numerous—up to a corresponding level, it cannot be too patriotically believed that we have nothing to learn from the Germans, tolerant as they are of uglinesses and stupidities, that we cannot teach ourselves much better for our own purposes.

The performance of Die Walküre improved as it went on. The first act was bad—very bad. Sieglinde was a cipher. Alvary began by singing out of the key. Later on he found the key, and merely sang out of tune. He posed with remarkable grace and dramatic eloquence: I can imagine no finer Siegmund from the point of view of a deaf man; but he may take my word for it—the word of a critic who has highly appreciated some of his performances—that he will have to get much nearer the mark in point of pitch, and assimilate his vocal phrasing much more to his admirable pantomime in point of grace, if he intends to hold his own within two minutes' walk of Jean de Reszke.

The white-armed Klafsky herself, in spite of her dramatic passion, which produced all its old effect in the more tempestuous passages, often betrayed the influence of a low standard of accuracy in intonation and distinction in phrasing. In the more violent passages she sang in tune or out of tune just as it came; and throughout the performance her "in tune" only meant commonly—seldom or never exquisitely—in tune. The only one of the principals who was free from the touch of provincialism given by this sort of laxness was Mr Bispham.

Wiegand was a rather inert Wotan, grumbling, crusty, and distinctly lazy; but he woke up at the end and finished well. He made a few inessential alterations here and there to avoid the highest notes; but happily he did not, like Theodore Reichmann, for whom the part lies too low, ruin the second act by cutting out the first half of the narrative to Brynhild. This, one of the finest passages in the drama, was powerfully supported by Klafsky, who, having nothing to do but listen, did so with a dramatic intensity that helped Wiegand out very materially.

Sieglinde, a part which requires an artist of the first rank, did not have one on this occasion, to the great detriment of the first act. Fricka was more fortunate in the hands of Olitska, who played very well, and could easily have sustained the interest of the pages which were cut. Herr Lohse, the conductor, was energetic; but he failed to get really fine work out of the band, partly, perhaps, because the men were overworked with the Richter concerts and the Handel Festival, and partly, I venture to guess, because they were sulky about the low pitch.

One circumstance struck me as curious in connection with the stress laid on the fact that Drury Lane is "the National Theatre." One at least of the Valkyries was an English lady, Mrs Lee. But the playbill of the National Theatre drew the line at "Mrs." In Klafsky's case it wavered between Frau and Fräulein; Pauline Joran was Miss one day and Mdlle the next; "Mr" was tolerated in the case of Mr Bispham; but Mrs Lee was always Madame Lee. May I suggest in a friendly way that it is time to drop this old-fashioned nonsense?

4 July 1894

IN this oppressive weather, with the season advanced to a point at which each successive concert brings a heavier burden of fatigue than the one before, it is hard to have a Handel Festival hurled at one like the stone of Polyphemus. Like all our national institutions, the Handel Festival has a great deal of nonsense about it, and is applauded for its nonsense much more than for its sense. As, for example, the size of the thing, though, after all, it is only about quarter as large as the London police force, about which nobody makes any fuss. Mr Manns is much praised for the Napoleonic feat of conducting nearly four thousand performers, as if that were fifty times as difficult as conducting the seventy-five or eighty who constitute his band at an ordinary Saturday concert.

Of course such a calculation is pure folly: you cannot get artistic magnitude by the multiplication of nobodies, although you can get, on any given note in the performance, enough suburban amateur choristers singing right, and enough country parsons, surgeon-majors, and young ladies playing their fiddles right, to extinguish the irresolute and unconcerted efforts of the minority who are singing and playing wrong. This advantage apart, the bigness of the affair is a heavy drawback except in so far as the vastness of the audience impresses the principal singers, and stimulates them to rise to what they conceive to be a great occasion. The multitudinous choristers, singing what is to them the easiest and most familiar music in the world, taken so slowly that there is plenty of time for them to consider what they are about, have only to observe the simplest mechanical conditions of their art: that is, accuracy as to the notes, clearness of pronunciation, and an occasional reduction of their chronic *forte* to *piano*.

The number of effects they can produce could be counted on the fingers of one hand even by an average worker at a circular saw; so that in half an hour the interest of their performance is quite exhausted. There remains, of course, the interest of Handel's work, as far as it can be realized under such circumstances; but this limitation is so serious that I do not hesitate to say that whoever has heard an oratorio of Handel's at the Handel Festival only has never heard it at all.

The other day Mr de Lange's Amsterdam choir of thirty-odd singers had to leave London abruptly because they were not inclined to allow the British public the customary ten years or so which it takes to find out a superlatively good thing. That choir was worth ten Handel Festival choirs piled one on top of the other. Even in mere volume and penetrating force of sound it was superior: its imposing *fortissimo*

struck home in a way unknown at the Crystal Palace, where
the attempt to produce gigantic explosion at such points
as Wonderful! Counsellor! in the Messiah invariably
fails, exactly as the simultaneous discharge of four thousand
muskets would fail to produce the boom of a single cannon.
In range and delicacy of gradation, in power and subtlety
of expression, in short, in artistic capacity, it differed from
the Handel choir as a living creature differs from a machine.

If the sole useful function of a choral performance were
the perfect execution of the masterpieces of choral music,
then I should unhesitatingly recommend the dispersion of
the Handel choir by armed force, with or without a preliminary reading of the Riot Act. But in England it has another
function—a social one. Choral singing with us is not an artistic pursuit: it is a game of skill which we play just as our
athletic friends play cricket or football; and as a game of skill
we understand it, on the whole, very well. The degree of
connoisseurship which such entirely popular assemblages
as Festival choirs and audiences display in the recognized
points of the game often puts the professed musical critic to
shame.

Take an example from the present year's Festival. The
hero of the occasion among the soloists was Mr Santley. The
roar of applause which followed each of his songs was stupendous. Now this was not by any means a mere ignorant
hero-worship of Mr Santley. He is a popular favorite, no
doubt; but Mr Lloyd, Madame Albani, Mr Ben Davies,
Madame Melba, and the rest are also popular favorites; and
yet none of them got quite the same cheer that followed
Honor and Arms and Nasce al bosco. It was not the loveli-
ness of the songs either: Nasce al bosco cannot touch an
audience like Ombra mai fu, which Albani gave us, nor
charm them like Love in her eyes sits playing, which Mr
Lloyd sang to perfection.

As to the hackneyed Honor and Arms, it is, from any point
of view that includes common sense as a factor in human
utterance, an obsolete absurdity. In a modern opera it would

be received with shouts of laughter. And there is something else to be explained. Mr Santley, in spite of all the applause he wins—in spite of the fact that, as I shall presently shew, he wins it by a genuine objective superiority which is intelligently appreciated by the audience—has told us in one of the most sincere and unaffected autobiographical sketches we possess, that the English public never supported him in his efforts to complete his artistic activity and develop his powers to the highest degree as a dramatic singer. The only encouragement he got was at the Italian Opera under the old régime, where "artistic activity" consisted in playing Don Giovanni for the first time after one rehearsal, at which the tenor (the illustrious Mario) did not take the trouble to appear until it was half over.

All this is inexplicable to the Wagnerian amateur who judges all music as tone poetry, and all singing by its expressiveness. But the Handel Festival enthusiasts care nothing for poetry or its expression: they are absolute materialists in music. They know the points of a good voice, and the rarities of vocal execution; and they like familiar music that shews off those points and demands those rarities. In Honor and Arms the phrase Though I could end thee at a blow is set sensibly to eight notes in a way to which neither Gluck nor Wagner could take the smallest exception; but it is not at all preferred to the single word "glory," set to a "division" consisting of no less than thirty-six notes.

Santley's singing of the division of Selection Day was, humanly speaking, perfect. It tested the middle of his voice from C to C exhaustively; and that octave came out of the test hall-marked: there was not a scrape on its fine surface, not a break or a weak link in the chain anywhere; while the vocal touch was impeccably light and steady, and the florid execution accurate as clockwork. The phrase Though I could end thee at a blow was admired, not for its rational setting, but for the irrationality of the repetition of the eight notes a sixth higher, compelling the singer to sing up the scale from his low G to the G above, and immediately afterwards from E flat to E flat, thereby exhibiting his whole compass (barring the top E natural and F, which were repeatedly in evidence under more difficult conditions in Nasce al bosco) in such a way as made it impossible for him to conceal any blemish, if there had been one.

Everyone else broke down under these Handelian tests except Mr Lloyd, whose voice, homogeneous as it is from top to bottom, and charming as its color is, has not quite the beautiful firmness and purity of tone which the public has learnt the value of from Patti and Sims Reeves as well as from Santley. Madame Melba might perhaps have held her own on this point had she risen to the immense care and vocal conscientiousness of those three artists; but she underrated her task, and all but came to grief in the (for her) only really difficult "division" in Let the bright Seraphim, which she seemed to me to be reading at first sight. Albani's voice, wonderful enough, in spite of its obvious pulsation, from E to B natural at the top, is conspicuously deficient in the middle.

Mr Ben Davies, when remorselessly compelled in Waft Her, Angels, to walk his voice slowly up from A to A so deliberately as to allow every step to be scrutinized, had to confess to a marked "break" on F sharp, or thereabouts; and this was promptly scored against him, according to the rules of the game, though it is only fair to him to add that a strong contrast of registers often produces very charming effects, which Handel, however, certainly did not lay his music out for.

And so, though all the artists I have named were hugely applauded, Santley, having scored the most points, was the hero of the day, all the more popular because his method, which many of our young baritones carefully avoid (rather an easy thing to do, by the way), has stood the wear and tear of forty years' work; for Santley began to sing in public at about the date when I began to cry in private, and more than twenty years before Albani was heard of in this country. That is a remarkable record; and a noteworthy feature of it is that he sang at this Festival better than he did at the one three years ago, and must therefore be considered to be still improving.

The fact that the British public understands the game of singing so well as its appreciation of Santley, Patti, and Sims Reeves proves, shews that we are a musical and sporting nation, not in the least that we are an artistic one. Santley might have perpetrated almost any conceivable artistic atrocity at that Festival without losing the most infinitesimal part of his popularity. He might have interpolated the vulgarest claptrap cadenzas, or achieved the finest strokes of poetic insight, without rebuke in the one case or encouragement on the other.

To the Briton with a turn for music he is just what Dr Grace is to the Briton with a turn for cricket; and when he gives us more than is implied in that, he gives it for its own sake, knowing that its existence will be a secret between himself and a very few people, and that this great lumping oratorio public, with all its apparently unerring discrimination and enlightened loyalty to old favorites, is really a people walking in exceeding darkness. And that is all I need say about the Handel Festival, except just to note that the sopranos were the weak point in an otherwise very fine chorus, and that the Festival was at all points as good as the Palace authorities could possibly have made it.

The real musical problem of the day, however, is not the multiplication of the sound-producing power of the musical individual by five thousand. He already makes noise enough, with his iron-framed piano, to bring him under stringent police regulation in Germany, and to make him an almost impossible neighbor in London. Why is it that the closer we get crowded together and piled up, in flats costing from two hundred to two thousand a year, the louder we make our musical instruments? In older times, when space was so cheap that no man was tempted to knock down his house and cut up his grounds into building lots, we played the viol instead of the violin, and the lute or the virginals instead of

270

the piano. We played "fantasies" and "concerts" instead of transcriptions of the Tannhäuser overture and the Walkürenritt. When we got in a good new instrument it did not cost us from £80 to £250 net, nor did it take several strong men to get it upstairs, leaving marks, as of a discharge of grape, at every corner and on every doorframe, and finally causing an extensive settlement of the floor. A virginal or a clavichord is more portable than a housemaid's dressing-table, and takes up no more room.

A first-rate clavichord from the hands of an artist-craftsman who, always learning something, makes no two instruments exactly alike, and turns out each as an individual work of art, marked with his name and stamped with his style, can be made and sold for £40 or less, the price of a fourth-rate piano (No. 5768 from Messrs So-and-so's factory), which you can hardly sell for £15 the day after you have bought it. Above all, you can play Bach's two famous sets of fugues and preludes, not to mention the rest of a great mass of beautiful old music, on your clavichord, which you cannot do without great alteration of character and loss of charm on the piano.

These observations have been provoked by the startlingly successful result of an experiment made by the students of the Royal College of Music. They, on having their ears and minds opened by Mr Arnold Dolmetsch's demonstrations to the beauty of our old instruments and our old music, took the very practical step of asking him to make them a clavichord. It was rather a staggering request to a collector and connoisseur; but Mr Dolmetsch, in the spirit of the Irishman who was invited to play the fiddle, had a try; and after some months' work he has actually turned out a little masterpiece, excellent as a musical instrument and pleasant to look at, which seems to me likely to begin such a revolution in domestic musical instruments as William Morris's work made in domestic furniture and decoration, or Philip Webb's in domestic architecture. I therefore estimate the birth of this little clavichord as, on a moderate computation, about forty thousand times as important

271

as the Handel Festival, or even the production at Covent Garden on Saturday last of Mr Cowen's Signa, of which I hope to treat at befitting length in my next article.

11 July 1894

THIS is certainly an amazingly prolific opera season. Last Wednesday Sir Augustus Harris produced his sixth new opera, L'Attaque du Moulin, and shewed that his resources were still unexhausted by promising yet another by no less a composer than Bach. I presume this means the celebrated Bach, the composer of Irmengarde, and not the poor old Leipzig cantor, John Sebastian of that ilk, who used to pass current as "Bach" pure and simple. L'Attaque du Moulin followed hard upon Signa, separated from it only by Mirette at the Savoy. Mirette was interesting enough from the critical point of view. I have made a careful analysis of it, and have formed the following opinion as to the process by which it was produced. First, it was decided, in view of the essentially English character of the Savoy enterprise, to engage a French librettist and a French composer. Then came the appalling difficulty that Frenchmen are often clever, and are consequently in danger of writing above the heads of the British public. Consequently Messager was selected as having learnt by the financial failure of his Basoche at the Royal English Opera (now a music-hall) how very stupid the English nation is. Carré was warned to ascertain the exact British gauge by a careful preliminary study of the works of Mr Weatherly, the most popular of English providers of words for music. Both composer and poet followed their instructions conscientiously and adroitly. Never has the spirit of Mr Weatherly, never has the depth of his poetic passion, the breadth of his view of life, and the peculiar amenity of his literary touch been more exactly reproduced than by Carré. As to Messager, he has hit off Sir Arthur Sullivan, in Sir Arthur's worldliest moods, with a quite exquisite felicity. The only drawback to this double success is that the result, however curious to experts in theatrical manufacture, is not particularly delectable as an opera. In fact, if I were a private individual, and could escape from the public responsibility which forbids a critic to tell the truth, I should say flatly that Mirette goes, in pointlessness and tediousness, to the extreme limits compatible with production at the Savoy Theatre. I have the less hesitation in allowing the acute reader to guess this private conviction of mine since Mr D'Oyly Carte, apparently realizing that the opera was open to misconstruction, circulated on the first night a managerial note explaining that it was not on Gilbert-Sullivan lines, but was rather like Il Barbiere, L'Étoile du Nord, Carmen, and Basoche. Also that the book dealt with a subject which has interested the world for some thousands of years. It gave me quite an uncanny sense that the order of nature was being suspended and even reversed without a word of warning when I found the subject which had enjoyed this prolonged popularity falling perfectly flat on me. And for the life of me I could not see where the resemblance to L'Étoile du Nord came in. Further, Mr Carte is anxious lest the comic man should stamp the opera as a comic opera in the English sense. "This personage," says the managerial manifesto, "falls into a pond and gets wet [as a matter of fact he adhered closely to stage tradition by falling into a pond and *not* getting wet], displays cowardice, and dances: actions which may possibly be laughed at again as they have been since plays were first written. He also gives utterance to certain anachronisms." I wonder what the anachronisms were. The gentleman sang in a duet about Noah, and gave us a song about special editions; but neither of these seemed at all out of place, perhaps because of the extreme difficulty of referring the events or personages of the opera to any conceivable period of human history. Surely the plain fact of the matter (unless I dreamt that special-edition song and other cognate features) is that an attempt was made in manufacturing Mirette to repeat the Haddon Hall experiment of combining sentimental opera in the style of Balfe with topical extravaganza

273

in the style of Mr Gilbert. I can quite well understand how Mr Carte, when he saw the result, felt impelled to urge that the work should not be criticized from that point of view; but he can hardly suppose that it would mend matters if I were to criticize Mirette as an attempt at a work of the class of Carmen. I cannot even wholly endorse his modest plea that "it is a very simple love story, not too exciting or absorbing, but which may please." The story, briefly told, is as follows: Mirette, who is adored by Picorin, adores Gerard, who adores her, but is adored by Bianca. This is disagreeable for Picorin and Bianca, and not particularly pleasant for Gerard and Mirette, who are separated by a considerable difference in social position. Finally, Mirette very sensibly concludes that it would save no end of trouble if she were to marry Picorin and Gerard to marry Bianca. Gerard falls in with the suggestion at once; and down comes the curtain. I do not deny that this is "a very simple love story": my only doubt is whether it is not rather too simple to give even that mild degree of pleasure which Mr Carte hopes for. Perhaps, in view of my scepticism and in justice to M. Michel Carré, I should state that the exact account of the authorship given in the program is "The book by Michel Carré; English lyrics by Fred. E. Weatherly; English dialogue by Harry Greenbank." This may mean either that Mr Greenbank has supplied dialogue to M. Carré's scenario, or that he has translated M. Carré's dialogue. But I am afraid it does not greatly matter.

Of the music I need only say that at the very outset Messager announced, *fortissimo*, that he was going to be as commonplace as he possibly could; and he kept his word in the main, though he could not help once or twice lapsing into habits of distinction and refinement formed in his own unhappy country. Miss Maud Ellicot, as a Bohemian girl who dwells in marble halls in the second act, and so does not need to dream about them, proved herself a very capable young lady, with a ready fund of dramatic feeling and musical talent, backed by a voice which, if not particularly re-

markable for richness of color or purity of tone, is vigorous
and serviceable, and has in the middle and lower registers a
not unattractive peculiarity which answers perhaps to a
touch of swarthy color in her complexion. The other parts
are in the hands of old friends, none of whom have any
opportunity of adding to their reputations: indeed Mr Scott
Fishe has to exert all his tact to keep Prince Gerard from
having an unintended success as a wild burlesque of Lucia
di Lammermoor. The opera is staged with all the taste and
thoroughness that distinguish the Savoy: nothing is missing
except Mr Rutland Barrington and a good work for him to
appear in.

Mr Cowen's Signa can hardly, I think, be said to have a
fair chance either of success or failure at Covent Garden.
When a four-act opera is cut down to two acts, the composer
is entitled to claim suspension of judgment as to the merit of
his work as a whole. I have seldom been so taken aback as
when the three leading persons in the opera, whose acquaintance we had barely made on quite amiable terms, suddenly
pulled out daggers and ended one another's existences on
no discernible provocation.

I can understand that Ancona, in stabbing Madame de
Nuovina, may have yielded simply to an irresistible impulse
to finish the opera and go home; but why on earth did Mr
Ben Davies, regardless of his growing portliness, not only
stab himself, but immediately afterwards gather himself together and launch himself on all fours into the air, exactly as
an inexperienced bather goes off a spring-board for the first
time, descending on the prostrate form of the lady with a
crash that overpowered the full force of the orchestra? When
the curtain went up to enable him to acknowledge the
tempest of applause evoked by this singular feat, he, taken
unawares, was discovered apparently picking portions of
the stage out of his knees; whilst, amazing to relate, Madame
de Nuovina, erect and apparently without a single broken
bone, smiled and bowed with Spartan fortitude.

On the whole, the opera rather missed its chance—such

275

as that chance was. A pretty tune with guitar accompaniment was sung villainously out of tune by a handful of tenors from the chorus, these gentlemen, like all thoroughly bad singers, being able to hit a note accurately only on condition of being allowed to bawl it at the utmost stretch of their throats. Madame de Nuovina, a lady with genuine talent for the stage, has unluckily contracted a habit of sending her voice on edge through the house with a recklessness equally destructive to itself and to the peace of mind of the audience. This does not do for Mr Cowen's music, nor, indeed, for any composer's music; and if Madame de Nuovina wishes to establish her reputation in London, and to realize the full value of her striking appearance and personal force, she must resolutely face the fact that the expression of dramatic passion by music and its expression by physical violence are incompatible. She must touch our ears and hearts, not tear them. Ancona, in the part of a homicidal elderly farmer, displayed his fine voice at great length.

Mr Ben Davies made almost the only hit of the opera by his singing of a song in the first act, which was the most effective number in the work as it stood; but his success would have been greater if a somewhat smarter physical training had made him less obviously a popular and liberally fed London concert singer. The music of Signa, judging by the samples presented, suffers from Mr Cowen's old fault of presenting themes which are nothing if not flowing and popular, and then checking them, just as they are getting into full career, by some rather pettily self-conscious interval or progression from which they never recover. After half a dozen such disappointments, one is apt to lose interest in a work, if not to lose patience.

Nevertheless, Signa is freer from these checks than Mr Cowen's previous works; and in one instance, that of the tenor song in the first act, he has succeeded in bringing off a fairly big climax without a hitch. The only respect in which there is no improvement is in the orchestration. This is pretty enough within the limits of the old-fashioned symphony orchestra; but the trombone and percussion parts are stuck on in a flagrantly inorganic fashion. With the exception of Ancona, none of the performers, either in the rank and file or among the principals, can be said to have done their best for the work.

L'Attaque du Moulin was a good deal better supported. Madame de Nuovina had more scope for her power of acting, and had perhaps been warned to use her voice more mercifully. At all events, she rent the air only once or twice, in pressing emergencies. There had been great talk of Madame Delna's Marcelline; but, frankly, it was not a bit good, Madame Delna being a lady of an essentially urbane charm, much more likely to have two daughters well married in society than two sons as rankers in the Army, and quite out of the question as nurse and housekeeper to a country miller. Her voice, a bright mezzo-soprano, is a little the worse for violent wear at the top.

Bouvet would have been very good if he had not forced his voice so furiously in the more exciting passages. It was clearly Bruneau's intention that at these points I, as audience, should be excited, and Bouvet, as actor, cool and efficient. As a matter of fact, it was the other way about. The music is like all Bruneau's music: that is, it has every sort of originality except musical originality. It is impossible not to admire the composer's freedom from technical superstitions. In his perfect readiness to play two tunes at once without exacting any harmonic coincidences or even community of key, and the almost Mozartian *sans-gêne* with which he makes the music go where he wants it, even if he has to step over all sorts of professorial fences and disregard all sorts of academic notice-boards in doing so, he shews himself not only a man of strong character, but a keen musical observer of what the ear will tolerate. He will combine a few hackneyed fanfares, or a rum-tum pedal bass with a few common place progressions and snatches of tunes, in such a way as to make people talk as if he had conquered a new musical domain.

But, for all that, his musical stock-in-trade is very limited, and entirely borrowed. Like Boito, he is ever so much abler and more interesting than some of the poor musical bees and silkworms whose honey and silk he manufactures; but he is himself barren: he invents novel combinations, but does not discover new harmonies—can keep an opera cast singing the whole evening, but could not, for the life of him, produce one of Sir Arthur Sullivan's ballads—stands, as artificer compared with creative artists, in the same relation to Gounod as Boito to Verdi, or as Berlioz to the whole romantic movement in music, from Gluck to the Eroica symphony and the operas of Meyerbeer and Spontini. I am very curious to see what rank these literary exploiters of music—these Delaroches and Kaulbachs of the orchestra—will take finally in the republic of art; for I have noticed that they generally make their living as musical critics; and I am not sure that I could not compose a little in their style myself. Will any impresario with a commission to give take the hint?

18 *July* 1894

THE production of Der Freischütz and Fidelio at the German Opera momentarily transferred the centre of operatic interest, for me at least, from Covent Garden to Drury Lane. It was amusing to find these two masterpieces arousing quite a patronizing interest as old-fashioned curiosities, somewhat dowdy perhaps, but still deserving of indulgence for the sake of tradition. As to the Freischütz, hardly anyone could remember its last performance in London; and I was astonished when the questions addressed to me on this point made me conscious that although the work is as familiar to me as the most familiar of Shakespear's plays, and counts, indeed, as a permanent factor in my consciousness, I could only clearly recollect two actual representations of it, one in Munich, and the other in my native town, which is not in England. I will not swear that I have not seen it oftener; for I have long since given free play to my inestimable gift of forgetting, and have lost count of the performances I have witnessed almost as completely as I have lost count of my headaches; but still, even in my case, it is somewhat significant that I should be unable to recall a representation of Der Freischütz in London. Such a doubt as to the abysmally inferior Carmen would be a ridiculous affectation.

Perhaps, therefore, the first question to answer is, "How has Der Freischütz worn?" To which I am happy to be able to reply that its freshness and charm delighted everyone as much as its unaffected sincerity of sentiment impressed them. I will not, of course, pretend that the hermit strikes the popular imagination as he did in the days when hermits habitually trod the stage, and were deferred to, at sight of their brown gowns, rope girdles, and white beards, by all the civil and military authorities, exactly as if they were modern French deputies exhibiting their scarves to the police in *émeutes*.

And it would be vain to conceal the fact that the terrors of the Wolf's Gulch and the casting of the magic bullets were received with audible chuckling, although Sir Augustus Harris had made a supreme effort to ensure the unearthliness of the incantation by making the stage a sort of museum of all the effects of magic and devilry known in the modern theatre. He had illuminated steam clouds from Bayreuth, and fiery rain from the Lyceum Faust; he had red fire, glowing hell-mouth caverns, apparitions, skeletons, vampire bats, explosions, conflagrations, besides the traditional wheels, the skulls, the owl, and the charmed circle.

And yet nobody could help laughing, least of all, I should imagine, Sir Augustus himself. The owl alone would have sufficed to set me off, because though its eyes were not red like those of previous stage owls, and it was therefore not so irresistibly suggestive of a railway signal as I had expected, one of its eyes was much larger than the other, so that it seemed to contemplate the house derisively through a single eyeglass. This quaint monocle notwithstanding, the scene

279

produced some effect until the other phenomena super-
vened. If they had been omitted—if the apparitions had
been left to our imaginations and to Weber's music, the
effect would have been enormously heightened. Owls, bats,
ravens, and skeletons have no supernatural associations for
our rising generations: the only function an owl or a bat can
now fulfil in such a scene is to heighten that sense of night in
a forest which is one of Nature's most wonderful effects.

But this change in public susceptibility makes it necessary to take much greater pains with stage illusions than
formerly. When the bat was a mere bogy to terrify an
audience of grown-up children, it was, no doubt, sufficient to
dangle something like a stuffed bustard with huge moth's
wings at the end of a string from the flies to make the pit's
flesh creep. Nowadays, unless a manager can devise some
sort of aerial top that will imitate the peculiar flitting of the
real flittermouse he must forgo bats altogether.

To appeal to our extinct sense of the supernatural by
means that outrage our heightened sense of the natural is to
court ridicule. Pasteboard pies and paper flowers are being
banished from the stage by the growth of that power of accurate observation which is commonly called cynicism by
those who have not got it; and impossible bats and owls
must be banished with them. Der Freischütz may be de-
pended on to suggest plenty of phantasmagoria without
help from out-of-date stage-machinists and property-
masters.

Except during the absurdities of the Wolf's Gulch, the
performance appeared to me to be an exceptionally successful one. The orchestra has improved greatly since the first
week; and though Lohse has one trick which I greatly dislike—that of hurrying at every crescendo—he is equal to
his weighty duties as Wagner and Beethoven conductor.
His handling of Fidelio was at many points admirable. Beethoven had not any bats or skeletons to contend with; but he
had what was quite as bad in its way: to wit, an execrable
chorus of prisoners who, on catching sight of the sentinels,

would break in on the German text with mistuned howls of "Silenzio, silenzio." In both operas there were moments when the singing was beyond all apology.

Alvary's Florestan, vocally considered, was an atrocious performance; and Klafsky did not finish the aria in the first act without perceptible effort. Weber's music was, of course, far more singable; and even Alvary, saving a few intervals the corruption of which must, I suppose, be put up with from him as part of his mannerism, sang fairly in tune according to his German scale, which, let me point out, not for the first time, is not precisely the southern scale dear to our ears.

But Wiegand, as Caspar, dropped all pretence of singing before he came to the coda of the Revenge song. He simply shouted the words hoarsely through the orchestration, and left the audience to infer that Weber meant it to be done that way—a notion of which I beg somewhat indignantly to disabuse them. Yet in spite of all this and more, these three artists, Klafsky, Alvary, and Wiegand, with Mr Bispham and Rodemund to help them, made Fidelio and Der Frei-schütz live again. Their sincerity, their affectionate intimacy with the works, their complete absorption in their parts, enable them to achieve most interesting and satisfactory performances, and to elicit demonstrations of respect and enthusiasm from the audience, which, nevertheless, if it has any ears, must know perfectly well that the singing has been at best second-rate, and at worst quite outside the category of music.

Klafsky is the best German leading soprano we have accepted here since Titiens; and though Klafsky has in her favor the enormous superiority of the era of Brynhild and Isolde to the era of Semiramide and Lucrezia, Titiens would certainly have been greatly disconcerted, if not actually terrified, had she, at Klafsky's age, been overtaken by as many vocal disasters in the course of an opera as Klafsky seems to take as a matter of course. It is a great mistake to assume, as these German artists evidently do, that their rough, violent, and inaccurate singing does not matter.

A very striking proof of this was forthcoming at the last concert at the Albert Hall, where Patti continued her new departure into Wagnerland by singing Elisabeth's prayer from Tannhäuser. Now, if I express some scepticism as to whether Patti cares a snap of her fingers for Elisabeth or Wagner, I may, after all these years of Una voce and Bel raggio, very well be pardoned. But it is beyond all doubt that Patti cares most intensely for the beauty of her own voice and the perfection of her singing. What is the result? She attacks the prayer with the single aim of making it sound as beautiful as possible; and this being precisely what Wagner's own musical aim was, she goes straight to the right phrasing, the right vocal touch, and the right turn of every musical figure, thus making her German rivals not only appear in comparison clumsy as singers, but actually obtuse as to Wagner's meaning.

At the first performance of Tristan at Drury Lane this season Klafsky, by sheer dramatic power, was really great in the death song which is the climax of the opera; but she did not sing it half as well as Nordica, who carries much lighter guns as a dramatic artist, has sung it here; and what is more, she completely perverted the music by making it express the most poignant grief for the loss of Tristan—the very sort of stage commonplace to which Isolde's sacred joy in the death towards which the whole work is an aspiration, ought to be the most complete rebuke.

If the song were beautifully sung, it simply could not take the wrong expression; and if Patti were to return to the stage and play Isolde, though she might very possibly stop the drama half a dozen times in each act to acknowledge applause and work in an encore—though she might introduce Home, Sweet Home, in the ship scene, and The Last Rose in the garden scene—though nobody would be in the least surprised to see her jump up out of her trance in the last act to run to the footlights for a basket of flowers, yet the public might learn a good deal about Isolde from her which they will never learn from any of the illustrious band of German Wagner heroines who are queens at Bayreuth, but who cannot sing a gruppetto for all that.

In offering these disparagements to the German artists, I am not for a moment forgetting that to them we owe the fact that we have any lyric stage left at all. When I turn from Klafsky playing Leonora, Agatha, Brynhild, and Isolde at Drury Lane, to Melba trying to revive Lucia at Covent Garden, or even to Calvé playing Carmen and scoring cheap triumphs with trashy one-act melodramas; and when I go on the same night from witnessing the discordant but heroic struggles of Alvary with Florestan to see Jean de Reszke gravely airing his latest achievement—nothing less than getting up the tenor part in Mr Bemberg's inanely pretty Elaine (Mr Bemberg being, as I am told, and can well believe, a rich young gentleman much better worth obliging than Beethoven or Wagner)—when I see all this, remembering what I do of the miserable decay and extinction of the old operatic régime under the sway of the two-hundred-a-night prima donnas, I am in no danger of losing sight of the fact that when singers sing so well that it no longer matters what they sing, they keep the theatre stagnant with all their might, the stagnation, of course, presently producing putrescence; whilst, on the other hand, the ambition of lyric artists who could not by mere charm of vocalization raise the receipts at any concert or theatre bureau by £5 makes strongly for dramatic activity and for the reinforcement of the attractions of the individual artist by those of the masterpieces of musical composition.

It is because Alvary is a much less attractive singer than Jean de Reszke that he has to summon Wagner to his aid, and play Siegfried or Tristan with infinite pains while De Reszke is giving his thousandth impersonation of such comparatively cheap and easy characters as Gounod's Faust or Romeo. This is not altogether creditable to Monsieur Jean: it makes him appear too little the chivalrous hero and devoted artist, and too much "the economic man" (sometimes supposed to be a figment of Adam Smith's, but actually one of the most real of ancient and modern types of humanity). I have appealed so often and so utterly in vain to De Reszke in these columns to do for the sake of art what Alvary does because he must, that I do not propose to waste any more ink on the matter.

To the Germans I would point out that their apparent devotion to the poetic and dramatic side of their art can claim no credit as long as it is forced upon them by the fact that they sing so badly that nobody would listen to them for their own sakes alone. The standard of beauty of execution in vocal music has fallen so low on their stage that we find an artist like Rodemund going through the music of Mime without taking the trouble to sing a single note in tune, and thereby losing all the elfin charm and doting pathos which Lieban's fine musical instinct enabled him to get from it. Yet Rodemund can distinguish the pitch of a note accurately enough, as he shewed in Beethoven's music and Weber's. In Wagner's he evidently believes it does not matter.

What the Germans have to learn from us is that it does matter. Wagner meant his music to be sung with the most exquisite sensitiveness in point of quality of tone and precision of pitch, exactly as Mozart did. In a day or two I shall be within the walls of the temple at Bayreuth, laying in a stock of observations for the further enforcement of this moral; for I am really tired of going to the theatre to hear the best music associated with the worst singing, and the best singing with the worst music.

25 *July* 1894

THE time has come when I must leave Handel Festivals, operas, and the more highly organized musical species generally, to glance for a moment over the crowd of concerts and recitals which have been devastating my afternoons for weeks past. Fortunately for myself I have not been to everything of the kind that has been given during this rather busy season. There are concerts which I shirk, and concerts which shirk me. There are concerts the promoters of which send me invitations without sending me programs, as if, at my age, I were likely to run the risk of walking into a public hall and finding myself at the same old miscellaneous concert that has been in stock for years— Popper's Papillons, Sognai, La mia Piccirella—no, thank you! Then there are the concerts fixed for the first night of some new opera, or on the afternoon of Selection Day at the Handel Festival, given by enthusiasts who write begging me to be present, and expressing a hope that I have no other engagement. There are concerts which I am too lazy to go to, or too busy to go to, or which I would rather die than go to, not to mention the concerts which are in the hands of sensitive souls who smart under injustices perpetrated in this column, and who mercifully lighten my season's work by not inviting me to their entertainments. But with all these deductions I lead a dog's life from May to July inclusive.

One new feature of the present season is the variety of concert-rooms. Instead of the old unvaried round of Steinway Hall, Prince's Hall, and St James's Hall, we have the large Queen's Hall, which is a happy success acoustically, and the smaller room at the top of the building, now much the most comfortable of our small concert-rooms, though, as I am unfortunately a bad sailor, its cigar shape and the windows in the ceiling suggest a steamer saloon so strongly that I have hardly yet got over the qualmishness which attacked me when I first entered it. Messrs Brinsmead, too, have set apart a room "in cellar cool," outside which the belated critic can sit cosily on the warm stairs and enjoy an excellent view of the platform through the banisters. The room in the basement of the Grafton Gallery has not been in evidence this season, as far as I know; but Messrs Erard have just opened a London "Salle Erard" in Great Marlborough Street, which is by a very great deal the best-looking room of the kind our great pianoforte houses have yet given us.

This Erard room was opened the other day with a reception at which Paderewski was the chief attraction. I was un-

able to go and be received on that occasion; but I seized an
opportunity to see the new room at a concert given there next
day by Clément, the tenor from the Paris Opéra Comique,
and Léon Delafosse, of whom I had not previously heard,
though I am not likely soon to forget him. He is a vigorous
and nimble-fingered young gentleman with remarkably high
animal spirits, in the ebullition of which he fell on Beethoven's Moonlight Sonata and left it for dead in the shortest
time on record. The Erard room has two defects: excessive
resonance, and painted windows which would pass very well
in a restaurant, but which are not at all up to the artistic standard set by the handsome proportions of the room and its
plain but elegant wainscoting. Everything in such a room
ought to be the best of its kind; and I strongly urge Messrs
Erard either to call in Morris and Burne-Jones and make
the stained glass in the room one of the sights to be starred
in Baedeker, or else, if that would cost too much, or if the
light is too scanty for good stained glass, to substitute plain
lattice windows like those in the halls of Barnard's or Clifford's Inn. It is a pity to spoil a good room by a single conspicuous touch of Philistinism; and I suggest to Messrs
Erard that it would be a prudent as well as a gracious act to
present the windows to some free library or municipal school
of music, so that those dreadful medallion portraits of great
composers, which are neither fine drawings nor good like-
nesses, might smile, in perfect harmony with their surroundings, on some gamboge-tiled staircase, with a bust of the
mayor on the landing. Having already heard Clément at St
James's Hall, I had great hopes that he would break the
windows with one of those strident notes of which he is so
proud. I must own that he did his best; but the glass was too
thick; and finally it was I who was sent flying into the street.
I would ask Clément seriously whether he thinks that the
English people have built up their nation through all these
centuries only to sit down now and hear a young man yell at
the top of his voice. That may do very well for the gallery at
the Opéra Comique, for the suburbs, for the provinces, for

Australia, for South Africa, for City dinners, for smoking concerts, and other barbarous places; but in the true artistic centre of London "people dont do such things," as Judge Brack has it. I have no doubt that Clément could sing very nicely if he wanted to; but, like most tenors, he doesnt want to. That is why great tenors are so rare, although good voices are so plentiful. Clément's concert at St James's Hall was a fashionable affair, because Plançon and Melba sang and Réjane recited. This was a very necessary diversion, since all the music was selected from the compositions of Mr Bemberg, who does not seem sufficiently alive to the fact that it is possible to have too much of a good thing. As far as I can judge, Mr Bemberg's ambition is to succeed to the business so long carried on in first-rate style by Gounod. It therefore concerns him to know that in this country we have found by our experiments with Mors et Vita and The Redemption that a whole concert of Gounod is insufferable. No doubt that is due to the imperfection of our own natures; but the fact, creditable to us or not, is indisputable; and if Mr Bemberg is wise he will in future be content with half an hour or so, and give Beethoven or some other composer a chance.

Another notable concert at St James's Hall was Miss Liza Lehmann's farewell to the concert platform. As Miss Lehmann's only reason for retiring is that she is getting married, I question whether her renunciation of the lucrative activity of public singing will be permanent. Though a bachelor, I venture to doubt whether matrimony is so absorbing a pursuit as she thinks at present; and I look forward to the time when Miss Lehmann will reappear as Madame, and once more sing Love may go hang rather more appropriately than she did on this occasion.

At all events, I decline to treat the farewell as a particularly solemn one; and when I say that Miss Lehmann sang very well, and seemed to have quite recovered the freshness and charm which at one time seemed to be wearing off under the influence of a trying course of sentimental popularity at the Monday Popular Concerts, I trust that my opinion may

287

derive authority from the certainty that, if she unhappily had
not sung well, I should have said so without the smallest re-
morse, farewell or no farewell. Madame Alice Gomez, who
also sang, rather confirmed an impression which she gave
me at the last Patti concert, that she is singing with somewhat less refinement than before, and that her voice is a little
roughened in consequence.

Mr J. Robertson sang a couple of songs, in gratitude for
which I will tell him exactly why his singing, in spite of the
care he takes of his voice, and his sensitive and entirely praise-
worthy repudiation of violent methods, is unsatisfactory. He
sings out of time—that is the whole secret. You never once
feel the swing and form of the melody, never get rocked or
lilted by it: he pulls it to pieces as thoughtlessly as a child
pulls the legs out of a fly. A week at the music-halls would
teach Mr Robertson a good deal in this respect. If Miss
Marie Lloyd, or Miss Katie Lawrence, or Mr Dan Leno
were to spoil a tune in such a fashion, their popularity would
be gone in one turn.

Among the concerts which more particularly interested
me was one at the Chelsea Town Hall, where I found Sir John
Stainer gravely conducting a setting of Rossetti's Blessed
Damozel by Lady Ramsay, of Banff. It was very pretty; and
it was quite original in the sense of having evidently been
composed by Lady Ramsay entirely and sincerely on her
own impulse and in her own way. But if Lady Ramsay were
to ask me how much she knows of composition, I should
reply, "Just enough to write a barcarolle."

The Blessed Damozel consists of that barcarolle, with re-
miniscences (quite unconscious) of Mendelssohn's I waited
for the Lord and Molloy's Dresden Shepherdess, and a few
pages of occasionally quite irreparable part-writing. The
barcarolle is the vital part; and it is no worse than any other
barcarolle, and much more refined in feeling than some. But
a barcarolle, if Lady Ramsay will only consider it attentively,
is nothing more than the see-saw of two chords, like an im-
provisation on the accordion. Lady Ramsay varies and pretti-

fies her see-saw by shifting it from key to key with sugary little modulations, and occasionally see-sawing from the tonic to some sentimental old chromatic chord—Neapolitan sixth or the like—instead of from tonic to dominant; but from the harmonist's point of view she is always like a child in a swing: the motion is delightful and becoming, and enables the child to pretend to itself that it is flying; but it is really only an exploitation of the force of gravitation, and the child can only go where the swing takes it, and back, over and over again.

The harmonization of a chorale by Bach or Wagner (Wach' auf in Die Meistersinger, for example) is, in comparison, like the march of an army round a province. These master-harmonists can, without once repeating themselves or leaving the key, move freely through a circle of dozens of progressions back to their starting-point, while Lady Ramsay—or, not to confine the lesson invidiously to her, Auber or Offenbach—can make but one oscillation across and back. And that is why The Blessed Damozel is not what Sir John Stainer would call a great cantata; though whether Sir John has had the artistic probity to say as much to a lady who sings so very well, and is otherwise so attractive as Lady Ramsay, is best known to himself.

I have been at some excellent concerts of good chamber music given by Miss Emily Shinner, Miss Fillunger, and Mr Leonard Borwick, and by Miss Amina Goodwin, Madame Lilian Griffiths, and Mr Paul Ludwig at Queen's Hall —two independent sets of high-class concerts which were well worth the subscription. Herr Zeldenrust's pianoforte recital proved him to be very neat, smart, and vigorous with his fingers, and gifted with a high degree of musical intelligence; but he failed to convince me that his evident enjoyment of his skill in playing was accompanied by much love of what he played; and so the impression he left was not very deep. Miss Douste de Fortis and her sister, Miss Jeanne de Fortis, who has now become an accomplished concert singer, have been active as usual: I heard them at a *matinée* given at

Brinsmeads' by Miss Edith Nalborough, whose pianoforte
playing I am not able to judge from the little I heard of it—
though that was satisfactory as far as it went. One gentleman, Mr Sidney Dark, invited me to a vocal and dramatic
recital at which he alternated various bass songs, from Qui
sdegno to A Friar of Orders Grey, with recitations from
standard authors, from Marlowe to Rudyard Kipling. I
heard Mandalay, Fuzzy Wuzzy, and the Friar, and am
bound to say that Mr Dark acquitted himself, both as elocutionist and singer, very handsomely, and with a certain
personal ability not too common in his profession. A different sort of combination of the orator with the musician
was that effected by Miss d'Esterre Keeling in her lectures
on great composers. As a rule I detest lady-lecturers on
music, because they never even pretend to say what they
think; but Miss d'Esterre Keeling relied on her mother-wit,
and made it go as far as a ton of clergy. I disagreed with some
of her observations, and gathered from a certain severity of
style on her part towards her audience that she had a low
opinion of our intelligence, which was doubtless justified;
but I was not bored; and the playing was adequate. Probably Mr Isidore de Lara started a Parisian fashion in opening
his recital on the 17th by a lecture from Paul Milliet, the
editor of Le Monde Artiste. I say probably, since my pil-
grimage to Bayreuth, of which I shall presently have plenty
to say, prevents me from answering for anything that happened last week.

1 *August* 1894

WHEN I ran across to Bayreuth the other day I was
fully aware that the cost of my trip would have
been better spent in bringing a German critic to
England. And I greatly regret that this article is not written
in German, and for a German paper, since it is now evident
that, as far as any musical awakening and impulse can come
from one country to another, it must come for the present
from England to Bayreuth, and not from Bayreuth to

England.

First, as to the wonderful Bayreuth orchestra, to the glories of which we have been taught to look with envious despair. I beg to observe here, in the most uncompromising manner, that the Bayreuth orchestra, judged by London standards, is not a first-rate orchestra, but a very carefully worked up second-rate one. The results of the careful working up are admirable: the smoothness, the perfect *sostenuto*, the unbroken flow of tone testify to an almost perfect orchestral execution in passages which lend themselves to such treatment. But there are two factors in the effect produced by an orchestra: the quality of the execution, and the quality of the instruments on which the execution is done. How much this may vary may be judged by the wide range of prices for musical instruments, even leaving out of account the scarcity values reached by certain exceptionally desirable old fiddles and bassoons.

Take, for example, the cheapest and most popular wind instrument in the orchestra—the cornet. Heaven knows how low the prices of the vilest specimens of cornet may run! but between the cheapest orchestrally presentable cornet and a first-rate one by Courtois or a good English maker the variation in price, without counting anything for electroplating or decoration of any sort, is from about thirty-five shillings to eight or ten pounds. Fiddles range from a few shillings to the largest sums any orchestral player can afford to give for them; and the scale of prices for wood wind instruments varies from one to three figures.

Now, if there were such a thing as an international musical parliament, I should certainly agitate for a return of the prices of the instruments used in the Bayreuth and Crystal Palace orchestras respectively; and I should be surprised if the German total came to as much as half the English one. In the brass especially, the peculiar dull rattle of inferior thin metal at once strikes an ear accustomed to the smooth, firm tone of the more expensive instruments used in England. There is a difference in brightness too;

but that I leave out of the question, as possibly due to the difference between Continental and English pitch, a difference which is all to the bad for us.

In judging the wood wind I am on less certain ground, since the tone is so greatly affected by the way in which the reed is cut. I have heard in the street what I supposed to be an execrable cracked cornet, and on coming round the corner have found an old man playing a clarinet with an old slack reed as easy for his feeble jaws as the reed one cuts for a child in a cornfield. The tone produced by such ancient men and that produced by Lazarus in his best days (which was, I think, purer, if less rich, than Mühlfeld's) mark the two poles of my experience of clarinet-playing; and I have always found that in German orchestras the standard tone leans more to the man in the street than to Lazarus.

Unfortunately, I am not expert enough to discriminate confidently between the difference due to the cutting of the reed and that due to the quality of the instrument; but except in the case of unusually fine players, who generally take the first chance of coming to England and settling here, the German wood wind player is content with a cheaper tone than the English one; and Bayreuth is no exception to this rule. The oboe there is as reedy as the *cor anglais* is here. The strings, as compared with ours, are deficient in power and richness; and even in the case of the horns, which we somehow or other cannot play, whilst the Germans can, the tone is much rougher and more nearly allied to that of the Alpine cowhorn than what may be called the standard tone here.

I rather harp on the word standard, because the facts that so many of our best orchestral players are Germans, and that Mr August Manns, the conductor whose band, in the wind section, puts the Germans most completely to shame in point of fineness of tone, is himself not merely a German, but a Prussian, conclusively prove that the inferiority of the German orchestra to the English is not an inferiority in natural capacity, but an inferiority in the current national standard of musical beauty—that is, an inferiority in the higher physical culture, and consequently in the quality of the demand to which the orchestral supply is a response.

That this inferiority is no new thing, and was well weighed by Wagner himself, is clear from the stress which he laid on the superiority of the instruments used by our Philharmonic band, and also by the fact that he always cited the Conservatoire concerts in Paris as the source of what he had learned from actual experience as to fineness of orchestral execution. All the other points he so strenuously urged on conductors have been mastered at Bayreuth; and the superficialities of the Mendelssohnian system have disappeared.

But the material of it all—the brute physical sound of the instruments which are so ably handled—still remains comparatively cheap and ugly; and the worst of it is that no German seems to care. As far as I can make out, the payment of an extra five pounds to an instrument-maker for the sake of a finer tone would strike both conductor and player as an unreasonable waste of money.

And yet this German indifference to the final degrees of excellence in instrumental tone is conscientiousness itself compared to their atrocious insensibility to the beauty of the human voice and the graces of a fine vocal touch. The opening performance of Parsifal this season was, from the purely musical point of view, as far as the principal singers were concerned, simply an abomination. The bass howled, the tenor bawled, the baritone sang flat, and the soprano, when she condescended to sing at all, and did not merely shout her words, screamed, except in the one unscreamable song of Herzeleide's death, in which she subsided into commonplaceness.

The bass, who was rather flustered, perhaps from nervousness, was especially brutal in his treatment of the music of Gurnemanz; and it struck me that if he had been a trombone-player in the band, instead of a singer, the conductor, Levi of Munich, would have remonstrated. Indeed, I

presently heard a trombone-player, who was helping with
the fanfares outside the theatre between the acts, pulled up
by the sub-conductor for being "a little too strong." Accordingly, having the opportunity of exchanging a few words
with Levi afterwards, I expressed my opinion about the bass
in question. Levi appeared surprised, and, declaring that
the singer had the best bass voice in Germany, challenged
me to find him anyone who would sing the part better, to
which I could only respond with sufficient emphasis by
offering to sing it better myself, upon which he gave me up
as a lunatic.

It had to be explained to him that I was accustomed to
the "smooth" singing popular in England. That settled the
question for the Bayreuth conductor. Good singing there is
merely "glatt," obviously an effeminate, silly, superficial
quality, unsuited to the utterances of primeval heroes. The
notion that this particular sort of smoothness is one of the
consequences of aiming at beauty of tone and singing in
tune is apparently as strange in Germany as the notion that
it is more truly virile to sing like a man than like a bullock.

If I had passed the whole season listening to Alvary,
Klafsky, and Wiegand at Drury Lane, no doubt I should
not have noticed any great deficiency in Grengg or Rosa
Sucher. Even as it was, after the first three performances my
ear became so corrupted that the second performance of
Parsifal did not infuriate me as the first one did. I had become accustomed to second-rate intonation, especially after
Tannhäuser, in which from beginning to end there was not
a vocal note placed, I will not say as Melba or Miss Eames
or the De Reszkes would have placed it, but as any tolerable
English concert singer would have placed it.

This inveterate carelessness of intonation is only partly
due to bad method. It is true that German singers at Bayreuth do not know how to sing: they shout; and you can see
them make a vigorous stoop and lift with their shoulders,
like coalheavers, when they have a difficult note to tackle, a
pianissimo on any note above the stave being impossible to

them.

But this system is nothing like so injurious to them as that of many of the operatic singers to whom we are accustomed. Their voices, it is true, get stale and rough; but they last astonishingly in that condition; the singers themselves are as robust as dray horses; and sixty appears to be about the prime of their shouting life. The thin, worn, shattered voice, with its goat-bleat or tremolo, and its sound as if it had taken to drink and wrecked its nerves and constitution, all shockingly common here, even among quite young singers, is not to be heard, as a rule, at Bayreuth. Singing there, in fact, is exactly like public speaking in England—not a fine art, but a means of placing certain ideas intelligibly and emphatically before the public without any preoccupation as to beauty of voice or grace of manner.

The music-dramas are, so to speak, effectively debated; and the exposition of the poetic theme has all the qualities of a good Budget speech; but there is just about as much charm of voice and style as there is at a conference of the National Liberal Federation. The English political speaker learns his business by practice, and has neither the vices of the artificial elocutionist nor the fascinations of the cultivated artist. Nobody will listen to his voice for its own sake; but he does not break it: it lasts him until he is old enough to retire; and his general health is improved by the vigorous exercise of his lungs.

And that is just exactly the case of the German singer. Unfortunately, this disqualifies him from presenting the works of Wagner as completely as Sir William Harcourt is disqualified from playing Hamlet—a matter which will appear more fully when I come to describe the fate of Parsifal and Tannhäuser in the hands of German singers as compared with that of Lohengrin as performed by Belgian, Roumanian, American, and English singers. For I shall require more than one article to make myself sufficiently unpleasant to help those German lovers of music who are in revolt against the coarseness and laxity of German taste in this matter, and who are struggling to awaken the national conscience to the impossibility of a school of art in which the first lesson is one of callous indifference to beauty.

8 August 1894

SITTING, as I am today, in a Surrey farmhouse with the sky overcast, and a big fire burning to keep me from shivering, it seems to me that it must be at least four or five months since I was breathing balmy airs in the scented pine-woods on the hills round Bayreuth. If I could only see the sun for five minutes I could better recall what I have to write about. As it is, I seem to have left it all far behind with the other vanities of the season. I no longer feel any impulse to describe Lohengrin and Tannhäuser as I promised, or to draw morals for Frau Wagner on the one hand, or Sir Augustus Harris on the other. For months I have held the whole subject of musical art in an intense grip, which never slackened even when I was asleep; but now the natural periodicity of my function asserts itself, and compels me to drop the subject in August and September, just as hens moult in November (so they tell me here in the farmhouse).

What I feel bound to record concerning the Bayreuth Lohengrin—remember that this is the first time the work has been done there, and probably the first time it has ever been thoroughly done at all, if we except the earliest attempt under Liszt at Weimar—is that its stage framework is immensely more entertaining, convincing, and natural than it has ever seemed before. This is mainly because the stage management is so good, especially with regard to the chorus. In Lohengrin there are only two comparatively short scenes in which the chorus is not present and in constant action.

The opera therefore suffers fearfully on ordinary occasions from the surprising power of the average Italian chorister to destroy all stage illusion the moment he shambles on the scene with his blue jaws, his reach-me-down costume, his foolish single gesture, his embarrassed eye on the prompter, and his general air of being in an opera chorus because he is fit for nothing better. At Covent Garden he is, in addition, generally an old acquaintance: it is not only that he is destroying the illusion of the opera you are looking at, but that he has destroyed the illusion of nearly all the operas you have ever seen; so that the conflict of his claim upon you as one of "the old familiar faces" with the claims of the art which he outrages finally weakens your mind and disturbs your conscience until you lose the power of making any serious effort to get rid of him. As to the ladies of our opera chorus, they have to be led by competent, sensible women; and as women at present can only acquire these qualities by a long experience as mothers of large families, our front row hardly helps the romance of the thing more than the men do.

Now I am not going to pretend that at Bayreuth the choristers produce an overwhelming impression of beauty and chivalry, or even to conceal the fact that the economic, social, and personal conditions which make the Covent Garden chorus what it is in spite of the earnest desire of everybody concerned that it should be something quite different, dominate Frau Wagner just as they dominate Sir Augustus Harris, and compel her to allot to Elsa a bevy of maidens, and to Henry the Fowler a band of warriors, about whose charms and prowess a good deal of make-believe is necessary. The stouter build of the men, the prevalence of a Teutonic cast among them, and their reinforcement by a physically and artistically superior class of singers who regard it as an honor to sing at Bayreuth, even in the chorus, certainly help the illusion as far as the Saxon and Brabantine warriors in Lohengrin are concerned; but this difference in raw material is as nothing compared with the difference made by the intelligent activity of the stage-manager.

One example of this will suffice. Those who know the score of Lohengrin are aware that in the finale to the first act there is a section, usually omitted in performance, in which the whole movement is somewhat unexpectedly repeated in a strongly contrasted key, the modulation being unaccountable from the point of view of the absolute musician, as it is not at all needed as a relief to the principal key. At Bayreuth its purpose is made clear. After the combat with Telramund and the solo for Elsa which serves musically as the exposition of the theme of the finale, the men, greatly excited and enthusiastic over the victory of the strange knight, range themselves in a sort of wheel formation, of which Lohengrin is the centre, and march round him as they take up the finale from Elsa in the principal key. When the modulation comes, the women, in their white robes, break into this triumphal circle, displace the men, and march round Elsa in the same way, the striking change of key being thus accompanied by a correspondingly striking change on the stage, one of the incidents of which is a particularly remarkable kaleidoscoping of the scheme of color produced by the dresses.

Here you have a piece of stage management of the true Wagnerian kind, combining into one stroke a dramatic effect, a scenic effect, and a musical effect, the total result being a popular effect the value of which was proved by the roar of excitement which burst forth as the curtains closed in. A more complex example of the same combination was afforded by the last act of Tannhäuser, which produced the same outburst from the audience, and which was all the more conclusive because none of the enthusiasm could be credited to the principal artists, who had, in the first two acts, effectually cleared themselves of all suspicion of being able to produce any effect except one of portentous boredom.

Here, then, we have the point at which Bayreuth beats Drury Lane and Covent Garden in staging Wagner and every other composer whose works have been for some years in our repertory. I have over and over again pointed out the way in which the heroic expenditure of Sir Augustus Harris gets wasted for want of a stage-manager who not only studies the stage picture as it is studied, for instance, at the Savoy Theatre, or at any of our music-halls where ballets form part of the entertainment, but who studies the score as well, and orders the stage so that the spectator's eye, ear, and dramatic sense shall be appealed to simultaneously.

298

I have sometimes had to point out, in the case of old stock operas, that there is often reason to suspect that the stage-manager either does not even know the story of the opera he has in hand, or has become cynically convinced that an opera is in itself such a piece of nonsense that an extra absurdity or two cannot matter much. This is of course quite a tenable view argumentatively; but it is not the understanding upon which the public pays for its seats. The moment you take a guinea, or half-a-crown, or whatever it may be, from an individual for a performance of an opera, you are bound to treat the performance as a serious matter, whatever your private philosophic convictions may be.

At Bayreuth they do take the performance seriously in all its details: the heroine does not die in the middle of the street on a lodging-house sofa, nor does the tenor step out of a window with a rope ladder attached to it, and openly walk off at the level of the chamber floor. The rank and file are carefully instructed as to what they are supposed to be doing; and nobody dreams of taking any liberties with the work or with the public. It is quite a mistake to suppose that the makeshifts which circumstances force upon Covent Garden are unknown at Bayreuth, or that the stock works are as well rehearsed and prepared as the new works; but there is, at any rate, always the habit of discipline; and though things may be left undone for want of time or ill done for want of rehearsal, nothing is let slide on the assumption that it is not worth doing. I have been tortured there by bad singing, and bored by solemnly prosaic acting; but I have never been offended by wanton trifling.

I have sufficiently explained in my last article how Bayreuth's scrupulous artistic morality is heavily counterbalanced by the callousness of its musical sensibility. The cure for this, however, is not the writing of homilies about it, but the cultivation of the German ear by actual experience of something better than the singing they are accustomed to tolerate. Already the popularity of Van Dyck, a Belgian singer with none of the German bluntness about him, whose

299

charm of voice and style was sufficient, when he appeared as Des Grieux at Covent Garden, to produce on Jean de Reszke, who was at that time taking his supremacy for granted somewhat too lazily, the effect popularly known as "making him sit up," is rendering the Bayreuth stage more accessible to foreigners, who will finally, if the Germans do not realize their own deficiencies, make it difficult for a German singer to get an engagement there. This year we have Nordica and Miss Brema as well as Van Dyck; and it is probable that Frau Wagner will look for more help in the same direction —across the frontier, that is—on future occasions.

I am not quite done with the subject even yet; but as this farmhouse is beyond the sphere of the Post Office, I must conclude, in order to allow three or four days for the journey of thirty miles or so which my communication must make before it reaches London.

POSTSCRIPT 1931.—As it happened I *was* done with the subject. I had already resigned my post as musical critic to The World on the death of its editor Edmund Yates on the 19th May 1894. But his successor pleaded that it would seem a personal slight to himself if I did not go on under his editorship until the end of the season; and this, to save appearances, I consented to do. After the autumn recess my vacant place was filled by Mr Robert Smythe Hichens, who had trained himself as a musician, not knowing that he was destined to be a famous novelist.

I never again undertook regular duties as a critic of music.

INDEX

INDEX

INDEX

305

INDEX

INDEX

INDEX

INDEX

THE END